CAN RELIGIOUS EDUCATION
BE CHRISTIAN?

THE MACMILLAN COMPANY
NEW YORK · BOSTON · CHICAGO · DALLAS
ATLANTA · SAN FRANCISCO

MACMILLAN AND CO., LIMITED
LONDON · BOMBAY · CALCUTTA · MADRAS
MELBOURNE

THE MACMILLAN COMPANY
OF CANADA, LIMITED
TORONTO

CAN RELIGIOUS EDUCATION
BE CHRISTIAN?

by Harrison S. Elliott

New York
THE MACMILLAN COMPANY
1947

268
EL5c

25291
ag. 49

To My Wife

Preface

THE ISSUES WHICH ARE DISCUSSED in this book are those which
have emerged because of the conflicts between the historic Protestant conception of religious education and a modern social and
experience-centered theory and practice. There have been important problems in this area ever since the inauguration of the
modern movement of religious education at the turn of the present
century. But the focus of the problems has shifted during the past
ten years. In connection with the liberalization of Christian beliefs
and of the program of the churches, attention was formerly centered upon the reinterpretations of Christian education and of the
Christian religion, necessary if the insights from psychology, sociology, and education were to be utilized. With the reaction against
liberalism and the emphasis upon the Christian religion in its more
consistent historical formulations, the conflicts between the historic
Protestant conceptions of religious education and modern educational theory and practice have become more clearly defined.
These are the issues which are discussed in this book.

The material on which the book is based was submitted as a
dissertation in the field of religious education for the degree of
Doctor of Philosophy at Yale University, but it has been rewritten
for publication and for general use. The author is under special
obligation to Dean Luther A. Weigle and Dr. Hugh Hartshorne
of Yale University Divinity School for their counsel and criticisms.
He also wishes to express his appreciation to President Henry
Sloane Coffin and Dr. Erdman Harris of Union Theological Seminary and to Chairman Clyde M. Hill and Professor John S. Bru-
bacher of the Department of Education, Yale University, for read-

vii

ing the manuscript and making suggestions. The manuscript in an earlier form was read by Professor Robert L. Calhoun of Yale University Divinity School and has profited by his criticisms. Certain parts of the manuscript have also been read by Professors Frederick C. Grant, Eugene W. Lyman, and Reinbold Niebuhr of Union Theological Seminary, for which appreciation is expressed to them. The author is especially indebted to his wife, Grace Loucks Elliott, for the invaluable cooperation she has given in the preparation of the book.

HARRISON S. ELLIOTT

Union Theological Seminary,
New York City.

Acknowledgments

ACKNOWLEDGMENT IS HERE MADE of the courtesy of the following publishers and authors who have granted permission for the use of selections taken from the books listed below:

The Abingdon Press, New York: Frederick C. Grant, *The Growth of the Gospels*; Wilfred Evans Powell, *Education for Life with God*.

Cokesbury Press, Nashville: Edwin Lewis, *The Faith We Declare*.

Thomas Y. Crowell Company, New York: Henry N. and Regina Westcott Wieman, *Normative Psychology of Religion*.

Harper and Bros., New York: The Commission on Appraisal, William Ernest Hocking, Chairman, *Re-Thinking Missions, A Layman's Inquiry after One Hundred Years*; Hendrik Kraemer, *The Christian Message in a Non-Christian World*; James Moffatt, *The Moffatt New Testament, A New Translation;* Reinbold Niebuhr, *An Interpretation of Christian Ethics*.

Houghton Mifflin Co., Boston: Ellwood P. Cubberley, *The History of Education*.

International Council of Religious Education, Chicago: *Christian Education Today*.

The Lutterworth Press, London and the Macmillan Co., New York: Emil Brunner, *The Divine Imperative* and *The Mediator*.

Religious Education Association, Chicago: E. G. Homrighausen, *The Real Problem of Religious Education*, from Religious Education.

Charles Scribner's Sons, New York: Karl Barth, *The Knowledge of God and the Service of God*; Emil Brunner, *The Theology of Crisis*; George Albert Coe, *A Social Theory of Religious Education* and *What is Christian Education?*; Hugh Hartshorne, *Character in Human Relations*; Arthur Cushman McGiffert, *A History of Christian Thought*, Vol. I; Reinhold Niebuhr, *Beyond Tragedy, Moral Man and Immoral Society*, and *Reflections on the End of an Era*; Paul Tillich, *The Interpretation of History*.

University of Chicago Press, Chicago: William Clayton Bower, *Character through Creative Experience*.

Willett Clark and Co., Chicago: John Bennett, "The Causes of Social Evil" in *Christian Faith and the Common Life*, An Oxford Conference Book; J. W. D. Smith, "The Crisis in Christian Education" in *Church, Community and State in Relation to Education*, An Oxford Conference Book.

Contents

CAN RELIGIOUS EDUCATION BE CHRISTIAN?

CHAPTER I

The Source of Basic Conflicts

RELIGIOUS EDUCATION is not a modern phenomenon. In some form, it is as old as religion itself. But the term has come to have in this present century a specialized meaning, particularly in the United States and Canada. It has come to be used to designate the utilization of modern educational principles and methods, not only in the teaching of religion but also in the development of religious faith and in the realization of religious experience.

Because the modern educational approach was first adopted in the churches by those responsible for the program with children and adolescents, religious education in the minds of many has no bearing upon the long-established practices of the church in which adults predominate in number. This is similar to the situation in the general field where education was considered to be a matter which concerned the young and immature only. But the leaders of the modern religious education movement have no such limited conception. For example, the first convention of the Religious Education Association in Chicago in 1903 had, among the four hundred delegates, forty college and university presidents, twice as many well-known teachers, and scores of pastors and Sunday School workers. This association enlisted in its membership college and university teachers and administrators, public school teachers and officers, secretaries of denominational boards, secretaries of the Young Men's and Young Women's Christian Associations, and ministers and lay workers in churches. It was composed of representatives of the three great faiths, Protestant, Catholic, and Jewish. Its purpose was stated to be: "To inspire the educational forces of our country with the religious ideal; to inspire the religious forces of our country with the educational ideal; and to keep before the public mind the ideal of Religious Education, and the sense of its need and value."[1] Thus, religious education represents a concern for the inter-relation of education and religion in all areas and at all age levels. In the more recent developments within the churches, as within general education, special attention is being given to the program for adults. Religious education represents an educational emphasis and approach in the entire program of the church or synagogue, and has within its scope of interest the long-established practices of worship and preaching as well as the specialized program for children and adolescents.

The utilization of educational insights and methods in the teaching of religion and in the realization of religious experience would seem, on first thought, to raise no basic questions. It would seem just ordinary good sense to use the best available methods in the program of the churches and synagogues. Actually, the efforts to apply educational theory and methodology to the work of these institutions during the present century have resulted in basic conflicts. To many in the Christian churches, this modern movement of religious education seems to be based upon assumptions which deny the fundamental tenets of the Christian religion. They say it is character and not religious education, and that it is not and by its very assumptions cannot be Christian education.

The issue is a basic one. There is no question but that modern religious education represents in certain regards a different approach and emphasis from that of the historic program of the

---

[1] The Religious Education Association, A Brief Statement of the Purpose, Plan, History, and Results, with a List of the Officers, for 1905.

churches. The conflicts have arisen because attempts have been made to introduce an educational program into churches and denominations which had already developed various practices such as preaching, worship, Bible teaching, and evangelism with a very different origin from modern education. Not only have these practices developed in the long history of the churches, but church doctrines have been the controlling factor in the determination of these practices. Program and methodology have been developed which are consonant with these doctrines and which furnish a medium for making the beliefs effective in personal life and experience. Thus a theological approach has been taken to the problems of program and methodology. This is seen in theological seminaries in the title of "Practical Theology" for the department responsible for teaching in the practical field. Since Protestants have emphasized going directly to the Bible for religious beliefs, attention has been focused upon preaching and teaching as methods by which particular interpretations of the Bible and of the Christian religion can be brought to the people. This does not mean that no attention was given to the improvement of methodology before the modern period. It indicates rather that attention was centered on how the message of the church could be more effectively presented.

The leaders in modern religious education have taken a diametrically opposite approach to the problems of program and methodology. Instead of beginning with the beliefs of the churches and thinking of education as a methodology for the transmission of Biblical and doctrinal teachings, they have centered their attention upon the children, young people, and adults who were to be educated. While leaders in religious education have not been unmindful of the insights regarding human beings in the Bible and in the doctrines of the churches, they have believed that program and methodology should be based upon the best scientific knowledge available in regard to the nature of man and the conditions for his growth. Therefore they have taken seriously the data from the sciences of psychology, sociology and anthropology and from the developments in general education. Indeed, religious education has been fundamentally influenced by the developments in general education and has been a part of the modern educational movement. But this, as will be later discussed, had its origin outside the churches and developed independently of the theological conceptions of the church. It was a product of the confidence in man and of the scientific attitude which originated in the Period of the Enlightenment. Thus empirical data and educational insights, rather than theological conceptions, have been the controlling factors in the development of program and method in religious education.

Had modern religious education represented merely an improved methodology for bringing the message of the church to children, young people and adults, no serious conflicts would have developed. It is because it represents a different approach from that which has characterized the historic program of the churches and because it has implications which challenge the theological assumptions of the churches that the problems are so difficult. For example, the central concern of theology has been God, his relation to man and man's relation to him. The doctrine of man has been based upon the doctrine of God. The psychology has been a theological psychology. Commencing with the omnipotence and sovereignty of God, there has been, upon the whole, an emphasis upon man's sinfulness and inadequacy, his submission to God's will and his dependence upon God's saving grace. There has been a low estimate of "natural" man and of his possibilities. In contrast, and on the basis of the empirical data, educators have tended to emphasize the possibilities of human beings and this estimate religious educators have shared.

The Protestant doctrines, on which the church's practices have been based, not only had the support of a long history, but they also carried the authority of divine revelation, however differently that term was interpreted. Therefore, in the historic program of the churches, the interpretations in the Bible and in the teachings of the church have been assumed as given, and attention has been focused upon the transmission of these truths to the people. In modern religious education, the Biblical and theological interpretations themselves are examined, rather than being made the presuppositions of the educational process. While there has been no lack of emphasis upon the experience of God, the conceptions of God have been considered to be the fruition of the educational process rather than the presupposition with which it commenced. Religious experience has been considered to be integrally related to religious education rather than a work of God apart from the educational process. Thus it is seen that the issues are not superficial ones as to whether one type of method is more effective than another. They concern important questions in the philosophy of religious education.

This brief review makes evident that important problems facing the churches grow out of the fact that two separate and distinct streams of influence meet in the work of the churches. The historic practices of the church belong primarily to the first stream and religious education primarily to the second. The efforts to adjust or integrate the two in the program of the churches causes serious problems, particularly since there are disagreements both in regard to basic assumptions and in regard to the approach to be made to the solution of the differences. These conflicts have taken different practical forms. In churches with more than one professional leader, they have often been manifested in differences between the minister who represented by training and conviction the regularly established practices of the church, and the director of religious education who had been trained in the newer educational approaches. But even where there was no director of religious education, there were often distinct differences in approach and method between the church school or young people's society and the longer established services of public worship and preaching. Often these differences have been found within the church school itself or within the educational societies of the church. Some defended, others opposed graded lessons, week-time activities, and other aspects of the religious educational emphasis. In some denominations, it has been a conflict between an evangelistic approach with the emphasis upon God's part in the transformation of human beings, and an educational approach in which stress has been laid upon nurture in the Christian life.

Confusion and conflict arise when there are found in the same local church or within the same denomination two parallel and conflicting programs based on different assumptions. The confusion is increased because usually there is not a clear-cut distinction between the two approaches and programs, but elements of both are intermingled. Public preaching and worship, the mid-week prayer meeting, and the pastoral work of the churches have been influenced to a greater or less extent by educational insights. The modern program of religious education, as found in nationally developed courses and plans or in the program of the local church, has elements of both approaches.

The conflict is often found within the life of the religious leader himself, be he minister, director of religious education, or lay worker. Often he belongs to both streams of influence. As a leader in the church, he recognizes his relationship to a religion with a long history and he knows that the religion of religious education is not some vague generality but is the Christian religion. As an educator, on the other hand, he feels his relationship to the modern educational movement and he has a sense of obligation to embody in the work of the churches the educational insights which have grown out of that movement. But too often he has not made an integration of the two in his own philosophy and methodology and they remain for him two parallel and sometimes conflicting approaches and points of view.

The professional training of the minister has usually given him little help on the integration of these contrasting approaches and may indeed have accentuated the conflict. In his theological education, he has taken courses in the Bible, church history, systematic theology, philosophy of religion, and Christian ethics. For the most part, these courses are taught for the purpose of acquainting the student with the history of the church and of Christianity and with the Bible and its interpretation for today. The emphasis is upon the message of the minister. In some cases, psychological, sociological, and educational approaches and insights are utilized in the courses, but often they are taught without reference to the contribution which these sciences might bring to the understanding and interpretation of the Christian religion and of religious experience. In many theological seminaries, there are also courses in religious education, psychology, and sociology, paralleling those in the historical and philosophical fields, in which the attention is focused not only upon an educational emphasis in the program of the church, but also upon the contribution of these subjects to the understanding of the Bible, the interpretation of the Christian faith, and the realization of Christian experience. In some seminaries, particularly in those in a university center, there is as definite a conflict between the assumptions and teachings of these two aspects of the student's training as there is in the two parallel programs in the churches, and little or no provision is made for an adjustment or integration of the conflicting viewpoints. In this situation, some students commit themselves to one approach, some to the other. More students attempt to follow both and go from the seminary with two parallel points of emphasis in regard to religion and religious experience and in regard to the program of the church. Very few make a real synthesis of the interpretations of the historical and philosophical departments with those of religious education. When the theological graduate attempts to follow both types of emphasis in his work as a minister, there is the same confusion within his own life and leadership as is found in the program of the church.

An examination of the program of leadership training for lay workers in the churches shows that they contain the same conflicts that are found in the courses for the education of ministers. There are courses on the Bible and on Christian belief and practice which are based, on the whole, on a historical and theological approach; and there are parallel courses on child psychology, educational methods, and psychology of religion which are similar to courses for teachers and other educational leaders. There is little or no provision for adjustment or integration of the conflicting viewpoints, and lay leaders tend to have the same conflicts within themselves, often unrecognized, as do the ministers.

The development of parallel programs and points of view in the work of the churches was probably inevitable. New viewpoints and programs are usually first developed by a minority—a sect within the church—and must demonstrate their usefulness before they become adopted by the majority. In any case, they usually do not replace the majority viewpoints, but influence them in the direction of partial or fundamental modification; and, in turn, these viewpoints are themselves modified in the process. It looked for a time as if this gradual and mutual modification and inter-relationship would go on within the churches in a constructive manner. The interpretations of the Christian religion, at least by the so-called liberal groups in the churches, were influenced, on the one hand, by the literary and historical criticism of the Bible and by a broader perspective on the history of the church, and on the other hand, by the scientific approach to nature and human life and by educational and social movements. The leaders in religious education were recognizing the limitations involved in an over-attention to method and were giving more consideration to the distinctive characteristics of religious and Christian education, as compared with general education, and to the place in the educational process of the historical formulations of the Christian faith in the Bible and in the history of the church. Further, leaders in general education and in social agencies had come to recognize the importance of religious problems and the difficulties in an education which had been secularized because of fear of religious differences and controversies. The liberalizing of theology and the development of educational processes seemed, to many, complementary factors, making for the greater effectiveness of the churches.

This process of adjustment and integration has been greatly retarded in recent years. Both liberal theology and the "Social Gospel" have been under severe attack. There has been an increasing tendency in the Protestant churches to return to the historical formulations of the Christian religion and to repudiate the adjustments which had been made under the influence of modern scientific and social developments. Instead of being called the savior of the churches, as religious education was previously designated by many, the developments of modern religious education are often attacked as a menace to the churches and an evidence of secularization. This situation has brought into the open and accentuated the conflicts which had never been fully resolved.

The issues have become acute because of the present emphasis upon Protestant Christianity in its more consistent historical formulations. The conflicts therefore are focused in the differences between those who are emphasizing a neo-orthodox [2] interpretation both of the Christian religion and of Christian education and those who maintain their belief in modern religious education and who are usually "liberal" in their theology. These conflicts, however, are of a distinctly different type from those which have occurred in the past between "Fundamentalist" interpretations and religious education. The neo-orthodox leaders in Protestant Christianity have accepted modern knowledge as thoroughly as have the "liberals." Often they belong to a radical school of Biblical criticism. They do not look to the Bible for scientific knowledge and therefore do not feel a conflict between science and religion. They believe in and often are active participants in scientific, social, and political movements. But they emphasize the lack of pertinence of such developments to Christian faith and experience. Since Christianity is a revealed religion, for them it does not depend upon human knowledge or human processes. Therefore, the issues at present have elements which are different from those of any previous period of Protestant religious education.

It is the basic issues in theory and practice, particularly as they are found in contemporary Protestantism, that are to be explored. The problems, however, are not peculiar to churches with these particular theological interpretations. These are but particular manifestations of basic conflicts which have been and are now being faced wherever a scientific educational approach is introduced into either churches or synagogues with their long-established practices based on historical religious beliefs. Therefore,

---

[2] The term "neo-orthodox" is used in the following chapters of the book to designate those described in this paragraph, who are emphasizing Protestant Christianity in its more consistent historical formulations. They have sometimes been designated as "radical-orthodox."

the discussion should throw light upon the wider problems. The purpose is to discuss the educational rather than the theological issues, and theological viewpoints are considered only as they are involved in educational philosophy and practice. The discussion is therefore in the field of philosophy of religious education rather than in philosophy of religion. The churches belong to a historical tradition and their work cannot be carried on without due regard to their historic beliefs and practices. At the same time, the churches have to face the modern world and it would be inadvisable for them to attempt to develop program and methodology as if there had been no contributions from education, psychology, mental hygiene, sociology, and other similar work. Therefore, a philosophy of religious education should offer a way for adjusting these two points of emphasis. Particularly must there be consideration of the challenge of those who hold that modern religious education is not and by its very assumptions cannot be Christian education.

CHAPTER II

Protestant Influence in American Religious Education

IT WAS SUGGESTED in the last chapter that the issues in regard to religious education have become acute because of the present emphasis upon Protestant Christianity in its more consistent historical formulations. On first thought, this is difficult to understand, for some of the neo-orthodox theological interpreters emphasize a return to the teachings of the Reformation, from which they say both liberal theology and religious education have departed. It would seem that to go back to the Reformation would raise no basic issues for religious education, but would indeed bring added support to an educational approach. The influence of the Reformation upon popular education is well known. The elementary schools for the common people are perhaps due more to the influence of Luther and others of the Reformers than to any other single influence. In substituting the authority of the Bible for that of the church, it became important that the people should be able to read the Bible for themselves. Further, large dependence was placed upon pamphlets in spreading the ideas of the Reformation. This was notably true of Luther who kept the printing presses running almost continuously. It was the invention of printing, contemporaneous with the Reformation, which made this use of the Bible and other religious literature possible.

The right of the private interpretation of the Bible was a cardinal principle of the Reformation. That every Christian should be free to test a doctrine for himself was also emphasized.

Certainly such points of emphasis open the way for the use of an educational process in the examination of current beliefs and in the reinterpretation of the Christian religion by any individual or group. If the neo-orthodox theological interpreters were emphasizing the liberty of the individual believer, of which Luther wrote and on which the Reformation was inaugurated, the present issues in regard to religious education in the Protestant churches would not be so serious. A modern educational approach is not in conflict with this original spirit and emphasis of the Reformation. But these neo-orthodox interpreters are asking a return to the authoritarian doctrinal emphasis which developed later among the Reformers and which especially characterized Protestant scholasticism. With such an emphasis, modern religious education is in basic conflict.

Two elements in the educational emphasis which developed out of the Reformation need to be kept in mind in understanding the present issues. The first was the gradual substitution of interpretations of the Bible for the authority of the Bible itself. Luther was pushed into this by his contests with the Church of Rome, in which he needed some external authority to use in opposition to the ecclesiastical enactments. He was himself independent and free in using the Scriptures and did not hesitate to make his own selections of that which he considered authoritative. But this did not change the fact that he increasingly worked out interpretations to which he gave the authority of the Bible. Along with the translation of the Bible into the German vernacular—a translation which has set a standard for the German language—he prepared catechisms which embodied what were for him the accepted doctrines. His controversies with others in the Reformation movement and particularly with Zwingli led him to abandon in practice his declared principle that every Christian has the right to test a doctrine for himself and to put increasing emphasis upon the interpretations which to him had the support of the Bible.[1] For Melanchthon, there was no such independence in the use of the Bible as Luther manifested. He not only quoted it as if all the parts were of equal authority, but he made saving faith depend upon the acceptance of all the truths of divine revelation as found in the Bible and as interpreted by the three ecumenical creeds and by the teaching of Luther. Thus sound doctrine as formulated by the true Church was made the authority, and the basis was laid not only for Protestant scholasticism but for the authoritarian doctrinal emphasis which has been so prominent in Protestantism.[2]

The basis for the authoritarian element in Protestantism is also found in the teachings of Zwingli and Calvin. Zwingli thought of the Christian life as obedience to the divine will as revealed in the Scriptures, and the Bible for him was "an authoritative code for the government of Christian life and thought."[3] Calvin, like Zwingli, emphasized the divine will as revealed in the Scriptures, but he was more rigorous than Zwingli in his application of this principle. The Christian must be held strictly to the observance of the divine law. Calvin, like Melanchthon, emphasized the importance of the correct interpretations of the Bible as found in sound doctrines.[4] This emphasis upon authoritative interpretations of the Bible was carried still further in Protestant scholasticism.[5]

[1] See McGiffert, Arthur Cushman, *Protestant Thought before Kant*, Chapter II; also his *Martin Luther*.

[2] *Ibid.*, p. 77.

[3] *Ibid.*, p. 70.

[4] *Ibid.*, Chapter V. See also Hunt, Robert N. Carew, *Calvin*, and Harkness, Georgia, *John Calvin; The Man and His Ethics*.

[5] For example, the *Formula of Concord* in 1580 not only asserted the authority of the Bible but also that the authoritative interpretations of the Scriptures were found in the three ancient creeds (the Apostles', the Nicene, and the Athanasian), the Augsburg Confession, Melanchthon's Apology for the Confession, the Smalcald Articles, and Luther's two Catechisms. *Ibid.*, p. 144.

It is thus seen that the authoritarian emphasis in Protestantism had its origin in the Reformation period. In place of private interpretation of the Bible and personal testing of beliefs, there developed an emphasis upon the authority of sound doctrines as embodied in the true interpretations of the Bible. The pulpit became the center of Protestantism because it was from the pulpit that the Bible was authoritatively interpreted. The basis was laid for the conception of religious education as a methodology for transmitting authoritative and saving truth.

A second development within the Reformation period is important in understanding the Protestant influence in American religious education. Religious liberty in the sense in which that term is now used in this country was not characteristic of the Reformation, despite the principle of the right of private interpretation of the Bible. The contest with the power of Rome was settled in the German states by providing that each prince should decide between Catholicism and Protestantism and that his subjects should accept the faith of the ruler. In the Protestant states, Protestantism was the official religion and it was the Bible in its Protestant interpretations which was taught in the schools. The decision as to the true religion was thus in the control of the temporal power. Calvin, on the other hand, attempted to place the decision, both as to doctrines and as to morals, in the control of the church and insisted that the civic authorities should enforce the church decrees. The civic authorities thus became the agents of the church in enforcing church practices and in regulating the morals of the people. Out of this theory of the relation of church and state there grew the conflicts between Calvin and the civic authorities and the difficulties in enforcing the decrees upon those who refused to conform. The Reformation, which was a protest against the corrupt rule of the Roman Church, resulted in the substitution of a new form of church authority over both religious and civic affairs. In this conception, education had the double function of supporting the doctrines and practices of the church and the moral and civic enactments as decreed by this church-state combination. Thus within the Reformation an authoritarian pattern for education developed. It represented the subordination of education to the authoritative interpretation of the Bible and this was made effective through civic or state control.

Most of the early settlers in America came from lands which had adopted the Protestant faith. The various Puritan congregations who settled in New England were ardent Calvinists and each attempted to set up a town religious government on the model of Geneva or other subsequent governments in Scotland or Holland. Since in these towns civil and religious affairs were inter-related, as in the Geneva republic, the schools had the two-fold function of providing that all children were taught "to read and understand the principles of religion and the capital laws of the country." The material for instruction was predominantly religious. The religious sects were so numerous in the middle Atlantic region in the Colonial period that no single religious school was possible. There, in so far as education was available, it was provided in parochial schools, privately supported and under the control of the church. The curriculum, as in New England, was predominantly religious. The clergymen were usually the teachers. In Virginia, the practice in England was followed and education for the most part was a privilege of the landed class. But aside from Virginia, the Protestant emphasis in education was dominant.

While these groups of settlers—Dutch, Germans, English, Scotch, Calvinists, Lutherans, Anglicans, Presbyterians—developed in America great variety in the form of religious organization, in the type of education, and in the kind of social observances, the various groups were alike in their insistence upon an authoritative interpretation of religion and upon schools which supported the accepted religious views. Thus the practice of making education the agent of religion was predominant in colonial America.[6]

It is not within the function of this discussion to review the history of education in the United States out of which has emerged the present public-supported school system—up to and including the tax-supported universities—and the resulting complete divorce of general education from the control of the church. Certain factors in this change need to be noted because it is necessary to keep them in mind for an understanding of the special problems under consideration. The first of these is the achievement of religious liberty in the United States. While freedom to worship God according to the dictates of one's conscience was a primary motive in bringing various groups to settle in America, there was intolerance by the Protestants toward any whose interpretation of the Bible and of religion was different from that held by the particular group. They left Europe to escape the efforts to make them conform to religious beliefs and practices with which they did not agree; and, as so often happens, they repeated the very coercion they had risked the perils of the wilderness of America to escape. It is true that there were notable exceptions: Roger Williams, Mrs. Anne Hutchinson, Samuel Groton, and others who fought the Massachusetts authorities and set up in what is now Rhode Island settlements in which there was freedom of

[6] "One learned to read chiefly that one might be able to read the Catechism and the Bible, and to know the will of the heavenly Father. There was scarcely any other purpose in the maintenance of elementary schools. . . . Such studies as history, geography, science, music, drawing, secular literature, and organized play were unknown. . . . Religious matter constituted the only reading matter, outside the instruction in Latin in the grammar schools. The Catechism was taught, and the Bible was read and expounded." Cubberley, Ellwood P., *The History of Education*, pp. 374–375.

belief and worship; George Calvert, the first Lord Baltimore, and his son, the second Lord Baltimore, both Roman Catholics, who, in order to make a success of their colony in Maryland, opened it to all religious groups and insisted on religious liberty in the colony; and the Quakers in New Jersey, Delaware, and Pennsylvania, notably William Penn in Pennsylvania, who guaranteed religious freedom to all law-abiding citizens. But the early history of the settlements in America was, upon the whole, characterized by intolerance and the attempted coercion of those who held beliefs and who attempted to set up worship different from those of the group which formed the settlement. In other words, they followed the Protestant theory that a "state" should be free to choose its religion, but, once chosen, it must be accepted by all. At the time of the opening of the War for Independence, Congregationalism was the dominant religion in three of the New England colonies and Anglicanism in New York and in five of the southern colonies.[7]

The agitation during the Revolutionary War on the part of the Baptists in Massachusetts for the separation of religion from the control of the state was unsuccessful; and the Massachusetts constitution, adopted in 1779 in the midst of the Revolution, made it the "right and duty" of the legislature to "authorize and require . . . suitable provision . . . for the instruction of the public worship of God."[8] Religious freedom did not come in Massachusetts until 1833; in New Hampshire in 1817 and in Connecticut in 1818. Early in the War, this freedom was achieved in those colonies in which the Episcopal Church was dominant—in Maryland and New York and in the southern colonies with the exception of Virginia. The Baptists were the only sect which demanded religious liberty before the Declaration of Independence. But with

---

[7] Sweet, William Warren, *The Story of Religion in America*, p. 274.
[8] *Ibid.*, p. 275.

the close of the Revolution, two other dissenting bodies, the Presbyterians and the Methodists, joined in the efforts to secure complete religious liberty. The contest lasted for several years in Virginia and religious liberty was not attained until 1786. Thomas Jefferson, who framed the bill as finally adopted, considered this so important that he directed that it should be one of three achievements recorded on his tombstone, along with his authorship of the Declaration of Independence and his founding of the University of Virginia. A few years later religious freedom became a part of the fundamental law of the land through the first amendment to the Federal Constitution.[9] This guarantee of religious liberty made the problem of religious education very different from that of the colonies or of Reformation Germany and Switzerland.

The needs of the state under the new conditions of independence had led to a shift in the emphasis in public education, even before religious liberty was achieved. The conviction had grown that "the life of the Republic demanded an educated and intelligent citizenship, and hence the general education of all in common schools controlled by the state."[10] But the maintenance of religious freedom made it necessary that the publicly supported schools should not be sectarian, even if particular beliefs represented the faith of the majority. Otherwise, the rights of minorities could not be safeguarded. This two-fold influence led to the orientation of the schools in training for responsible participation in the life of the nation. While in theory religion was still recognized as an important element in such training, direct religious teaching became difficult because of the sectarian divisions. That this question of sectarian teaching was no imaginary issue became evident in the efforts of Horace Mann to provide moral and reli-

[9] *Ibid.*, pp. 275–279.
[10] Cubberley, Ellwood, *The History of Education*, p. 692.

gious training in the schools and at the same time keep them non-sectarian. Horace Mann was concerned lest, in the effort to protect children from religious proselytism through the statute of 1826,[11] they should be deprived of all religious education. In his first report to the Board of Education of Massachusetts of January 1, 1838, he called attention to this danger. He thought the problem might be solved, not only by reading of the Bible, but also by the use of books which set forth the "beautiful and sublime truths of natural religion" and by providing in the normal schools for teaching "the principles of morality and piety common to all sects of Christians."

The issue came to a focus in the effort of the Massachusetts Board of Education to recommend books for school libraries which would contain non-sectarian religion. Frederick A. Packard, the Recording Secretary and Editor of Publications of the American Sunday School Union, sought to have included books from the "Select Library" of the Union, books which were manifestly Calvinistic or at least "evangelical" in emphasis. When Mann said they were sectarian and would offend both Unitarians and Universalists, Packard and others carried on an agitation against the State Board of Education. In the attacks, it was claimed that Mann's "natural religion" was really Unitarian and thus sectarian and that it was only through "revealed" religion that the provision of the statute that the minds of children and youth should be impressed with the "principles of piety, justice, and sacred regard for truth, etc.," could be carried out. In any case, it was held that any community had the right by majority vote to determine what type of religion should be taught in the schools. Thus, the issue was joined by a reaffirmation of the Reformation position that there should be in each state an official

[11] This statute provided that no school books should be used in any of the public schools "calculated to favor any particular religious sect or tenet."

religion and that this religion should be taught in the schools. A majority of the orthodox as well as of the liberal ministers rallied to the support of the religious liberty guaranteed by the statute and, when the matter came before the legislature in 1840–41, the Board of Education was vindicated and religious liberty maintained.[12]

The issue in Massachusetts was in a state at the time overwhelmingly Protestant and concerned the divisions among Protestants. Further, it did not have to do with the public support of parochial schools. With the Irish immigration to the United States in the forties and the consequent increase of the Roman Catholics, the question became one of the division of the school funds. The church schools in many eastern states, particularly those in areas in which parochial schools had been established by the Protestants, had shared in the public school funds. The request of the sectarian agencies for a division of the public funds led the New York City Council in 1825 to refuse to grant public money to any religious society. The Roman Catholics carried the issue to the State legislature in 1840. The difficulty of dividing funds between rival religious sects led the legislature in 1842 to create for the city a board of education, to establish real public schools, and to stop "the debate on the question of aid to religious schools by enacting that no portion of the school funds was in the future to be given to any school in which 'any religious sectarian doctrine or tenet should be taught, inculcated, or practiced.'"[13] The issue was faced in other states, but in no case was demand for a division of the funds successful after 1840. Legislatures now began to propose constitutional amendments, forbidding a division or diversion of the funds. All states admitted to

[12] A fully documented account of this controversy will be found in *Horace Mann and Religious Education in the Massachusetts Public Schools* by Raymond B. Culver, on which this brief summary is based.

[13] Cubberley, Ellwood, *The History of Education*, p. 694.

the Union after 1858, with the exception of West Virginia, contained this provision in the first state constitution.[14]

The secularization of public education in the interests of religious freedom made the problem of religious education for Protestants in this country an entirely different one from that faced by the Protestants of the colonial period in America where religious education was a primary function of the schools. In this situation, the Protestants adopted the Sunday School, which had already been established, as the medium for the religious education of their children and youth. The first Sunday School was organized in the United States in 1785[15] and Sunday Schools were established in various centers in the eastern part of the country during the next thirty years. The first Sunday Schools in America for the most part followed the pattern established by Robert Raikes in Gloucester, England, in that they were an effort to provide the rudiments of education for the children of indigent parents, but they were soon broadened in their scope. The Sunday School was at first a lay organization independent of denominational relationship or ecclesiastical control and was developed before the denominations took up the work of the Sunday Schools in a large way. But by 1830 denominational boards had been organized, and gradually the Sunday School came to be

[14] *Ibid.,* p. 695. For a summary of the provisions in the various states, see Jackson, Jerome K., and Malmberg, Constantine F., *Religious Education and the State.*

[15] This was the first Sunday School of the Robert Raikes type. George Stewart says that "the use of Sunday for religious instruction in Connecticut not only sprang up independently of Raikes' work but in certain cases schools held for religious instruction on Sabbath days actually antedated his efforts. Rev. Joseph Bellamy conducted a school for religious instruction on the Sabbath in 1740." Stewart quotes the testimony that Bellamy was accustomed to meet the youth "not merely for a catechetical exercise but for a recitation from the Bible, in connection with which he communicated, in a way admirably adapted to the capacities of the young, much important instruction." Stewart, George, *A History of Religious Education in Connecticut,* p. 318.

recognized by the various denominations as the primary instrument for the religious education of their children and youth.

The Sunday School carried on the authoritarian tradition which developed in the Reformation and which was prominent in the colonial period in the United States. The purpose was to ground children in those interpretations of the Bible and of the Christian religion on which the particular denomination believed that salvation depended. To be correct in doctrine was the important consideration. Consequently, the Bible and the catechism formed the chief curriculum material and the catechetical method the chief form of instruction. Indeed, the catechism often occupied a more prominent place than the Bible because it was in the catechism that the accepted doctrines were stated. This was perhaps inevitable because the denominational aspects of the Sunday School movement developed in what Professor Sweet calls "the restless thirties and forties," when so many divisions took place within the denominations and when each denomination began to emphasize its own peculiar interest.[16] But there were many in the Sunday Schools who felt that the Bible should occupy the central place in the curriculum, and by the middle of the century it was generally recognized as the primary curriculum material, although the catechism still occupied an important if a secondary place. Memorization of Bible verses now became prominent as formerly had been the memorization of the catechism. As the inadequacy of a memorization system became evident, question books on the Bible were introduced. These were considered superior because they provided for a more systematic knowledge of the Bible and because they facilitated the work of untrained teachers.[17]

Some progress had been made in the non-denominational

[16] Sweet, William Warren, *The Story of Religion in America*, Chapter XVII.
[17] Betts, George Herbert, *The Curriculum of Religious Education*, p. 105.

American Sunday School Union toward "selected uniform lessons" for all Sunday Schools. But when the denominational publishing houses entered the field about 1830, this movement for uniformity was checked. Each denomination felt the obligation of supplying its Sunday Schools with lessons which emphasized its particular doctrines and aims, and each denominational publishing house saw in the lessons for its denomination an important publishing field. The period from 1840 to 1870 has been called the "Babel period" in the Sunday School curriculum.

The movement for uniform lessons based on the Bible was initiated again in 1865 by John H. Vincent, a Methodist minister in Chicago, in the employ of the Chicago Sunday School Union, an interdenominational organization. This culminated in the adoption by the convention of 1872 of the National (later known as the International) Sunday School Association of a resolution, introduced by B. F. Jacobs, a Baptist layman and Sunday School leader. This resolution authorized the convention to appoint a committee of five clergymen and five laymen to "select a series of Bible lessons for a series of years not exceeding seven," which should embrace "a general study of the whole Bible, alternating between the Old and New Testaments." The resolution also placed the convention back of a recommendation of these lessons to the Sunday Schools of the country. The denominational problem was met by the provision that this committee should choose the topic, the Scripture passage, and the Golden Text for each lesson; but lesson helps, usually in the form of quarterlies, were edited and published by the respective denominations.

The uniform lessons were immediately popular and soon became the dominant material in the Sunday Schools. While the plan provided for covering the Bible in a seven-year cycle, nothing like a systematic study of the Bible was secured, even when the Daily Home Readings were included. Nevertheless, this provision for the study of the same lesson on a particular Sunday in the Sunday Schools in all parts of the United States, and indeed a little later in all parts of the world, marked a distinct advance over the chaos which had prevailed, even though it fastened upon the churches a system which it has been difficult to supplant because of its simplicity.

The important fact to be remembered as the basis of understanding the present issues is that the change from catechism to Bible and from a chaotic to a uniform study of the Bible did not mean a change in the basic viewpoint. During the entire period from the inauguration of the Sunday School movement in the first quarter of the nineteenth century down to the close of the century, the controlling purpose was to make the doctrinal message of the Bible known to children and youth. It was knowledge of the word of God essential to salvation which dominated the Sunday School. The Sunday School was subject-matter-centered and the Biblical and theological approach to religious education was dominant.

Another characteristic of the Sunday School of this period must be kept in mind if the contrast in the present educational approach is to be fully understood. Conversion at the age of accountability was the purpose of the Sunday School, and little or no attention was given to nurture of Christian life and conduct either before or after conversion. In other words, the goal was entirely in line with the Reformation emphasis upon the depravity of human nature and the lost state of every child until he had been justified by faith and been reconciled to God through the atoning work of Christ. It is true that those who were in the tradition of the Pietists, either directly or by way of the Wesleyan Evangelical movement, placed particular emphasis upon conduct, and differed from those more directly in the Reformation tradition in their stressing of regeneration; but they trusted the change of nature in the second birth of conversion to bring about Christian conduct. Prominent in all denominations was the emphasis upon salvation as necessary for future blessedness. The dominant purpose in teaching the catechism and the Bible in the Sunday School was to give a basis for the faith on which alone salvation was considered to be possible.

Those who had been under the instruction of the Sunday School were considered a particularly fruitful field for the revival methods which were so generally used. These revival methods had their origin in the two "great awakenings" of the eighteenth century. The first occurred on the Atlantic seaboard toward the middle of the century under the preaching of Jonathan Edwards in New England and through Pietist influences among the Pennsylvania Germans, in the Dutch Reformed Churches, and among the Presbyterians in the middle colonies. George Whitefield's evangelistic tours, chiefly in the middle colonies, "stirred all classes and churches." The second great awakening came at the close of the century. Following the spiritual deadness among all the churches in the period after the Revolution, there was a renewed interest in religion in the East and a growth of the churches in interest and vitality. It was in the new frontier, formed by the movement of population westward, that the revival movement was characterized by strong emotion and various physical manifestations.[18] The excesses of the western revivals aroused opposition in the various denominations, particularly the Presbyterian, and schisms resulted. But upon the whole, on the basis of the experience of these two great awakenings, it may be said that revival methods had come to be recognized as a means of securing the conversion of individuals, particularly of adults; and this method was utilized among chil-

[18] Sweet, William Warren, *The Story of Religion in America*, Chapters IX, X, and XV.

dren, especially those who had been under Sunday School instruction.[19]

That the aim of religious instruction in the Sunday School was to show children their lost condition and to lead them to accept the saving work of Christ and that revival methods should be used in securing their conversion when they reached the age of accountability were generally accepted beliefs. There was, however, a notable challenge to these viewpoints, made by Horace Bushnell near the middle of the century. In an article entitled "Spiritual Economy of Revivals of Religion" in the *Christian Spectator* of 1838, the material of which was published in his *Views of Christian Nurture* in 1847,[20] Bushnell criticized the term, "revival of religion" and the overemphasis upon revivals. He objected to the assumption that the Spirit of the Lord was especially present in revivals as compared with other periods in the life of individuals and of the church. While recognizing the place of revivals in the economy of the church, he held that other periods were equally under the direction of the Spirit, since God is omnipresent and working in various ways. He also felt that the effort to maintain revival fervor was unhealthy for the spiritual life. Particularly did he object to the oft-repeated statement that the "great business of the gospel and of Christian effort is to convert men." He declared: "As well might it be said that the great business of travelers is to set out on journeys."[21] Holding that the great business of the gospel is to form men to God, he stressed the danger of focusing effort on getting conversions and failing to give attention to the cultivation of the Christian life in those already converted.

[19] Note examples in Stewart, George, *A History of Religious Education in Connecticut*, pp. 324 and 328–329.

[20] See Bushnell, Horace, *Views of Christian Nurture and of Subjects Adjacent Thereto* (Edwin Hunt, Hartford, 1847), pp. 123–146.

[21] *Ibid.*, p. 141.

In the next published article by Bushnell in this general area in the *New Englander* in October, 1844, under the title, "The Kingdom of Heaven as a Grain of Mustard Seed," [22] there was one section in which he set forth his views on the possibility of children being nurtured in the Christian life in the relationship with their parents in the life of the family, a viewpoint which was contrary to the current emphasis upon conversion. This raised questions in the ministerial association to which he belonged and he was invited by its members to discuss the subject of Christian training. Accordingly, he prepared two sermons on this subject for his congregation and read them to the ministerial association.[23]

In opposition to the common assumption "that the child is to grow up in sin, to be converted after he comes to a mature age," he affirmed that the true idea of Christian education is "that the child is to grow up a Christian." He made clear that he did not affirm "that every child may in fact and without exception, be so trained that he certainly will grow up a Christian," but that this should be the "aim, effort and expectation." [24] He did not

[22] This article was later renamed "Growth not Conquest the True Method of Christian Progress" and appeared in the 1847 volume on *Christian Nurture*, pp. 147–181.

[23] There was no dissent from his views and unanimous request was made for the publication of the addresses. While preparing them for the press, he received a request that they be offered to the Massachusetts Sabbath School Society for publication. They were accordingly published by this Society in 1847 with the statement on the title page, "Approved by the Committee on Publication." These *Discourses on Christian Nurture* received some favorable reviews, but a letter addressed to Dr. Bushnell from Bennett Tyler, President and Professor of Christian Theology in the Theological Institute of Connecticut, was read before the North Association of Hartford, strongly attacking the discourses because of their dangerous tendencies. This letter was published with the approval of the Association and was industriously circulated. (See Dr. Tyler's letter to Dr. Bushnell on Christian Nurture, privately published in 1847.) Frightened by this opposition, the Sabbath School Society withdrew the publication, and the two discourses together with other material were published by Edwin Hunt, Hartford, in the same year. Cheney, Mary Bushnell, editor, *Life and Letters of Horace Bushnell*, pp. 178–180.

[24] Bushnell, Horace, *Views of Christian Nurture and of Subjects Adjacent Thereto*, p. 6.

base this hope upon a conception of the "radical goodness of human nature," but on the belief that a child could have a "new heart" better than an adult. It seemed to him "unnatural and pernicious" to believe that "the plastic nature of childhood must first be hardened into stone, and stiffened into enmity towards God and all duty, before it can become a candidate for Christian character." [25] Bushnell had earlier (in 1844) in the article in the *New Englander,* which was published in this volume, emphasized the dilemma in which this practice placed childhood.

> If it may not grow in holy virtue,—if it must grow up in sin, till it comes to some definite age, before it is a candidate for repentance and a new life, then, during that interval, is it seen to lie under some doom more dismal and hapless than any other we are acquainted with in this world. Capable of sin—incapable of repentance.[26]

Thus, his objection emphasized the fact that in the practice of the church there was no philosophy for childhood. He says that "it would certainly be very singular, if Christ Jesus, in a scheme of mercy for the world, had found no place for infants and little children; more singular still if he had given them the place of adults; and worse than singular, if he had appointed them to years of sin as the necessary preparation for his mercy." [27]

In his *Views of Christian Nurture,* Bushnell showed how the current practice made Christian instruction ineffective and indeed worse than useless. Children were given to understand that these lessons could not be expected to be effective until they grew up.[28] But his conception of Christian nurture included more than instruction. He based it upon the degree to which the life of a little child is bound up with the life of his parents and he develops his attitudes and his practices, not so much from instruction as from his experience with his parents and in the home.[29]

[25] *Ibid.,* pp.14–15.
[26] *Ibid.,* p. 168.
[27] *Ibid.,* p. 39.

[28] *Ibid.,* pp. 11–12.
[29] *Ibid.,* p. 13.

He also emphasized the gradual development from complete dependency upon the parents into a will and individuality of his own. It is this period of growth from complete irresponsibility to maturity that is the period of Christian nurture.[30]

The center of Christian nurture, according to Bushnell, is the life and attitudes of the parents. Unless they are Christian in spirit and conduct, they cannot expect their children to grow up as Christians.[31] He held that the reason that many persons, remarkable for their piety, "have yet been so unfortunate in their children" was not difficult to understand. They are "yet very disagreeable persons, and that too, by reason of some very marked defect in their religious character. They display just that spirit, and act in just that manner, which is likely to make religion odious—the more odious the more urgently they commend it. Sometimes they appear well to the world one remove distant from them, they shine well in their written biography, but one living in their family will know what others do not; and if their children turn out badly, will never be at a loss for the reason. Many persons too have such defective views of the manner of teaching appropriate to early childhood, that they really discourage their children." [32]

He insisted also that at times the church made Christian nurture by parents difficult. "It is rent by divisions, burnt up by fanaticism, frozen by the chill of a worldly spirit, petrified in a rigid and dead orthodoxy. It makes no element of genial warmth and love about the child, according to the intention of Christ in its appointment, but gives to religion, rather, a forbidding aspect, and thus, instead of assisting the parent, becomes one of the worst impediments to his success." [33]

These points of emphasis of Bushnell sound more like the

---

[30] *Ibid.*, pp. 19–22.
[31] *Ibid.*, p. 41.

[32] *Ibid.*, p. 35.
[33] *Ibid.*, p. 37.

words of a psychologist in a modern child guidance clinic or of a present-day advocate of a social theory of education than like those of a theologian of the middle of the last century. But, unfortunately for the Christian education of the churches, the discussion of this book centered in its challenge to the theology of the time, while its practical suggestions in regard to Christian nurture have waited more than three-quarters of a century to be fully recognized in the theory and practice of religious education. Bushnell's emphasis challenged, and indeed outraged, those who followed the dominant Protestant belief that an individual could become a Christian only by the work of God through Christ in a definite experience of conversion when the age of accountability was reached.

The chief attacks upon the book were made by Bennett Tyler who objected to Bushnell's emphasis on the part parents might play in the development of the Christian life of children.[34] This seemed to him a denial of the fact that the heart of man, depraved throughout, could only be renewed by the sovereign act of God, independent of all human instrumentality.[35] He recognized the importance of parents instructing their children, but held that this was for the purpose of bringing them to conversion, and that the results of their labors, like those of the minister, were determined by God.[36] "That God is able to renew the heart of an infant," he recognized, but held that the question was whether "if parents are faithful, he will, as a general thing, renew thus early, the hearts of their children."[37] He held that Chris-

[34] Tyler, Bennett, *Letters to the Rev. Horace Bushnell, D.D., containing Strictures on his book entitled "Views of Christian Nurture and Subjects Adjacent Thereto."*

[35] *Dr. Tyler's Letter to Dr. Bushnell on Christian Nurture*, p. 4.

[36] *Ibid.*, p. 6.

[37] Tyler, Bennett, *Letters to the Rev. Horace Bushnell, D.D., containing Strictures on his Book entitled "Views of Christian Nurture and Subjects Adjacent Thereto,"* pp. 14–15.

tian history seemed to show that individuals were usually converted when they reached the years of accountability and implied that this was the plan of God. This he supports by various examples from the Bible and later history.[38] He feared that the adoption of Bushnell's viewpoints would lead parents to be complacent about the lost state of their children and lead the children to assume that they were Christians when they had never been convicted of sin or converted by the work of God. To him, bringing children up in the "nurture and admonition of the Lord" meant that they should be instructed as to their lost state and their need of salvation, and in no sense implied the type of Christian nurture which Bushnell had described. Princeton Seminary, in the person of Dr. Charles Hodge, objected that Bushnell had resolved the whole matter into organic laws, explaining away both depravity and grace, and that he took recourse to naturalism in explaining the whole subject.[39]

It is thus seen that while Bushnell claimed that he believed in the depravity of human nature and that Christian experience was the work of God, he had a conception of both very different from that held by those who opposed his views. His conception of God as omnipresent and at work in nature and all aspects of life—which he developed more fully in his later writings—gave him the theological basis for the nurture of children in the Christian life in and through the life of the family. The differences were fundamental ones in the conception of man and of God, and particularly of God's relation to human life and destiny. The issue between an "evangelistic" and an "educational" emphasis, brought to a head by Bushnell's writings, has continued down to the present time and is one form of the conflict now in evidence.

[38] *Ibid.*, Letter VI. He also attacked Bushnell's idea of spiritual growth and said that conquest of stubborn wills was necessary if the work of God was to be accomplished.

[39] Stewart, George, *A History of Religious Education in Connecticut*, p. 355.

While the discussions which grew out of Bushnell's writings tended to increase the recognition of the importance of Christian education and while perhaps he may be said to be the "father" of the religious education movement, unfortunately the conflict centered upon the theological issue of the *possibility* of Christian nurture rather than upon the educational question as to *kind* of nurture which was to be given. Therefore, while Bushnell's writings helped to reinforce those who wished an emphasis upon Christian education in the churches, his practical suggestions in regard to the kind of nurture which would be effective seemed to have had little influence at the time. Even though his suggestions were in direct contrast to the kind of religious instruction which prevailed in the Christian education of the churches, this continued to be the prevailing method.

CHAPTER III

The Development of an Educational Approach

A DIRECT EDUCATIONAL challenge to the program of the Protestant churches came in the latter part of the last century. While there had been opposition to the uniform lessons ever since their adoption in 1872, little or nothing was said about the educational unsuitability of one lesson for all ages. The opposition was on other grounds: "(1) that they were fragmentary, skipping here and there about the Bible and giving little or no continuous study of it; (2) that there was no opportunity for the denominations to teach their own particular doctrines; (3) that the lessons ignored missions and social-reform movements; (4) that they did not sufficiently recognize and emphasize the church year." [1]

Two factors were important in the opposition to the uniform lesson system with its inadequate educational methods. One was the historical criticism of the Bible, the so-called "higher criticism." While this was bitterly fought at first by the conservative leaders in the churches, nevertheless there came to be increasing recognition of the fact that Bible study and teaching involved more than moralizing on isolated texts or passages, irrespective of the authorship of the books and of the historical setting of the events. Historical criticism showed the inadequacy of the common method in Sunday Schools of reading individual verses and trying to discover their meaning and application; and it also made of Bible study a more serious matter than was assumed in most of the uniform lesson quarterlies.

[1] Betts, George Herbert, *The Curriculum of Religious Education*, pp. 130–131.

34

It is interesting that the first graded lessons that were successful rivals of the uniform system grew out of this historical approach to the study of the Bible. They were prepared by Erastus Blakeslee, who had been a former student of William Rainey Harper at Yale and who had learned and accepted Dr. Harper's method of inductive Bible study. As a Congregational minister in New England, he had tried to apply an educational method to the uniform lessons without success. Being unable to secure any coöperation from the International Lesson Committee for the development of graded lessons, he prepared a system of his own known as the Blakeslee lessons.[2] Since these lessons were backed by many prominent educators, college presidents, ministers, and others, they became successful rivals of the uniform lessons of the denominations.[3]

A second influence which reinforced the emphasis upon the need for more thorough study of the Bible grew out of the attention given to an educational approach and method in general education. The educational ideas of Pestalozzi, Froebel, and Herbart were influencing public school education. Particularly

[2] The Bible Study Publishing Company of Boston commenced the publication of these lessons in 1891, and in 1893 the Bible Study Union was formed in New York for the promotion of the Blakeslee lessons as embodying better methods of studying and teaching the Scriptures than were available elsewhere. These lessons were later taken over by Charles Scribner's Sons, New York, and embodied in the system of graded lessons developed by that firm. Betts, George Herbert, *The Curriculum of Religious Education*, pp. 131–132.

[3] Other graded series were also developed: The Lutheran Graded Series in 1895; Constructive Studies in Religion, in the development of which President William Rainey Harper of the University of Chicago took the lead and which were published by the University of Chicago Press; The Beacon Course, prepared by the Unitarians; The Christian Nurture Series of the Protestant Episcopal Church; and the graded series of Bible study, initiated by Henry B. Sharman for use in voluntary Y.M.C.A. groups in colleges and universities and published by the Association Press. Since our interest is in tracing the development of an educational approach in the general stream of Protestant religious education, these special series are not included in the survey. They had, however, a definite influence on the developments and were in turn a product of these developments.

was this true in the latter years of the century when Herbart's plan of teaching subject matter was widely adopted. Normal schools and other teacher training institutions were giving large attention to Herbartian psychology and methodology and the working out of lesson plans on the Herbartian procedure was an important part of the training. The haphazard lessons and teaching in the Sunday Schools made a poor showing alongside these developments in public schools.

The discussion in the churches was centered in the demand from various quarters for a system of graded lessons to replace or to be used as an alternative to the uniform system. Various experiments were tried and books written, all of which had their influence. But the greatest opposition to the uniform system of lessons came, as might have been expected, from the primary leaders and teachers, for it was in the material for the earlier years that the unsuitability of a uniform system was most seriously felt. As early as 1884 a group of women had organized themselves into the National Primary Union and had demanded of the International Lesson Committee the provision of lesson material better suited to younger children. In various ways primary workers in the ensuing years brought pressure to bear with only partial success;[4] but this demand finally reached the stage of effective action under the leadership of Mrs. J. Woodbridge Barnes, who was the Superintendent of the Elementary Division of the International Sunday School Association. Speaking, as they knew she did, for a large number of primary and other leaders in the churches, she obtained in 1906 from the International Executive Committee permission for coöperative action in planning graded lessons for the primary and junior departments. On the basis of this action, Mrs. Barnes organized what was

---

[4] See Brown, Arlo Ayres, *A History of Religious Education in Recent Times,* pp. 101–103, and Betts, George Herbert, *The Curriculum of Religious Education,* pp. 136–147.

known as the Graded Lesson Conference which took responsibility for outlining the International Graded Series. By the action of the Lesson Committee itself in 1908, this "conference" was made in effect a sub-committee for the preparation of the outlines for the new lessons.

A system of graded lessons thus came to be officially recognized by the International Lesson Committee as a parallel series to the uniform lessons. The denominational problem was solved in the same manner as in the uniform lessons by leaving to the denominations the preparation of the actual lesson material on the basis of the outlines furnished by the interdenominational committee. In turn, the support of the enterprise by the Sunday School editors of several of the leading denominations was an important factor in its success.

In the adoption of graded lessons the Protestant churches in North America recognized an educational approach as of major importance in their religious education. Both in subject matter and in method the lessons were to be suited to the age and attainment of the pupil. Further, the idea of nurture of children in the Christian life was made fundamental. It is true that these lessons were planned to look forward to children's own decision for Christ and church membership at about twelve years of age, but such decisions were considered a normal stage in the educational process.[5] For those adopting the graded lesson principle, nurture through instruction in home and church came to be considered the normal method of ensuring that children should grow up as Christians and take their places in the adult membership of the church. Dependence, however, was not placed upon this alone. It was expected that children and young people should participate in the religious practices of church worship and prayer and that

[5] The Lutheran Graded System, adopted in 1895, and the Christian Nurture series, projected in 1912 by the Protestant Episcopal Church, both provided for training in church doctrines and practices and looked forward to confirmation at about fourteen years of age.

these should be supplemented by the "family altar" and a personal devotional life. But such parallel religious practices were not looked upon at this period as fundamentally a part of the educational process and were not in any way challenged by the new educational developments.

The Herbartian procedures, still in vogue at the time in the public schools, were adopted in the preparation of the new lessons. Herbart's rather than Pestalozzi's and Froebel's educational ideas were more influential in this period because they demanded a less drastic change in education. The Herbartian procedure offered an improved methodology by which subject matter could be taught, and therefore enabled the public schools to continue to make subject matter the main element in the educational process. It was but natural that in the development of these new lessons, a Herbartian method should be used, since such an approach seemed especially suited to the lesson purposes. This method was centered in subject matter, and therefore was suited for study of the Bible. It built on the information and ideas the child already possessed— the "apperceptive mass," as it was called—and therefore was suited to a graded series. It aimed to supplement information already possessed and to present new information, not for its own sake, but for a moral purpose. The steps of the Herbartian process led up to a generalization or general principle which was to be applied in life. This was suited to the moral and religious purpose of Bible study in church schools. It also made possible the use of the results of historical criticism and therefore seemed ideally suited to the status of Bible study itself. The new lessons were aimed to bring to children of various ages the truths from the Bible and from extra-Biblical material which were suited to the needs, interests and attainments of various grades of pupils.[6]

[6] In her first report to the International Lesson Committee, Mrs. Barnes said: "We are agreed upon the needs and interests of pupils in the grades concerned, and the corresponding truths to be embodied in the lessons selected." Quoted by Brown, Arlo Ayres, *A History of Religious Education in Recent Times*, p. 109.

The shift from an emphasis upon the truths which were essential to conversion to those which were useful in the actual Christian life of children and young people, the grading of material to make it suitable to the age and advancement of the pupils, and the development of improved methods for making this knowledge and truth intelligible to children of various ages, all marked a distinct advance over the uniform lesson system. But in understanding the present issues, it is necessary to recognize that the graded lessons did not fundamentally challenge the authoritarian Biblical approach and emphasis which had characterized Protestant religious education during the nineteenth century. These lessons merely offered a better selection of material and provided a more effective method for understanding and applying the Biblical and other truths. In the Herbartian procedure, the outcome expected is stated in the aim, and the teaching plan consists of steps by which this predetermined outcome is to be reached. Therefore, the procedure is ideally suited for teaching authoritatively doctrines or interpretations of the Christian religion. As a matter of fact, instruction in the Bible and in the truths of the Christian religion was trusted even more completely in churches using the graded lessons than it had been in churches with the evangelistic emphasis when Christian education was considered a preparation for conversion. Where there was fundamental opposition, it came from those who still held to the "evangelistic" emphasis, thinking of the Sunday School as preparation for the supreme experience of conversion and trusting to revival methods to secure these crucial decisions.[7] These opponents criticized the graded lessons because of their failure to recognize sufficiently the need of divine transformation of the individual child through conversion or a similar experience. The opposition was based, therefore, as was that to Horace Bushnell, on theological

[7] There was, it is true, an issue around the use of extra-Biblical material; but those who wished such material to be used recognized the primacy of the Bible.

rather than on educational grounds. None of this opposition to the graded lessons was aimed at confidence in instruction in the Bible and in Christian truth. Rather, it was aimed at the purpose of such instruction.

A fundamental criticism of the authoritarian conception of religious education, which persisted even in the new graded lessons, has developed during the present century. This has grown out of the general educational movement known as progressive education. But this development, as has already been indicated, originated outside of the churches and was free from authoritarian theological domination. Modern religious education is a part of progressive education. It is out of the challenge in this movement to the authoritarian conceptions of Protestant religious education that the present conflicts have arisen. In order to understand the present issues, it is necessary to review this educational development in its bearing upon the theory and practice of religious education.

The development known as progressive education has been influenced by Pestalozzi and by one of his famous disciples, Froebel, more than it has by Herbart, another of Pestalozzi's followers, whose influence upon religious education has already been indicated. Pestalozzi received his inspiration from Rousseau's *Emile*. He followed Rousseau in rejecting the religious aim for education and the teaching of mere words and facts, and he built his proposals on Rousseau's emphasis that sense impression is the basis of human knowledge. Discovering the impracticability of Rousseau's suggestions through his efforts to apply them in the education of his own child, Pestalozzi started to observe and study children, for he believed that education must be based on the nature of the child and the natural laws for his development, and, therefore that education was a "drawing out instead of a pouring in." Teaching, he felt, must proceed from the concrete to the abstract, and he considered that the "environment or experience of the child is the most valuable means and materials of his instruction. Observation and investigation instead of memorizing and class discussion, and thinking instead of reciting, characterized his work." [8] Pestalozzi was opposed to the brutal discipline, which had characterized the schools and which was based on the belief in the depravity of the child, and attempted to substitute for it a "loving discipline." When his school was described as not like a school but a family, Pestalozzi considered this the highest praise which could have been given.

The name of Friedrich Froebel is associated with the development of kindergartens in the United States. The term itself was of Froebel's coining and kindergartens have been more widely developed in the United States than in any other country. But the basic ideas of Froebel, which could most easily be embodied in the newly formed education for little children, have been influential beyond the kindergarten in American education. These include such ideas as that "self-activity, determined by the child's interests and desires and intelligently directed, is essential to the unfolding of the child's inborn capacities," [9] that self-realization takes place through social participation or coöperation, and that learning takes place by doing. [10] He was a potent factor also in bringing about the appreciation of the significance of play and of hand-work in the education of children. John Dewey sought to embody the principles of Froebel in the experimental school which he conducted at the University of Chicago. This experiment was widely influential.

John Dewey has perhaps been the most influential interpreter of an approach and emphasis which are in the tradition of Pesta-

---

[8] Knight, Edgar W., *Education in the United States*, p. 314.
[9] Cubberley, Ellwood P., *The History of Education*, p. 767.
[10] Knight, Edgar W., *Education in the United States*, pp. 519–520.

lozzi and Froebel. Fully accepting the scientific outlook on life, having a pragmatic type of philosophy which emphasized the function of theory as an interpretation of and a guide to practical activities, and being concerned with educational and other social movements of the day, he developed an educational philosophy which embodied the most significant of the contributions of Pestalozzi and Froebel. But his philosophy contained distinctive contributions of his own in which he interpreted the possibility and the function of education in the development of significant living in present-day society. Emphasizing that education must be based on an understanding of the nature of the child and the way children grow, he felt that, since they must live not in a school but in a society, the work in the school should have direct connection with the activities outside of the school. The school must be in a sense the world in miniature in which children by participation would learn not only the skills and attitudes which were essential to social living, but would also come to an intelligent understanding of the world in which they lived. Knowledge was therefore not an end in itself, but was useful only as it brought understanding of the world about one and furnished resources for the control and direction of one's activities. He felt that the child learns to participate intelligently in life and to utilize the experience which is embodied in accumulated knowledge only as he is given opportunities to use his mind in relation to the activities in which he participates. In this process of living, the goals of endeavor are to be just as much chosen in the process as are the means for realizing those goals. "Learning by doing" to Dewey, is no mere method by which whatever adults wish is learned, but rather takes on true social significance because it is to him the way in which children learn to participate in the society of which they are a part. For him the experience process of living is similar to the educational process, and the nearer the school can approximate the conditions of life experience, the more significant will the school become.

The educational principles of Pestalozzi and Froebel, particularly as modified and amplified in the interpretations of Dewey, became very influential in the United States. But the emphasis upon "learning by doing," upon growth in and through social experience, upon the use of knowledge as a guide to activity, and upon the use of the intelligence in determining goals and in making choices, is very different from those ideas which had dominated general and religious education. Religious education built on these principles could in no sense be a method for bringing saving truth to children, but would be a process through which growth in Christian life and experience took place and in which the Christian goals and beliefs were determined. Such points of emphasis were not only diametrically opposed to an authoritarian conception of religious education, but they had developed independently of the church and of direct religious influences. They were distinctly educational in their origin and emphasis.

Another potent though related influence came in the development of educational psychology at the beginning of the century. In its bearing on education, psychology has had two main aspects: first, a study of the nature of the child and of the differences between children; and, second, an examination of the educative process itself or how children and adults learn and grow. The conception of child nature was based on the observation and study of children. While G. Stanley Hall's methods have not fully met the test of later, more scientific study, his life-long work in collecting data regarding children, culminating in his work on adolescence, really marked the inauguration of this approach and emphasis in the United States. Although himself a philosopher, William James opposed the scholastic psychology and attempted to describe the inborn capacities and instincts of man which education must take into account. Building on William James and on his own work in animal psychology, Edward L. Thorndike published in 1913 the volume in his three-volume *Educational Psychology* on "The Original Nature of Man." Later it will be necessary to examine these conceptions of original nature, but it is sufficient at this point to indicate that this attempt to discover the nature of those to be educated by a scientific study of human beings represented a different approach to the problem from the conceptions of man as derived from theology. It further resulted in a conception of human beings which emphasized the possibility of the modification and development of inborn capacities through education rather than one which stressed the depravity of human nature and the necessity for a special act of divine grace.

The study of the educative process, of how individuals learn and grow, was also important. William James in his *Principles of Psychology* and particularly in his widely influential *Talks to Teachers* had worked out a practical educational psychology; and G. Stanley Hall, in the now repudiated recapitulation theory, according to which the growth of the individual recapitulates the stages of development of the race, furnished a theory of individual growth which had large influence, particularly in organizations with programs of activities. But the scientific study of the learning process may be said to have been inaugurated in America by Edward L. Thorndike, who was invited to Teachers College, Columbia University, to be the first instructor in educational psychology in this country. Called, as he was, to help teachers improve the educational procedures for which they were responsible by giving them a better understanding of how learning takes place, Thorndike carried on experimental research in connection with the three main subjects of the public school curriculum—reading, writing, and arithmetic. He also studied the development of mechanical skills, such as typewriting. Out of this experimental work Thorndike formulated what he called the "laws of learning," the essence of which was that an individual learns what he practices with success and satisfaction.[11]

While these researches were not within the area of moral and religious education, the results challenged the assumption of Protestant theology that a change of heart was necessary before there could be a change of conduct. It seemed that a change of heart accompanied and was dependent upon a change of conduct. The results of these researches also formed a fundamental challenge to the Herbartian assumptions as to how learning takes place and as to how moral conduct is determined. Study of the actual processes of learning seemed to show that the individual did not first master the knowledge and the principles and then apply these in action, as Herbart had assumed, but that these two aspects of the learning process went on together and were integrally inter-related. For example, in learning to use English correctly in speech and writing the child did not first learn the rules and principles of grammar and then apply these to sentence construction. Instead, the experimental work confirmed common sense observation that mastery of writing English correctly grew out of practice in actual writing and that the principles and rules of correct usage were best learned in direct relation to such practice.

While these experiments had been carried on in connection with public school subjects and ordinary life practices, there seemed no reason why the laws of learning did not apply to moral conduct as well as to intellectual and mechanical skills. There seemed to be confirmation of Bushnell's emphasis upon the practice of Christianity within the home circle and under the

[11] Thorndike, Edward L., *Educational Psychology*, Volume II.

influence of parents as the basis for the development of individuals who were both in practice and conviction Christians. But such an idea directly contradicted the conception of a depraved nature which had to be transformed by the work of God. It gave a psychological basis for nurture, but was out of harmony with the traditional approach to the problem.

These earlier researches had been in areas of "secular" learning and did not directly touch the question of morals and religion. But on the initiation of leaders in religious education through the Religious Education Association, an extended study was financed by the Institute of Social and Religious Research and conducted through Teachers College, Columbia University, by Dr. Hugh Hartshorne and Dr. Mark May, under the general supervision of Professor Edward L. Thorndike.[12] This was known as the Character Education Inquiry and was directly within the areas of concern to religious education. As the result of testing hundreds of children, there was found to be little or no relationship between the moral knowledge of right and wrong on the part of the pupils and their actual conduct in definite situations, where there was opportunity for the practice of honesty or dishonesty and the like. More than this, there seemed to be no general characteristics of honesty in these children, but rather varieties of conduct dependent upon factors in the particular situations. A slight change in the situation seemed to modify the conduct. Those who conducted the research came to the conclusion that the moral education which these children had received had resulted in no general moral standards which controlled their conduct. They concluded that their moral knowledge was unrelated to the situations in which it would be used and had as a

---

[12] Character Education Inquiry, May, Mark A., and Hartshorne, Hugh, *Studies in the Nature of Character:* I Studies in Deceit; II Studies in Service and Self-Control; III Studies in the Organization of Character.

result little or no effect upon conduct. Thus, this extensive and costly research within the very area of moral and religious education appeared to confirm the challenge that had come through the experimental work in public education as to the effectiveness of instruction in morals and religion based on the Herbartian procedure.

Paralleling these experimental researches, searching analyses of the educative process were being made by leaders in the philosophy of education. In 1910 John Dewey published *How We Think,* in which he said that reflective thinking is not a formal logical process, in which deductions are made from accepted assumptions, but rather a method of finding one's way in a problematical situation where a problem is faced and various possible answers are explored in the search for the true solution. This description involved a direct criticism of the Herbartian procedure of commencing with generalizations or princples and then deducing applications. He pressed this searching analysis further in other writings on education, notably in *Democracy and Education,* in which he insisted that the educational process was similar to that of learning in ordinary life situations (the educational process is the experience process), the only difference being that in organized education aid and direction were given to the experience. He criticized the dualism involved in thinking of subject matter as something to be learned and later to be used in life. He said that it represented instead the record of accumulated experience in meeting the situations of life which might be used to advantage in meeting present situations to which it is pertinent. Following this viewpoint would involve a different organization of the Biblical material from that followed in the current Sunday School lessons.

The laws of learning were also fundamentally analyzed in their bearing upon moral and religious education. William H.

Kilpatrick, in his classes at Teachers College, Columbia University, and later in his book, *Foundations of Method,* pointed out that the learning process is a more complicated and vital matter than has sometimes been assumed by those who accept the conception of learning what is practiced. He held that in every learning situation, there is not only the direct response to the matter in hand—the arithmetic table, the passage to be read, the poem to be learned, the Bible verses to be memorized—but there are associated responses both to the material and to other factors in the situation, such as the teacher and the other pupils. As a result, there are what he called concomitant learnings: the motives or purposes which are operative, whether to please the teacher, to avoid punishment, to surpass some other pupil, or to see the significance of what is being studied; and there are the feelings about the process, whether of liking, distaste, or resentment. Kilpatrick held that these associated responses and these concomitant learnings are of prime importance because they represent the fundamental motives and attitudes which are being developed and which will be more determinative of future conduct than the actual lesson which is mastered. Particularly did he emphasize that, in moral and religious education, these motives and attitudes are important. He showed that these never could be learned directly, as was so often assumed, but that they are determined by the conditions under which the child's school, church, or other experience is carried on.

A still further exploration of the learning process was made by what are known as the Gestalt psychologists. The laws of learning had been developed on the basis of what Thorndike had called the S-R bond psychology, which held that habits and skills were developed through Stimuli (S) to which Responses (R) were made. On the basis of experiments in learning, chiefly with animals, Thorndike held that learning was largely a trial and error process in which the responses which brought success and satisfaction were gradually learned and those which brought failure and dissatisfaction were avoided.

Wolfgang Köhler, who was interned in Africa during the Great War, carried on experiments with apes.[13] He had the apes in a more natural situation than had been furnished for Thorndike's monkeys, and his experiments seemed to show that, while there was an element of trial and error in the efforts of the monkey to reach the fruit, there seemed to come a time when the ape saw the relation between the boxes and his ability to reach the fruit on the trees, or between the sticks and reaching the fruit outside of the enclosure. He held that in the learning process, where the elements were in a Gestalt or configuration, there was a capacity to see the relation between means and ends and to short-cut the trial and error learning by insight into the relation of means to the end. Psychologists of this school repeated the experiments of Helmholtz and others in perception, with the result that they insisted that the response is not to a stimulus, but to a situation which is a configuration with something in the foreground as the focus of attention but influenced by the background of which it is a part. Further, they insisted, as Kilpatrick had already in part pointed out, that the response is not a simple matter but a response of the entire organism. The Gestalt viewpoint gave psychological formulation to the emphasis which had already been made by Dewey and others as to the possibilities of learning in and through meeting problematical life situations.

These developments in general education and in educational psychology had an influence upon the leaders in the churches, particularly those who had taken their theological training in centers where there were schools of education. The educational

[13] See Köhler, Wolfgang, *The Mentality of Apes.*

principles, as set forth in the educational courses and as embodied to a greater or less degree in demonstration or experimental schools, were very different from the kind of religious education which was found in the churches, even where the denominational graded lessons with their improved Herbartian procedures had been adopted, and those who took this educational training felt the contrast. Some of those trained in the newer educational principles took places as denominational or inter-denominational secretaries or on the boards of the denominations, and brought their criticisms to bear.

Because of these influences and because of the practical difficulties in carrying out a Herbartian plan of teaching, modifications had actually been made in the practice of many religious educators. In the practical use of the Herbartian plan of teaching, both in public education and in religious education, it had been found that the use of knowledge which the pupils already had for the first step of preparation did not bring interest and vitality in teaching, and consequently incidents or situations out of life experience were often used for what came to be called the point of contact in teaching. Often use was made of this same incident or situation in applying the principles arrived at through the steps of presentation, comparison and generalization. Consequently, in practice, a Herbartian plan, modified in the direction of life situations and experience, was often used. Some had gone even further and made a more fundamental modification in the plan of teaching a lesson or conducting the discussion of a group. The writer, influenced by John Dewey's analysis of the process of reflective thinking in his book, *How We Think,* had developed in his work with student and other Bible and discussion groups what he termed a life situation approach. In this plan, the actual life situation being faced was described and explored in the group, the possible alternatives of action were defined, these were compared on the basis of their probable consequences in the situation, if put into effect; they were evaluated on the basis of points of emphasis in the Bible or other Christian teaching, and the group was led to make either individual or group decision as to what to do in the situation or what attitude to take in the solution of the problem. Discussion followed on plans for putting the decision into effect in the life situation. In this plan, Biblical and other experience was studied historically in what was in fact a life-situation approach to secure perspective and emphasis for meeting the present situation.

The idea of learning in and through activity had also been developed to a certain extent in the churches and the allied agencies. The Christian Associations and similar agencies had come to believe that activities had character-training value. At times there was an almost naïve faith in the effect of physical activities, for example, in developing fair play and sportsmanship; but, nevertheless, this recognition that activities themselves had character value was an important advance. Under the influence of these allied agencies and also through their own experience, the churches came to see that recreational and social activities, which had at first been introduced into the churches with the idea of holding children and particularly young people to the church, had significance of themselves in the educational process.

On the basis of the conception that one learned what he practiced, what was known as the project principle or the project method had been developed in general education, and had come to be adopted to a certain extent in the religious education of the churches. A project, according to William H. Kilpatrick, one of the chief exponents of this development, is a purposeful activity, in which the purpose guides the process and furnishes the drive.[14] Since among the enterprises which were recognized were those in

[14] Kilpatrick, William H., *The Project Method.*

which individuals and groups might set themselves to study subject matter, the project principle was used in the churches chiefly as a way of attempting to motivate study and other enterprises which were either already a part of the program or were chosen by the teacher, rather than as endeavors which children and teacher together initiated and planned. Nevertheless, this emphasis did lead to the development of some real projects in churches and helped to shift the work of religious education from formal instruction to significant enterprises and activities in which children participated in a responsible manner.

As in the case of the discussion of the possibility of Christian nurture which was precipitated seventy years earlier by Horace Bushnell's *Views of Christian Nurture,* the issue in regard to the type of religious education which prevailed in the churches was focused by a significant book. A recognized leader of the religious education movement, one of the founders of the Religious Education Association, published in 1917 *A Social Theory of Religious Education,*[15] in which he interpreted the newer psychological and educational developments in their particular bearing upon religious education. Indeed this book antedated some of the developments which have already been reviewed. In this book he insisted that the "first concern of education is not a textbook or anything that printer's ink can convey." Instead, "the central fact of the educative process is a growing Christian experience in and through the pupil's social interactions." On the basis of the conception that "where love is, God is" he expressed the belief that it was possible to have a religious education which is fundamentally religious. He said that it will consist "in providing for children conditions in which love is experienced, practiced, wrought into steady and deliberate living by the help of both intellectual analysis and habit formation, and developed into

[15] Coe, George Albert, *A Social Theory of Religious Education.*

a faith that illumines the crises and the mysteries of life." [16] This seemed to Coe to give the basis for a "most vital theory of Christian instruction. For now instead of attempting to transfer to the child mind certain truths that we hope will enter into his experience in a vital manner at some indefinite future time, we help him to define, understand, and improve something that he is already doing and enjoying. There is no longer the deadly separation of knowing from doing, or of Christian doctrine from Christian experience." [17] In the procedures which had been followed, he said that "the very attempt to exalt the Bible devitalized it, concealed it, by making it a thing *per se,* to be first known apart from experience and only afterward applied in experience." [18] Further, "if the curriculum is fundamentally a course in Christian living, the Bible will be used at each turn of the child's experience in such a way as to help him with the particular problem that is then uppermost." [19] He added: " . . . The theory of the curriculum is to be based squarely upon the idea of incarnation—that God makes himself known to us in concrete human life." Religious experience is awakened in children, according to his viewpoint through their contacts with persons who already have such experiences. The Bible with its record of religious experience "takes its place as a means that mightily assists in promoting, illuminating, and confirming these contacts, and in extending the Christian fellowship backward to Jesus and the prophets, and forward toward the fulfilling of the prophetic ideals." [20] As to the choice and arrangement of the Biblical material, "the changing social situations incident to the pupil's growth, with their inevitable problems of social adjustment, furnish a basis for the order and use of the material." [21]

---

[16] *Ibid.,* p. 80.
[17] *Ibid.,* p. 82.
[18] *Ibid.,* p. 103.

[19] *Ibid.,* p. 114.
[20] *Ibid.,* p. 113.
[21] *Ibid.,* p. 105.

These brief excerpts from the book show what is confirmed by careful reading, viz., that it contained a fundamental criticism of the kind of religious education which was found even in the denominational graded lessons and the new program of religious education in the churches. It proposed the organization of religious education around social experience and held that growth in the Christian life came in and through pupils' social interactions.

While this book precipitated the issue and doubtless had an influence upon later action which was taken by denominational leaders, practical difficulties made this action possible. While it had been expected that the new graded lessons would eventually supplant the uniform series, this expectation seemed not likely to be realized. As a matter of fact, not more than one-fourth of the churches ever adopted the denominational graded series; and with the advent of the graded lessons, those interested in the maintenance of the Uniform Series gave themselves to their improvement through the embodiment of the educational points of emphasis of the graded lessons in the adaptation of themes to the various age levels and in treatment of the lessons for the various ages. The Improved Uniform Lessons were successful competitors of the graded lessons. The difficulty of the closely graded lessons, that is, of lessons for every age or grade, led also to the proposal for Departmental Graded Lessons.

An equal if not a more important factor was the practical situation faced by the churches and their leaders in religious education. A demand had been placed upon religious education in the churches, which it had not previously had to meet, because religion and the church no longer occupied the former dominant place in the life of the community. In the more unified community life of another generation, children grew up under circumstances in which the tenets and practices of religion were accepted in all aspects of their lives in home, school, and church. The general community sentiment was on the side of religion and the "sinners" in the community were on the defensive. However important the church might consider its religious instruction to be, children were not in fact solely dependent upon it for their religious education any more than they were dependent upon the school for their general education. Growing up in situations in which every aspect of their experience was controlled by the assumptions of the Christian religion about life and destiny, they came to accept them as they did language and customs and other aspects of the common life.

It will be recognized at once that religious education in the churches has not in recent years had the advantage of any such unity in the experience of children and young people. The young are exposed to many and diverse influences, among which the assumptions of the Christian religion no longer hold the dominant place. Homes, even of church members, are less controlled by religious assumptions and practices. The schools are more completely secularized. Children are often exposed through radio, movie, and newspaper to experiences and points of view which are distinctly contrary to the Christian religion. In the community life itself, it often seems that it is the churches rather than the "sinners" who are on the defensive. In short, life for children and young people has not only become more definitely secularized, but explicitly anti-religious influences have been brought to bear upon it.

Not only has there been this change in the kind of experience to which children and young people are exposed, but there has also developed a keener recognition on the part of Christians of the gap between even the best assumptions and practices of community life and the demands of the Christian religion. It has come to be recognized that part of the reason that religious education was so much easier for another generation was because Christians identified "Christian" with what was accepted as decent, and did not recognize the degree to which even the best life of that time fell short of the ideals of the Christian religion. The problem which religious education and the church was forced to face was not that of inducting children and young people into the accepted culture and attempting to consecrate it by labeling it Christian, but rather of developing a quality of life and a type of experience which were often in conflict with the established mores and morals. It was in the face of this crucial practical situation that the inadequacy of the educational procedures in the churches became glaringly evident.

In view of this situation, the International Lesson Committee, the continuing body which since 1872 had been actually charged with the coöperative creation of lesson plans for the Protestant churches of America, appointed at its meeting in New York City, April 6 and 7, 1920, a commission of seven to study the lesson situation and recommend future policy with reference to the creation of lesson materials.[22] After two years of study of the situation, this commission recommended to the Committee on Education of the International Council of Religious Education at its meeting December 8, 1922, three basic types of course: (1) Group graded lessons in cycles of three years; (2) the Uniform lessons (without adaptations below the Intermediate Department); and (3) an entirely new course to be known as "The International Curriculum of Religious Education" to be built from the ground up and to include Sunday and week-day instruction. It further recommended that for the present the graded lessons be left without revision. A committee of eight members

[22] The writer is under special obligation to Dr. Wade Crawford Barclay of the Methodist Episcopal Board of Education for the loan of his complete file of minutes and other documents connected with this development, which have been used in this part of the chapter.

was appointed to undertake the construction of the new International Curriculum. Professor William C. Bower was made chairman. Not only were there on the committee members who, like Professor Bower, were acquainted with the newer educational developments and were leaders in progressive religious education, but this committee associated with itself an advisory committee of six outstanding leaders in the general field of education, in order, as the committee stated, "to place back of the work of the Curriculum Committee a thoroughly representative body of American educational opinion." Thus provision was made for the results of the general educational developments to be brought directly to bear upon the religious education of the churches. A distinctly educational approach was introduced into the work of the churches by the action of the denominational leaders themselves.

This Curriculum Committee set itself first to the formulation of a basic theory for the new curriculum. This work occupied it for two years and the formulation went through several revisions. The first basic statement in this theory of the curriculum is: [23] "Religious education should center in the experience of the child." In amplification of this it is stated that the teaching process not only "takes its point of departure from the experience of the child," but "it should seek to direct and enrich that experience in its religious aspects with a view to the adequate control of conduct and the development of a Christian personality." Such conscious direction of religious experience "presupposes an evaluation of the varying types of religious experience, the formulation of standards whereby these types may be evaluated and a study of the processes through which conduct may be controlled." Emphasis is placed upon the importance of the experience of the

[23] *Statement of a Theory of the Curriculum,* Second Issue for the Subcommittee on International Curriculum, January 25, 1924.

child in the educative process. "The experience of each child is of worth on its own account, and the best possible preparation for the future is to be had through the performance of functions normal to the present." But the experience of the child is not isolated or separated from that of adults. "Some of the most educative of these functions grow out of the fact that the child does not live an isolated life, but actually participates in the interests and activities of adult life."

Religious education is not only concerned with the direction of experience but also with its enrichment. It is stated in this theory of the curriculum that experiences may be enriched: "(1) by helping to bring about situations that are rich and desirable; (2) by helping growing persons to see the significance in elements and factors that might otherwise be overlooked, to lift his responses into more definite consciousness in such a way as to secure reflection upon them and so make them the objects of purposeful choice, and to feel regret at improper and undesirable responses, and so develop desirable responses into permanent attitudes and roles of conduct."

A different conception of subject matter from that current at the time is emphasized. "Subject matter of study should include not only historical and racially systematized knowledge but also problematic life situations to which actual responses must be made. Subject matter outcomes should analogously include habits, attitudes, ideals, skills and other elements of control involved in responding to situations as well as permanently systematized knowledge." Knowledge is not something separate from experience. On the contrary, it "arises within experience," and it has "its origin in the activities of individuals and groups, and its motivation in the furthering of their activities." Indeed, according to this theory of the curriculum, "the primary function of information is to enable individuals and groups to understand their experience and to control it." The sources of this information are "the accumulated stores of systematized experience to which the child should be directed for help in securing the knowledge required to interpret and control his own personal experience." In this storehouse of past experience, "the various forms of religious literature are valuable for religious education because they record the experience men have had of God and of other spiritual values. The Bible is the incomparable source of such material."

There is in this theory an emphasis upon a different type of organization of the church school. "Since subject matter is implicit in all the activities of the school, the school organization should, accordingly, provide for selecting experiences essential to Christian conduct." To this end "it should seek to set up in miniature an ideal Christian community in which the growing person increasingly participates."

As to method, it is stated that "the responses that are most educative are those in which the growing person in association with other mature persons and adults is thoughtfully active in bringing worthy ends to pass." Therefore, "the central requirement as to method is that the individual be led into whole-hearted activities that help to build the Kingdom of God." Such activities should be: "(1) suited to the individual's capacity; (2) loaded with problems that raise relations, functions, and responsibilities definitely into consciousness, that call for reflection, and that are capable of indefinite expansion; (3) social and shared; (4) continuous with the remainder of the individual's experience, so that his religious principles become a controlling factor in the whole of his conduct."

There is a closing note that "such an educational program as is contemplated in the foregoing statement of theory cannot be constructed by revising existing courses, whether by omission, addition, or enrichment, but only by formulating a new and comprehensive curriculum which shall embody these principles."

This "theory of the curriculum," after extended discussion and careful review, was later adopted by the Educational Commission of the International Council of Religious Education [24] for recommendation to the forty-one constituent denominations of the Council as the basis for a new curriculum of religious education.[25] While in the report of the committee it has been recommended that uniform, departmental graded, and closely graded lessons be continued, the theory for a new curriculum which the Committee formulated contained in fact a fundamental criticism of these parallel lessons. Acceptance of this theory would seem inevitably to lead to the conclusion that the new closely graded lessons as well as the uniform lessons were based upon an incorrect understanding of the educational process. There was in this new theory a recommendation of a fundamentally different viewpoint from that which was embodied in most of the lesson courses used in church schools. Further, in contrast with the traditional conception of presenting the truth essential for conversion when years of accountability were reached, the new theory embodied even more thoroughly than the graded lessons the idea of nurture or growth in Christian life and experience.

How drastic was the criticism of the current theory and practice of Christian education will be realized only as the Herbartian procedure, upon which the current lessons were based, is kept in

[24] The form in which the principles were adopted by the International Council is found in Section IV of Educational Bulletin No. 101, Revised 1930, entitled *The Development of a Curriculum of Religious Education*. For an extended exposition of this theory, see Bower, William C., *The Curriculum of Religious Education*.

[25] This theory in its essential features was reaffirmed in the report of the Committee on Basic Philosophies and Policies, entitled *Christian Education Today,* and this report was adopted by the Educational Commission and the Executive Committee of the International Council of Religious Education in joint session on February 9, 1940.

mind. An educational procedure, following Herbart's ideas completely, made a separation between knowledge and its application or use in life experience.[26] While Herbart made important distinctions as to how the mind is formed through knowledge, he did not break fundamentally from Locke's notion of the mind as a *tabula rasa*. Instead of its being a "blank tablet," it is in his thought something which is being progressively formed by knowledge, and new knowledge has to be given in terms of what is already known and understood by the mind. That this psychology was ideally suited to the situation in public and church schools may account in part for its persistency. Such schools are upon the whole isolated from the ordinary experiences of life and, if it were possible for them to furnish useful knowledge and guiding principles which so form the mind that they will be later used and applied to life situations, then no radical change in the set-up of such schools is necessary. They only need to improve their methods of instruction in subject matter for which the Herbartian procedures offered definite help. In so far as the description of how character is formed and of how Christian experience comes about as embodied in the new theory of the curriculum was taken seriously, it destroyed confidence in the effectiveness of Herbartian or other methods of formal instruction in subject matter in attaining these ends.

It will thus be seen that while the necessity of making a revision of the religious education of the churches grew out of the practical situation, the suggested theory of the curriculum was based upon the best data available from experimental research

---

[26] Even where the Herbartian procedure was not fully followed, this concept of the separation of knowledge and its application dominated religious education. As a matter of fact, the main attention in the church school was usually in getting the knowledge and principles; their application was seldom more than pointed out and there was confidence that if the pupil had the knowledge and the principles he could be counted on to use them in life for himself.

and searching analyses. The lessons and plans which had been developed in connection with the International Graded curriculum had been called "child-centered" in the sense that, even though the lessons were focused upon the study of Biblical and other subject matter, the material was chosen and the teaching plans were developed which were considered to be suitable to the particular age and attainment of children. The new proposals were called "experience-centered" in that they frankly recognized that learning takes place in and through life experience and that instruction is useful only as it is pertinent to such experience and is related to it.

The Bower Committee's report recommended a complete change in the orientation of religious education. In traditional Protestant religious education, the Bible and the accepted interpretations of religion are the organizing center, and religious education is conceived as an improved methodology for teaching the Bible and Christian truths; in the Bower report life situations are the organizing center and the Bible is utilized as an aid in meeting these situations on a Christian basis. In traditional Protestant religious education, Christian faith and practice are considered as already known, and education is a method of securing their acceptance and application; in the Bower report, what is Christian in faith and practice is to be discovered in and through the educational process. In traditional Protestant religious education, the teaching is a preparation for the experience of conversion; in the Bower report, it is assumed that Christian faith and experience are to be realized through growth from early childhood to adult years. In the general educational approach and developments, as applied to religious education in the Bower report, traditional Protestant religious education was fundamentally challenged from within the official Christian education of the churches themselves.

CHAPTER IV

Religious Education and the Interpretation of the Christian Religion

THE BRIEF HISTORICAL SURVEY of the last two chapters makes evident that a basic issue concerns the relation of religious education to the interpretation of the Christian religion. The issue is made clear by a comparison of the reports of two committees, one of the Federal Council of Churches of Christ in America and the other of the International Council of Religious Education.

In the section on religious education in the report of the Committee on the State of the Church to the 1938 biennial meeting of the Federal Council of Churches, there is a reaffirmation of the historic Protestant view of religious education as the utilization of pedagogical techniques for the mediation of an authoritative interpretation of the Christian faith. In what is evidently intended to be a criticism of educational developments within the Protestant churches, those who framed the report say that they "call upon the best minds in our churches to make a fresh approach to the problem of religious education from the standpoint of the Christian faith." They ask that "all the insights of recent educational philosophy in respect of human nature and the teaching art become the handmaid" of this new emphasis. In such an approach, "the pedagogical problem will not become less important, but more important." It will mean, however, that the "starting point should not primarily be a problem or an interest of the pupil, but the great realities of the Christian religion," and that "religious pedagogy will not attempt to determine the content of instruction" but will "brace itself to the task of mediating the common faith to different types of people and to different age groups in accordance with the best educational principles." In the report the conviction is expressed that "only by such an approach from God to the world, and not from the world to God, can religious authority be established and relatively transcended," and only in this way will pedagogy "fulfill its true function as the handmaid, not the mistress, of God's revelation in Jesus Christ." [1] This is in fact not a "new emphasis" or a "fresh approach," but the reaffirmation of the historic Protestant conception of the function of religious education. There is the assumption of a "common faith" which is authoritative because it is "God's revelation in Jesus Christ" and an emphasis upon religious education as an improved pedagogy for mediating the "great realities of the Christian religion" to different types of people and to different age groups.

In direct contrast to this report is that of the Committee on Basic Philosophy and Policies to the 1940 meeting of the Educational Commission of the International Council of Religious Education, representing forty-one denominations.[2] This report makes explicit that the function of religious education is not simply the transmission of an authoritative interpretation of the Christian religion, but the reinterpretation and enrichment of the Christian faith itself in and through an educational process. Education, according to this report, is "concerned, not merely with the transmission of a culture, a body of knowledge, or set of habits, as though these were ends in themselves." These "transmitted

[1] *The State of the Church*, pp. 8–9.

[2] *Christian Education Today*, prepared by the Committee on Basic Philosophy and Policies, Luther A. Weigle, Chairman, and adopted by the Educational Commission and the Executive Committee of the International Council of Religious Education in joint session, February 9, 1940.

factors" are to be used, not only "to develop persons fitted in character and ability to deal with new situations," but also "to add to the race's resources of knowledge, skill, and wisdom." [3] Education takes place, so the report states, where "historic culture and contemporary living meet." In the process, not only is "contemporary experience undergoing interpretation, appraisal, and re-direction in the light of our historic Christian heritage," but also "the accumulated traditions of the past are undergoing re-testing, re-appraisal, and reconstruction in the light of expanding experience." [4] The report says that "it is our obligation, as it was the obligation of our fathers in the Christian movement, to reinterpret Christian faith in terms of the living experience of our own day, to discover its wider and deeper implications, and to bring it into effectual relation with the issues of contemporary living." [5] It is explicitly stated that we should not seek "to bind our own conceptions of the Christian faith upon the future. Rather, we should by the understanding and appreciation of the great historic symbols seek to use them without being bound by them and to free those who will come after us to explore the depths and heights of Christian truth which belongs to the centuries and which cannot be fully stated within the limited framework of any given historic period." [6] This is a classic statement of an educational viewpoint. There is full recognition of the roots of the Christian religion in history and yet an emphasis upon the reinterpretation and the enrichment of that faith in any historic period.

The centrality of the Christian faith in the Christian educational process with provision for various interpretations of that faith is evidenced in the statement of *Objectives for Religious*

---

[3] International Council of Religious Education, *Christian Education Today*, A Statement of Basic Philosophy, p. 12.
[4] *Ibid.*, p. 15.   [5] *Ibid.*, p. 12.   [6] *Ibid.*, p. 12.

Education, as adopted by the International Council of Religious Education in February, 1930. These objectives were formulated on the basis of a research by Paul H. Vieth.[7] An examination of this statement of objectives [8] reveals the fact that there is no attempt to formulate certain fixed and authoritative beliefs at which the process of religious education must arrive. These objectives center upon the human scene—man's part in it and God's relation to human life. They call for the development of Christlike character and for the building of a Christian social order. They ask for a life philosophy on the basis of the Christian view of life and the universe, but do not insist upon any particular theological interpretation. They seek participation in the church as the organized society of Christians but indicate no particular theological interpretation of the church. They ask for the utilization of the best religious experience of the race as effective guidance for present experience. They ask for such understanding and appreciation of the personality, life, and teaching of Jesus as will have definite results for growing persons, but there is no insistence upon a particular theological interpretation of the meaning of Jesus Christ. Indeed, the only direct theological reference in this section is in the terms "Savior and Lord," but these have been widely interpreted.

There are three references to God's relationship to human life: "Consciousness of God as a reality in human experience; a sense of personal relationship to Him; the ability to see in life and the universe God's purpose and plan." Here again there is no insistence upon a particular conception of God or of the relationship of God to the world. They do rule out a mechanistic conception but leave the widest latitude of theistic interpretations. There

---

[7] Vieth, Paul H., *Objectives of Religious Education.*
[8] The International Council of Religious Education, *The Development of a Curriculum of Religious Education,* Educational Bulletin No. 101, Revised 1930, pp. 38–46.

might be considered to be an assumption of God as personal and transcendant, but the sense in which these would be implied is not indicated, and those who interpret God as impersonal (in the human sense) and immanent would have little, if any, difficulty in adopting these objectives. Many, if they were writing their own objectives, might phrase them differently and some would probably give them a less individualistic and more social emphasis. But, upon the whole, they are objectives which give direction and emphasis to the educational process, but do not present predetermined statements of its outcome. They assume various interpretations of Christianity and are therefore consistent with an experimental educational process.

The issue which is now being faced as to the function of Christian education in the interpretation of the Christian faith was set forth clearly ten years ago by George Albert Coe in his book, *What is Christian Education?*. He says that "the theory that has controlled Christian education almost universally, though not quite so, is that there is a body of most important truth—'saving truth'—which is to be handed on by the church from generation to generation to the end of the world." [9] The general assumption in religious education has been that it "spreads to others, and applies, what we already know, or what we hold as a conviction or a standard." [10] In contrast, he places what he calls "creative" education, in which it is recognized that in the educational process what is utilized from the past and the already known is actually changed. Even where the emphasis is on transmitting accepted beliefs, he holds that "in the personal relations between teacher and pupil the religion of the churches undergoes modification either slowly or rapidly," [11] and he suggests that this reconstructive process should be taken purposefully in hand and be made

[9] Coe, George Albert, *What Is Christian Education?*, p. 35.
[10] *Ibid.*, p. 21.   [11] *Ibid.*, p. 27.

central in Christian education. Thus, it is not "quantitative increase of something that is qualitatively finished and complete," but a recognition that "reconstruction, continuous reconstruction, is of the essence of the divine work in and through the human." [12] This emphasis should not only characterize the discovery and realization by individuals of the meaning of the Christian religion for themselves in the situations they face, but it should also appear in the focus of the Christian educational enterprise upon the unfinished tasks of the Kingdom of God where Christian conviction is divided or where it is not clear what Christian really means.

In direct contrast with Coe's analysis of the problem is that made by E. G. Homrighausen.[13] He is critical of religious education, not because it is too transmissive in its emphasis, but because he believes it has gone so far in its creative processes that it is now a "part of general education with no particular truth of its own." [14] "What is needed for religious education," he says, "is genuine return to, or progress toward, a religion of definite divine content, without giving up its concern for man's present life." He adds that such a proposal "would not involve a complete break with modern methods of religious education, although such a religion would have distinctive methods of its own. But it would mean that modern methods would have to be christened to a new purpose and directed from a higher vantage point." [15] The religion for Christian education, Homrighausen says, has been given by "divinely-initiated revelation, embracing a body of living, eter-

[12] *Ibid.*, pp. 31, 33.

[13] Professor of Christian Education, Princeton Theological Seminary. An analysis of the problem somewhat similar to Homrighausen's is made by Professor H. Shelton Smith of Duke University School of Religion. See Smith, H. Shelton, "Theological Reconstruction in Religious Education," in *Christendom*, Autumn, 1939, pp. 565–74.

[14] Homrighausen, E. G., "The Real Problem of Religious Education," in *Religious Education*, January–March, 1939, p. 14.

[15] *Ibid.*, p. 16.

nal truth through personality and history, capable of constant appropriation in and adaptation to the contemporary scene through faith and the Divine Spirit. . . . This . . . is found in the Hebrew-Christian tradition, and witnessed to in the Scriptures, finding its culmination in divine incarnation, the Word become flesh, and issuing in constant realization, through the Holy Spirit." [16] Thus, "Christianity has doctrines, definite concepts of man, God, sin, salvation, history, society, creation, and the like. These are not chosen by us, but God chooses them for us." [17]

It will thus be seen that, according to Homrighausen, the religion which is to be taught is authoritative because it is a direct revelation from God. The modern methods of religious education are to be used for the adaptation of this divinely revealed religion to the present scene and as an aid to its appropriation. The word "education" in the term "religious education" is thus conceived of as method by which a predetermined content is to be made intelligible and effective. He is basically in conflict with the theory of progressive education. He might use life situations as a more effective approach to teaching in a modified Herbartian procedure and he might use participation in the enterprises of the church as a way of building up the type of Christian conviction and experience to which he is committed, but he would find it impossible to carry through the process outlined in the Bower report or the creative education described by Coe; in reality he places himself in opposition to religious education of this type. Homrighausen believes in an improved type of authoritarian education. However much, by these improved methods, he succeeds in vitalizing the historic interpretations of the Christian religion, there is still no recognized function for religious education in the reconstruction and enrichment of the Christian faith itself.

This same emphasis upon an authoritative interpretation of

[16] *Ibid.*, p. 16.   [17] *Christian Education*, April, 1938, p. 243.

the Christian faith and upon religious education as a methodology for its mediation today is found in current theological writers. For example, the book by Edwin Lewis,[18] *The Faith We Declare,* carries in its very title his conception of the authority of the Christian faith. He is critical of modern religious education, holding that "the high promise of the educational program launched a short generation ago—a program which was to dispense with doctrine, with positive teaching, with the supposed necessity of a moral crisis in the growing life, and which was to produce a generation which would know how to meet 'life-situations' in a Christian way—this promise even the most ardent advocates of the program would admit has hardly been fulfilled." [19]

In his chapter entitled, "It Must Be Declared," he discusses the function of the preacher and the religious educator. The true preacher will "see in all the machinery and techniques of the Church no longer ends but means and he would know what ends they must serve." It is from the viewpoint of these definite ends of declaring the Christian faith that he will appraise the educational processes of the church. These processes must be in the hands of men and women whose Christian convictions are "clear and strong and evangelical." They must be "consciously and deliberately directed toward seeking to make boys and girls and youth and maidens and men and women" not only "participants in the Christian faith" but in that faith "as historically understood." [20] Earlier in the book he has made clear what he means by this last phrase. He insists that what he is setting forth as the faith to be declared has been the essential faith of true Christian-

[18] Professor of Systematic Theology and Philosophy of Religion in Drew Theological Seminary. He was formerly a liberal in theology, but at present he has become the advocate of what he calls the new or neo-orthodoxy.

[19] From *The Faith We Declare* by Edwin Lewis, p. 136. Copyright 1939. Used by permission of Cokesbury Press, publishers.

[20] *Ibid.,* p. 195.

ity throughout all of its history. Like Homrighausen, he claims that "on great questions like God and man and sin and the work of Christ and the new life and the soul's need and human brotherhood and the pathway to peace, the Christian faith is perfectly explicit. There is no need for vagueness, hesitation, compromise." [21]

Lewis admits that if the Christian faith is to be understood by any generation, it must be witnessed to in relation to the current life and problems and interpreted by means of current thought forms. Thus, adaptation for appropriation in any generation is implied as being the function of the educational process. But he insists that this does not mean that the interpretations are to be modified or adjusted to current human thinking. In other words, Christian education as well as the pulpit is to be used for bringing the message of the Christian faith as it has been understood throughout Christian history to bear upon the lives of children, young people, and adults. Christian education is to be the means for the propagation of an authoritative faith. This is in direct contrast with a type of Christian education which makes search for the meaning of the Christian religion and a progressive reconstruction of the Christian faith a primary purpose of the educational process.

Especially pertinent for understanding the basic character of the present conflicts is the viewpoint of Emil Brunner,[22] not only because of his recognized leadership on both sides of the Atlantic, but also because of his acquaintance with the American scene and, to some extent, with progressive education. An examination of his general educational viewpoint [23] shows that he is critical of formal instruction and recognizes that education takes place in

[21] *Ibid.,* p. 186.
[22] Professor of Theology, University of Zurich.
[23] See Brunner, Emil, *The Divine Imperative,* Chapter XLI.

and through life experience. He places large emphasis on what he calls community, in the relationships in the family and in the school district. He insists that it is the spirit which dominates the school and the school district which determines the influence of the school more than that which is formally taught. While it is evident that he conceives of "community" only in terms of relations between persons and does not have a truly social conception, nevertheless his general educational theory is not in basic conflict with a social and experience-centered religious education, even though it would fail to realize the full possibilities of such an approach. But it is in his discussion of the relation of the educational process to the Christian faith that his basic conflict with an educational approach to the work of the church becomes evident. That which makes education Christian, he says, is the Christian faith, and this is something which does not belong to the sphere of education which is human, but to that which is higher than education, viz., the life of faith. The Christian faith is not something which has been discovered by human instrumentalities nor can the Christian faith be interpreted through educational processes. The Christian faith has been revealed by God through the interpretations of Christ and his significance in the New Testament writings, and it does not come to be known or understood by "natural" processes of historical study of the Scriptures.[24] It is known only through faith, when one is enabled to see and understand by having the illumination of the Holy Spirit. The faith itself and the understanding of it are both gifts of God.

It is true, Brunner says, that human instrumentalities have to be used for the "proclamation of the Word of God"; therefore, educational processes must be used. Preaching the Gospel must

[24] For amplification of this viewpoint, see Brunner, Emil, *The Mediator*, Chapter VI.

observe the "pedagogical laws, which circumscribe the conditions of educational activity," and religious instruction (as he says it is wrongly called) to be effective "cannot ignore the general rules of the method of imparting instruction." Though the educational forms are used, it is not education in the accepted sense of the term. "The fact that the Word of God makes use of human forms, does not mean that it has itself become a human matter. Religious instruction . . . has, primarily, nothing to do with education; it is not cultural action, but it is the action of the Church." This is true, he says, even when laymen and not ministers are exercising the office. Even in the home, when the father prays with his children, reads the Bible with them, and exercises other forms of education and instruction, he is not an educator, but a "priest"; he is not in the "World," but in the "Church," even though he is using the forms of education. The church, even though it uses educational methods, is not an educational institution, but is the "community of the redeemed." [25]

For Brunner Christian education is but the human carrier for the proclamation of the "Word of God." [26] But the understanding and acceptance of the divine revelation and the Christian experience which is thus made possible are not dependent upon such an educational process. Indeed, what is happening in the experience of the individuals who have the "Word" proclaimed to them through an educational process is in an entirely different and separate realm. Thus, the issue between the historic Protestant emphasis regarding education and the viewpoint of pro-

[25] Brunner, Emil, *The Divine Imperative*, pp. 511–512.

[26] That human processes, such as religious education, are to be considered merely the carriers of the divine Word of God, Karl Barth also emphasizes even though he discusses it in terms of the preacher rather than of the religious educator. He emphasizes the threefold aspect of revelation: the *proclamation* by the minister of the *written record* in the Bible of the divine *revelation* in the Word of God made flesh. Barth, Karl, *The Doctrine of the Word of God*, pp. 98–140. See also his pamphlet, *Evangelium und Bildung*.

gressive religious educators is joined in its most clearly defined form.

The issue in regard to the relation of an educational process to the interpretation of the Christian religion is also evidenced by a comparison of three missionary documents which appeared within a little more than a decade:—the volume on Religious Education in the report of the Jerusalem Meeting of the International Missionary Council, 1928; Report of the Laymen's Inquiry, entitled *Rethinking Missions,* 1932; and one of the preliminary books for the World Missionary Conference in Madras, *The Christian Message in a Non-Christian World* by Hendrik Kraemer, 1938.

The first of these volumes, and particularly the preliminary paper prepared by Luther A. Weigle and J. H. Oldham, emphasizes the use of an educational process on the mission field for the reinterpretation and enrichment of the Christian religion. There is full recognition of Christianity as a revealed religion but the term is used in a sense which gives place for an educational process. "The Christian religion is based on, and inseparably bound up with, a historical revelation. It stands or falls with something that happened in human history." But the progressive discovery of the revelation of God is emphasized. The nature of the "world of spiritual values" is not only being progressively apprehended but also is being progressively revealed in human history. There is objection to the impartation of fixed religious truths without regard "to the right of each individual to find God for himself and in his own way." There is recognition that there have been various interpretations of the Christian religion and that the legitimate task of Christian education is to "assist growing persons to find and to understand those interpretations of Christian experience which the conscience and mind of the historic Christian community have found to be the richest, most adequate, and most satisfying." [27] Modern education "places at the service of the Christian educator not only better methods for the realization of such objectives as he already sees to be implied in the Christian purpose but instruments for the discovery of its ever-new ranges of application and depth of meaning." [28]

Especially pertinent in its bearing on the relation of an educational process to the interpretation of the Christian faith is the statement about the attitude toward non-Christian religions. There is no "denial or minimizing of the value of religious insights and religious achievements found in other faiths." Instead, there is joyful recognition and acknowledgment of "spiritual illumination, goodness, heroism, and love wherever they are found, believing that they have their source in God and are part of that same revelation which reaches its climax and completion in Christ." The expectation is also expressed that those who have been brought up in other faiths will be able "to contribute to the understanding and interpretation of the revelation in Christ." [29]

This emphasis upon the contribution of other faiths to the reinterpretation of the Christian religion is carried still further in the report of the Laymen's Inquiry.[30] In this report it is recognized that "the original objective of the mission might be stated as the conquest of the world by Christianity." In contrast with this attitude of earlier missionaries, it is recommended in the report of the Laymen's Inquiry that the necessity be recognized "that the modern mission make a positive effort, first of all to know and understand the religions around it, then to recognize and associate itself with whatever kindred elements there are in

[27] Jerusalem Meeting, I.M.C., 1928, *Religious Education*, pp. 37–39.
[28] *Ibid.*, p. 48.
[29] *Ibid.*, pp. 39–40.
[30] The Commission of Appraisal, William Ernest Hocking, Chairman, *Rethinking Missions, A Laymen's Inquiry after One Hundred Years.*

them." [31] This would involve recognizing that Christianity must build on the religious insight already developed in non-Christian lands. But more than an appreciation of the true and good in other faiths is involved. "So far from taking satisfaction in moribund or decadent conditions where they exist within other faiths, Christianity may find itself bound to aid these faiths, and frequently does aid them, to a truer interpretation of their own meaning than they had otherwise achieved." [32] The Christian will therefore "regard himself a co-worker with the forces which are making for righteousness within every religious system. If he can in any way aid or encourage these forces, he will regard it a part of his Christian service to spend thought and energy in this way." [33] Further, the missionary should rejoice in growth of the non-Christian religions under the influence of Christianity and indeed in any evidence of direct borrowing from Christianity.[34]

Even more important, the report states, is "deepening our grasp on what Christianity actually means" because of the contact with the non-Christian religions in mission lands. Not only should it be recognized "that the non-Christian religions do contain elements of instruction for us," but also that the Christian religion "cannot be handed on as a finished doctrine, without renewal of insight by those who undertake to transmit it." Indeed, "one great reason for the presence of Christianity in the Orient is an interest in its own developing interpretation, as it could hardly grow in America alone, through free intercourse with various other types of religious experience." [35]

The method which is suggested for "an important deepening of self-knowledge on the part of Christendom" is that of "a more thoroughgoing sharing of its life with the life of the Orient." By

[31] *Ibid.,* p. 33.
[32] *Ibid.,* p. 37.
[33] *Ibid.,* p. 40.

[34] *Ibid.,* pp. 42–44.
[35] *Ibid.,* pp. 45–47.

this is not meant sharing in the sense of "spreading abroad what one has." Instead of this conception, the report says that "sharing becomes real only as it becomes mutual, running in both directions, each teaching, each learning, each with the other meeting the unsolved problems of both." [36] The missionary should look forward to the "continued co-existence" of those non-Christian religions with Christianity, "each stimulating the other in growth toward the ultimate goal, unity in the completest religious truth." [37] Indeed, "the relation between religions must take increasingly hereafter the form of a common search for truth." [38] To facilitate "such cooperative religious inquiry through give and take between persons of various faiths," it is suggested that there be established "centers here and there as persons and occasions offer" for this purpose. "Out of these conversations and thoughts there should come, in the first place, a steady growth of mutual understanding and respect among these seekers of various faiths; then that deepening of self-knowledge which is inseparable from a better knowledge of others; and from time to time, as the supreme success, the birth of an idea which shall stir and strengthen religion in the race." [39] Thus, in *Rethinking Missions* an educational process is recommended, not only for the reinterpretation and enrichment of Christianity, but in a common search for truth beyond that already apprehended in any existing religious insights.

There is a radically different viewpoint in Kraemer's book.[40]

[36] *Ibid.*, p. 46.
[37] *Ibid.*, p. 44.
[38] *Ibid.*, p. 47.
[39] *Ibid.*, pp. 47–48.
[40] Kraemer, H., *The Christian Message in a Non-Christian World*. It must be remembered that Kraemer's book was a preliminary document for the Madras Conference and therefore is not an expression of the viewpoint of the Conference. In contrast with the Jerusalem report and that of the Laymen's Inquiry, which are both "official" reports, this is a private interpretation for which Kraemer alone is responsible. It was, however, one of the preliminary papers for the Madras Conference. At the Conference, it not only aroused discussion, but was also fundamentally criticized by many.

He rejects all notion that insights of the non-Christian religions are of the same sort or are a preparation for the revelation in Christ. They are an evidence of the religious need and yearning of all peoples, and are therefore to be treated with respect and understanding; but the religions which have come out of these human aspirations are "natural" religions and, therefore, have no connection with the self-revelation of God in Jesus Christ. The missionary should have a sympathetic understanding of these non-Christian religions not in order to discover their similarities to Christianity and to build upon their highest insights in the development of the Christian faith, but to show their complete inadequacy in approach and their error in comparison with the true revelation.[41] A study of comparative religion is valuable, not because it makes clear that in other religions on which Christianity may be built, but because it gives the basis for interpreting Christianity in the thought forms of other faiths. Contrast rather than similarity is the missionary's interest in understanding other religions.

In contrast with the emphasis in the Jerusalem report upon modern educational processes and in the report of the Laymen's Inquiry upon mutual sharing with those of other faiths, Kraemer defends evangelization, proselytism, and conversion as essential and primary in the missionary enterprise. "The recommendation of 'sharing religious experience' or of social service as the only valid missionary methods, are the offspring of a fundamental religious confusion. It is clear as daylight that once the cardinal fact is grasped that the apostolic theocentric apprehension is the only valid Christian apprehension, the Christian Church has not only the right but also the duty to take conversion and evangelization as prime necessities for mankind." [42] In his insistence upon an authoritative interpretation of the Christian religion and

---

[41] *Ibid.*, pp. 114–130.   [42] *Ibid.*, p. 295.

in his assertion that evangelization and proselytism are the core of the missionary method, Kraemer proposes a philosophy of missions which embodies in a thorough-going form an authoritarian Protestant type of approach and emphasis.

It seems abundantly clear that these critics of a modern educational approach to the work of the churches are reaffirming the historic Protestant viewpoint that there is a true interpretation of the Christian religion which has the authority of divine revelaton, and are reëmphasizing the function of religious education as furnishing an improved methodology for mediating this authoritative interpretation to children, young people, and adults. That there is this assumption of a single and authoritative interpretation of the Christian religion is not only implied in the viewpoints which have been reviewed, but it is expressly stated by these various interpreters. Edwin Lewis reviews the New Testament writings and gives certain examples from Christian history to support his contention that in the various efforts to make the Christian message relevant to the current scene, the essential message of Christianity has remained unchanged. He admits that attempts have been made to adjust the distinctive Christian message to current ideologies or knowledge, but he holds that when this has happened the vitality of Christianity has been lost and he rules these out as evidences of departure from true Christianity.[43] In his criticisms of those whose interpretations of the Christian religion are different from his own, Emil Brunner calls the roll of great theologians of the modern period and designates them as false interpreters of Christianity. Hendrik Kraemer draws a distinction between natural and revealed religion. Within natural religion he includes not only the sincere efforts in the non-Christian faiths to interpret the meaning of religion, but also all Christian interpreters who hold a different conception of revelation

[43] Lewis, Edwin, *The Faith We Declare*, Chapter V.

and who give a different meaning to the Christian faith from that which he sets forth as the true Biblical interpretation. Thus, those who are emphasizing a single authoritative interpretation of the Christian religion have taken upon themselves the rôle of the Reformers who, like Luther, defied councils and temporal power on the authority of their private interpretation of the Scriptures.

The difficulty in arriving at a universally accepted interpretation of the Christian religion is already evidenced, as it was in the Reformation, in the differences which have emerged among those who are at one in their insistence that there is an authoritative revelation in the Biblical interpretations. Barth in *Nein, Emil Brunner* has attacked Brunner for what to Barth are departures from the correct interpretations, with something of the vindictive passion with which Luther attacked Zwingli. The fact seems to be that the repeated attempts in Christian history to establish a single authoritative interpretation of the Christian religion have never succeeded. "Heresies" have developed and flourished and the efforts to prevent them have never met with success. These efforts were inaugurated in the second century. Within the Christian movement there were various schools of Gnostic interpretation of Christ, and the Gnostic experience had great appeal, particularly to the half-educated. But an even more serious threat to the primitive church was the movement initiated and led by the semi-Gnostic, Marcion. It was not alone that the Marcion heresy showed great vitality. More serious was the fact that Marcion sought to establish the authority of his teaching by forming a canon of authoritative Scripture.

It seemed to the church fathers in the second century that something must be done to prevent the development and spread of heresy. Evidently the trust that the early church had in present-day revelation could only lead to more and more divisions within the church. Something seemed necessary which would form the basis for drawing the line between true and spurious interpretations of the Christian religion. Particularly did this seem necessary when already a flourishing "heretical" section of the church based its doctrines on authoritative scripture. In opposition to the Marcion heresy, "Irenaeus followed by Tertullian framed a different canon composed of apostolic writings, a canon, as they claimed, more complete and accurate than Marcion's. This canon was authoritative not because it was inspired or because it had to do with Christ and contained his words and works, but because it was apostolic." [44] It is true that to include them in the canon, apostolic authorship had to be assigned to certain anonymous works which had won the confidence of the church and that on this same basis other writings considered of great value were finally excluded. But the important fact is that the question of heresy was met by establishing as authoritative only those interpretations of the Christian religion which had been made by the Apostles. "It was now believed that while the Apostles still lived, there had been direct communications from God; but after they passed from the scene there were no more. Under the pressure of heresy faith gave way to fear and the present was put under bondage of the past. Not new revelations were now counted upon, opening the way to fresh disclosures of God's will and truth, but a revelation given once for all in days long gone and never to be added to or altered." [45] Thus the apologetic for the authoritative understanding of the Christian religion was based on a *"New* Testament on the same level of inspiration as the *Old"* and one with a broader foundation than the limited canon of Marcion. [46] Further, it was "possible to reply more effectively than heretofore to the more damaging arguments of Jewish

[44] McGiffert, Arthur Cushman, *A History of Christian Thought,* Vol. I, pp. 154-155.
[45] *Ibid.,* p. 164.
[46] Streeter, Burnett H., *The Four Gospels,* p. 7.

opponents; for the difference between Jew and Christian was no longer a matter of the correct interpretation of the prophecies of the ancient scriptures, but of the recognition of the new."

The recognition of canonical Scriptures did not of itself solve the problem. Interpretations even of the teachings of these authoritative writings differed. Therefore, heresy was possible, if not indeed inevitable. Indeed the Gnostics and the semi-Gnostics like the Marcionites could and did defend their teachings on the basis of the canonical Scriptures. Accordingly, in refutation of the Marcion heresy, Irenaeus appealed not only to the apostolic writings but also to the apostolic tradition. For the latter purpose, he used, according to McGiffert, a "baptismal symbol in the church of Rome in his day," which was probably "the original of our so-called Apostles' Creed." He appealed to "a particular set of truths handed down from the time of the Apostles and formulated in a brief statement which he called the regula veritatis or rule of truth." [47] An interpretation of the apostolic writings in the form of a creed was thus introduced to support particular interpretations of those writings.

An authoritative creedal formulation of the interpretations in the authoritative apostolic writings did not prove sufficient to meet the problem. Even this briefer creedal statement could be interpreted so as to permit heresy, and this was what actually happened. Accordingly, "Irenaeus appealed both from apostolic Scripture and apostolic creed to the living voice of the bishops who presided over the churches." The source of the authority of the bishops was held to be the same as that of canon and creed; viz., their apostolicity. [48] The introduction of this interpretative and administrative function of bishops made it possible to deal

[47] McGiffert, Arthur Cushman, *A History of Christian Thought,* Vol. I, pp. 156–157.
[48] *Ibid.,* pp. 160–161.

with heretics more effectively and speedily than by the slower methods of persuasion.

The authoritative decisions of bishops still did not solve the problem. Bishops themselves often disagreed. So it became necessary to add the authority of councils. The action of councils was given apostolic authority on the ground that they were only interpreting and formulating "truths delivered by the Apostles and implicit from the beginning in the faith of the church." [49] While the bishops possessed an authority quite independent of the churches and "episcopal infallibility" was recognized, they were amenable to the councils as the final source of infallibility. Thus there grew up in the church a four-fold basis of authority: authoritative Scripture, authoritative interpretation in creedal formulations, authoritative bishops, and authoritative legislation by councils.

This four-fold system provided what McGiffert calls "a short and easy way with heretics." But while it furnished a method by which heretical teachings could be dealt with, it did not prevent basic differences of interpretation within the church. As a matter of fact, the divergent interpretations which developed each had so strong a following that political methods were resorted to in influencing councils, and the interpretation which was declared to be authoritative often won by a bare majority. The vitality of the heretical movements is seen in the fact that they often persisted even after the condemnation of this four-fold and impressive external system of authority. Indeed the Reformation itself was one of these heretical developments which has persisted down to the present time.

It is significant that the Reformers went back to the original source of authority of the second century and started this development of authority, which has been briefly traced, all over again.

[49] *Ibid.*, pp. 161–162.

They appealed to the Apostolic writings in the canonical Scriptures. But as already noted, the emphasis of Luther upon the right of private interpretation of these authoritative writings did not work. Even the Reformers had to reinstate the second step in the development of authority—the authoritative interpretation of these Scriptures in the formulation of creedal statements. These two did not solve the problem of acceptance of the correct interpretation of the authoritative Scriptures. So the fourth step of the original development was reinstated by the Reformers, and especially by Calvin, with the change that the civil government replaced the ecclesiastical authority in the enforcement of the decrees.

These methods have been characteristic of Protestantism in its authoritative form down to the present day. The Scriptures have been the authoritative guide to faith and practice, but the teaching of the Scriptures has been formulated in confessions of faith, articles of religion, or other creedal statements. Denominational assemblies have taken the place of councils in legislating in regard to the accepted beliefs. With the separation of church and state in this country, a judicial system was substituted for the action of ecclesiastical authorities in the Roman Church and of the civil government in early Protestantism. The person accused of heresy has had the right of trial, but such trials have been conducted on a strictly legal basis. The beliefs of the accused have not been examined as to their possible validity, but solely on the basis of whether or not they were in accord with the authoritative teaching as established by the legislative action of the church in its creedal formulations.

The attempts of the Reformers and their successors to establish a single authoritative interpretation of the Christian religion by means of a system of external control have not succeeded any better than the pre-Reformation attempts. Even within the Reformation period, differences commenced to develop as evidenced in the conflict between Luther and Zwingli and in the modifications in the orthodox Lutheran formulations by Melanchthon. Following the Reformation, there developed divergences from the Reformation teaching of opposite extremes. There were the radical sects like the Anabaptists and the Socinians, and there were the Pietist movement and the related though independent Wesleyan evangelical developments. The Socinians were really in the succession of the Pelagian heresy, although the influence out of which they grew was the humanistic emphasis of the day. Their radical divergence from Protestant orthodoxy was condemned by both the Reformed and Lutheran branches of the Protestant Church. The Pietistic movement was a protest against the lack of spirituality in the church because of the control by the civil government and centered, as the name indicates, in the quality of the spiritual life. In its Wesleyan form, it departed from the consistent Reformation teaching in its emphasis upon transformation of nature by the saving work of Christ. The divisions which had arisen in Europe were perpetuated in this country, and America has added its own quota to the formation of the more than two hundred denominations.

This authoritarian emphasis has not characterized all of Protestantism. Reference has already been made to the championship of religious liberty in the colonial days by the Baptists in New England and by the Quakers in the middle colonies. It should be remembered also that even within the authoritarian Protestant churches, there finally developed a tolerant attitude toward differences of theological interpretation. Under the influence of "liberalism" and "modernism," there came to be as much latitude in theological interpretation in the "authoritarian" as in the "free" churches. The "Fundamentalists" in these denominations forced the issue of rigid conformity to the creedal statements and attempted to enforce this conformity by legislative action. But upon the whole, these efforts have been defeated in recent times in the assemblies of these denominations.

The present neo-orthodox interpreters are denying this freedom which has been attained in Protestantism and are attempting again to go back to the original source of authority in the apostolic writings, this time by way of a previous major attempt in the Reformation. In the face of the impressive historical evidence of the impossibility of attempts to establish a single recognized interpretation of Christian faith and practice as authoritative for Christians, they are making this attempt. But if the evidence from Christian history is to be taken seriously, this effort will also fail. There has not been any single, clearly defined interpretation of the Christian faith in any period of Christian history. Christianity has been distinctive in the diversity of its interpretations, not because of the perversity of human beings in refusing to accept the true revelation but because of the vitality of the Christian religion. It has not been possible to confine the living experience of Christianity within any particular mould.

This issue is of vital importance. Modern religious education has been a part of the general "liberalizing" movement within the churches, in connection with which the freedom of the individual believer was safeguarded in authoritative as well as in free churches. It became evident in the historical survey, however, that this break with an authoritative interpretation of the Christian religion never was clearly formulated as the basis for the theory and practice of religious education until the report of the Bower Committee.[50] That report contains the theory and the methodology by which individuals and groups may for themselves interpret the Christian faith. "Christian education takes place through fellowship in Christian living and the sharing of

[50] See Chapters II and III.

the Christian faith." [51] But with an authoritarian interpretation of the Christian faith, such a process is possible only within rigidly defined theological limits. Attempt is made to draw the line between orthodox and heretical interpretations of the Christian religion and to rule out of the Christian fellowship those who do not hold the orthodox views. Further, earnest testimony as to one's faith and experience in a fellowship of sharing is turned into the attack and counter-attack of argumentation, and fellowship is destroyed. The dynamic possibilities of the educational process are not realized. The right to raise questions, to think for one's self, to come to one's own convictions and experience is denied. Religious education becomes authoritarian.

The difficulty may be illustrated by that which often happens in the local church when attempt is made to use an experience-centered and experimental educational process. The religious educator enlists young people in facing their own situations and their important problems and in a search for the Christian solution of those problems and for ways of meeting their situations which are true to fundamental Christian convictions. Then he introduces into the process as authoritative and final certain interpretations of the Christian faith out of the past. This stops the process of earnest search and changes it into an apologetic for the historic beliefs and an effort to get the individuals or the group to accept and apply them today. But in so far as the exploratory and experimental approach to present situations has been carried on thoroughly, it has raised vital questions in regard to the meaning of the Christian faith and it has uncovered doubts, which are prevalent even among church members, as to historic interpretations. It has not been a process which prepares for the acceptance and application of authoritative interpretations, and the religious

[51] International Council of Religious Education, *Christian Education Today,* p. 13.

educator who expected to secure a more meaningful acceptance of the convictions about religion in which he believes is disappointed.

The young people who had been enlisted in the process find themselves also, consciously or unconsciously, frustrated and baffled. They were started on what seemed to be a process of search and one in which there would be frank facing of problems and difficulties, but they find themselves facing the same efforts to get them to accept religion on adult authority which has characterized religious education with a different label. The use of an experimental educational process to teach authoritatively revealed beliefs about God and human life does not work out satisfactorily because such an educational process has as a basic assumption that the beliefs themselves are examined and reconstructed rather than adapted and appropriated in the process. A vital type of religious education can never be mere method in the service of another's theology.

Central in an educational approach is the original cardinal principle of the Reformation that if the possibilities of Christian education are to be realized, there must be opportunity not only for each generation but also for all groups and individuals to come to their own interpretation of the Christian faith. In this emphasis, there is no assumption that *what* a person believes makes no difference, if only he believes it hard enough to live by it. Beliefs determine the emphasis and the direction of life and are of crucial importance. But it is beliefs that are one's own and not those which have been authoritatively accepted which are dynamic. Therefore, in the interest of a vital faith, religious educators must take the risk which is involved in all vital education, and indeed in human freedom itself, that inadequate or false beliefs may become the convictions of individuals or groups.

In this emphasis, there is no assumption that individuals or groups would work out their Christian beliefs in a vacuum, as if there had been no Christian history. Historic Christian experience and convictions would be utilized to the full in the educational process. Neither is there thought that parents, teachers, and other adults must withhold all testimony to the faith which is to them vital and by which they live their lives. Such testimony is essential to an educational process. But it must be given, not as authoritarian truth, but as personal conviction. It is important to vital religious education that the resources out of history and experience shall be brought to bear upon the educational process but in such a way that the right and the obligation to reach personal convictions shall not be hindered or denied.

An examination of Christian history makes evident that every creative period has been marked not only by reinterpretations of the Christian faith but by wide diversity in those interpretations. We seem to be in the midst of one of those creative periods in which the Christian faith is being re-examined and reinterpreted, a period marked as have been other periods, by the variety and diversity of points of view. The full possibilities of this period of theological ferment will be hindered if the theologians are unwilling to enter fully into a creative educational process. In proportion as they resort to dogmatic assertion, reinforced by divine authority, will they cause the recurrence of that which is most to be regretted out of the Reformation period; viz., the crystallization of rival orthodoxies. The theologians must themselves be willing to enter into Christian fellowship with theologians of diverse and even contrasting points of view, in which they share their own convictions with earnestness and clarity and are willing to respect and listen to the convictions of others and even learn from them, that out of this educational process of Christian fellowship in which the Christian faith is shared there may emerge, not one single authoritative conception of the Christian faith, but varied and enriched interpretations for our day.

CHAPTER V

Religious Education and the Use of the Bible

THE USE of an educational process for the interpretation and rein-terpretation of the Christian religion was defended in the last chapter on the ground that there is not, and never has been, a single authoritative interpretation of the Christian religion and that the vitality of Christianity has depended upon its reinter-pretation as a part of the living experience of any individual or generation of Christians. That there have been many and diverse interpretations during Christian history, the neo-orthodox inter-preters would agree; but they would deny that this is an evidence of the vitality of Christianity. Rather it has come about because individuals and groups have misunderstood or modified the true interpretations as made by the Apostles and as recorded in the New Testament writings.

For the neo-orthodox interpreters there is in the New Testa-ment a single consistent interpretation of the meaning of the life and death and resurrection of Jesus Christ which is authoritative for today because it is uniquely God's revelation. There is in Christ, the Word made flesh, an absolutely unique revelation, which can never be repeated (*einmaligkeit,* onceness).[1] The char-acteristic truths of Christianity were not discovered by man nor could they have been discovered by him. They were made known to man in the way God chose, through his incarnation in Jesus

[1] Brunner, Emil, *The Mediator,* p. 25 n. See also Kraemer, H., *The Christian Message in a Non-Christian World,* pp. 63–68.

90

Christ. This unique revelation of God is not found solely or chiefly in the record of the earthly life of Jesus Christ, even though the Christian revelation did take place in history. The Word did become flesh. The faith which is expounded in diverse ways but with the same fundamental meaning in the records of the New Testament came after Jesus' death and resurrection and after Pentecost and is the interpretation of the pre-existent as well as the risen and ever-living Christ.[2] God did break into history and reveal himself in Jesus Christ, but at the same time the revelation was veiled and hidden. It is the Apostolic writers who, under the inspiration of God, have interpreted the meaning of Jesus Christ. Therefore, it is clamed that the interpretations of approximately the first century which are found in the New Testament are in an entirely different category from those of succeeding Christian history and are normative for Christianity today. The Reformation interpretations are emphasized because they represent a return to the apostolic teachings.[3]

An important issue in religious education is raised by this view of the Scriptures. It is already evident from the survey of the development of modern religious education that an historical approach to the study of the Bible has been an integral part of that movement and a major point at which it has differed from the traditional Protestant viewpoint. But in the historical approach to the Bible, no sharp distinction is made between the New Testament interpretations and those in later Christian history. It is assumed that the New Testament interpretations grew out of the experience of the primitive church and can be understood only in relation to the personal or corporate situations out

[2] Lewis, Edwin, *The Faith We Declare*, Chapter II. See also his *A Christian Manifesto*.

[3] "In Luther, Zwingli, and Calvin, the knowledge of God, not only in the 'dogmatic' but also in the 'ethical' sense did break in as at no other time since the days of the Apostles." Brunner, Emil, *The Divine Imperative*, p. 107.

of which they came. Some of them reflect the problems and experience of individuals and others are concerned with the relations of Christianity either to Judaism or to Hellenistic life and
thought. They are like the interpretations of later Christian history in that they represent the efforts of the leaders of the Christian movement to meet actual situations in the life of the Christian church or they grew out of the personal experience of
great souls. An historical approach is necessary also to understand
the Old Testament, not only the various editings of the history,
but also the development of the different codes, the growing conceptions of God, and other aspects of the Old Testament development. Thorough historical study of the Biblical records, utilizing
the best available results of historical criticism, is central in the
emphasis of modern religious educators, whether the purpose is
to recapture the experience recorded in the Bible or to use these
records for illumination and help on present-day situations.

Those with a neo-orthodox emphasis recognize the importance
of the historical and critical study of the Bible, but they deny the
pertinence of such a method for coming to understand the meaning of the Christian faith. There is as a result direct conflict
between them and modern religious educators as to how the
Scriptures should be studied and taught. It is true that the neo-
orthodox interpreters say that the New Testament records are
human documents and need to be understood in a human way as
do other historical records. It should be expected that the historical and critical study of these records "will clarify the whole
human form of the witness to Christ in the Old and New Testaments, throwing light on its linguistic, literary, historical and
religious-historical aspects." [4] The preparatory labors of the
Humanist historian should not be undervalued or omitted. But

---

[4] Barth, Karl, *The Knowledge of God and the Service of God*, pp. 66–67. See
also his *The Doctrine of the Word of God*, pp. 111–124.

the neo-orthodox interpreters insist that there is an entirely different category of historical interpretation necessary in the understanding of revelation. The meaning of that history in which God manifested himself in Christ is revealed only to faith. Those who depend upon an historical approach undertake a task which they are unable, being human, to accomplish. Even in the human realm, the efforts of historians to present a comprehensive and intelligible interpretation of events, because of human limitations, does not meet with success. This is especially impossible for religious interpretations, because there the human eye is diseased by sin and is not in a position to "comprehend reality as a whole, but only a certain superficial aspect of reality. Its depths, the secrets of God, are inaccessible to us as human beings; they can only be revealed to us through revelation, which cannot be perceived by the 'humane eye' . . . but only by those whose inward sight has been illuminated by the Holy Spirit."[5] Therefore, dependence cannot be placed upon the historical study of the Bible for understanding of the meaning of God's revelation therein found. "How could revelation be recognised as the divine content of that testimony except through revelation? But so to recognise revelation through revelation means to recognise it by revelation awakening one's faith. . . . Without that, the scientific study of the Bible will certainly miss the divine content of this testimony."[6] Even the literary testimony can only be understood by those who be-

[5] Brunner, Emil, *The Mediator*, p. 161.

[6] Barth, Karl, *The Knowledge of God and the Service of God*, p. 67. Kraemer makes the same emphasis. "Nowhere has the inherent correlation between revelation as the act of God and faith as the corresponding organ of human apprehension and as the gift of God been grasped so fully. . . . God was truly revealed in Jesus Christ, but at the same time He hid and disguised Himself in the man Jesus Christ. The universal revulsion from and protest against the Incarnation at all times is a clear indication of how completely hidden God's revelation remains from the natural eye of man." Kraemer, H., *The Christian Message in a Non-Christian World*, pp. 69–70.

lieve,[7] for "it is the 'humane eye' enlightened by the Spirit which is to see the meaning of this history."[8] This discussion clarifies the meaning of Brunner's emphasis, already noted,[9] that while human instrumentalities have to be used for the proclamation of the Word of God it has not thereby become a human matter.

Brunner says that he takes historical criticism of the Bible very seriously within its own limits and he insists that the historian must not allow his faith to keep him from pursuing his investigations as an historian with due regard for the canons of historical research.[10] He believes that faith can be combined with historical criticism, perhaps with a very radical form of criticism. Faith is not dependent upon the results of historical criticism for its certainty about the Christian faith, nor is it fundamentally affected by them. The Christian can watch the results of the most destructive criticism with equanimity because of his confidence that what is known through faith will be confirmed, and that the destructive results will eventually be overthrown. Thus, he makes faith not only the organ for the understanding of the revelation in the Bible, but also the test of the results of historical criticism.

Interpreters of the general viewpoint which has been under review also say that there is in the Bible a unified authoritative interpretation. The Old Testament is preparatory revelation. The New Testament contains the unique revelation which was made in Christ in the fullness of time. This revelation is expounded in diverse ways, but with the same fundamental meaning. Brunner admits that the historical study of the Bible has not resulted in the

---

[7] "It is to be feared that the scientific study of the Bible practised by superstition, error, or unbelief will perform its task poorly in its own sphere also. How can it see the form when it does not see the content? We may take it as true that these human documents on their human side also can only be rightly interpreted in the Church." *Ibid.,* p. 67.

[8] Brunner, Emil, *The Mediator,* p. 162.

[9] See pp. 72–73.

[10] Brunner, Emil, *The Mediator,* pp. 166–167.

development of a single interpretation, but rather in diverse and contradictory viewpoints. But he thinks that this is inherent in all human study of the Bible. It is only through faith and the illumination of the Holy Spirit that the unity of the revelation is seen.

Brunner reviews the results of the most recent historical criticism upon that which he considers the central problem so far as the Christian faith is concerned, viz., whether there is unity in the message of the New Testament in regard to Jesus Christ, the Word made flesh. He holds that the cleavage between the New Testament and the dogmas of the early church, which Ritschl and others sought to establish, has been shown to be untrue; and that the differences between Paul and John, which were previously emphasized, have been shown not to be fundamental. Especially does he feel that the latest historical criticism has shown that the conclusions of fifty years ago that there was a clear contrast between Paul and the earliest faith of the church have been largely denied, and Paul and the Primitive Church tend to come closer and closer together. This, he adds, does not mean that definite differences do not exist, but that there is agreement on the essential matters.[11]

His discussion of the places where he admits there are fundamental differences between the earliest and the later interpretations gives us the best clue to his method of dealing with the New Testament interpretations and establishing their unity. He admits that in the earlier tradition a settled doctrine in regard to the origin of the divine personality does not seem as yet to have been formed, such a doctrine as is found in the Logos formula of the Fourth Gospel. But he says that this is not surprising. It was to be expected, as the Reformers asserted, that there would be progression in the interpretations in the New Testament just as there

[11] *Ibid.*, pp. 173–181.

is in the New as compared with the Old. "Paul had a richer knowledge of Christ than the primitive apostles," and "it was reserved for the last of the Apostles, 'John,' to understand fully what had taken place in Christ and—with divine authority—to interpret this to others." Thus he makes the Johannine interpretation normative of the complete and final revelation. This conception he states quite clearly.[12] Incidentally it may be remarked that on this theory of progression, it is difficult to defend limiting progress in interpretations of Jesus to the New Testament period and writings, particularly when the way the canon was formed is taken into account. Certainly on such a theory there might be expectation that there would be later and still more authoritative interpretations.

Brunner says that the crux of the problem is found in the differences which he admits between the "message of Jesus Himself—a message which, in spite of many difficulties, we can to some extent reconstruct from the sources in the Synoptic Gospels —and the message of the Christian Church," which he holds "from the days of the original Apostles, in spite of all differences in detail, is in the main one and the same." This he solves in the same way that he does the differences between the Fourth Gospel and the earlier interpretations. "Jesus said nothing openly about His eternal being with the Father, and He did not connect forgiveness with the fact of His death" not because he was not conscious of these, but because he had not yet been crucified and risen again

[12] "The perception that 'John' alone taught the full doctrine of the deity of Christ—if we assume that it is right—need not be conceived in the sense in which it used to be understood, namely, that Christian believers drifted further and further away from the original truth, but it can—and from the point of view of faith must—be interpreted in the contrary direction: namely, that it was the task appointed to the Apostles by God, as witnesses of the Resurrection and of the foundation of the Church, to explain in an authoritative manner to the Church what had really taken place in Christ, just as it was the God-given task of the prophets to predict it—authoritatively, that is, in the word of revelation." *Ibid.*, p. 182.

and chiefly because he would have been misunderstood if he had attempted to explain them. The omissions, therefore, do not represent a contradiction but the fact that the "fullness of time" had not come for these revelations, which were reserved to the Apostolic interpreters under the inspiration of God's spirit.[13]

This brief survey shows the points at which there are issues in regard to the use of the Bible. First, while recognizing the value of historical criticism in the human study of the Scriptures, those with a neo-orthodox emphasis repudiate the historical method and approach as the way to come to an understanding of the New Testament interpretations, insisting instead that these can be understood only by the believer who has already accepted them as divine revelation and who is illuminated by the Holy Spirit. Second, they repudiate the efforts of liberal theology and of liberal religious education to recapture the historical Jesus as a basis of the interpretation of the meaning of Jesus for today, and insist that, instead, the apostolic interpretations, which take into account the death and resurrection of Christ, are authoritative, and that of these the Johannine contains the fullest and most complete revelation. Third, they insist on the unity in the New Testament and indeed in the whole Biblical revelation, accounting for the differences on a theory of progression. It will be seen from this review that the center of the issue, so far as religious education is concerned, is in the pertinency of an historical approach and method to an understanding, not only of the life and teachings of Jesus, but also of the interpretations of him which are found in the Scripture records.

The neo-orthodox interpreters of the Christian religion are at one with those who take an historical approach in recognizing that the Christian religion had its origin in an historical fact. For both, any proof that Jesus Christ never lived would be disastrous,

[13] *Ibid.,* pp. 182, 192–194. See also Chapter XIV.

not to religion in general, but to the distinctiveness of the Christian religion. Where they differ is in the importance which would be attached to the particular circumstances under which he lived and to what he said and did in coming to an understanding of him. For the neo-orthodox interpreter, the facts of the life of Jesus Christ are important in establishing his human existence, but his own viewpoints in regard to himself are not essential in interpreting him because he kept his thoughts about himself veiled. It is the interpretation of this life in the apostolic writings which is the authoritatve revelation, for the Apostles had the experience of the Resurrection and knew Christ in his fullness. For those with an educational approach, it is of first importance to know what in the records represents biographical material. Otherwise, they have no ground in the historical Jesus for coming to their own interpretations. This is not because they expect to confine their study of the New Testament to the actual events and teachings of the historical Jesus, as was the emphasis in the "back to Jesus" movement. To do this would be to ask each generation to start as if they were the first Christians in the world. But neither do they expect that the Christ of present experience shall be realized simply through the acceptance by faith of the Christ of the apostolic writers and of the early church. Since they expect that through the educational process individuals and groups will come to their own experience of Jesus and will have the opportunity to come to their own interpretations of Jesus' meaning for them, and since they also believe that this interpretation and experience should be based, as was the experience and interpretation of the apostolic writers, upon the historical Jesus who lived and taught in Palestine, an historical study of the Jesus of Nazareth seems basic in an educational process.

The "Christ of experience" should have vital connection with the Jesus of history. Looking at his life historically, Jesus was a devout Jew, thoroughly at home in the Old Testament Scriptures and profoundly concerned about the status of his people. He believed he had a distinctive contribution to make, but what he thought that contribution to be seems impossible to understand except in relation to the historical circumstances, and even then it is not entirely clear. Two important religious developments of the Old Testament were manifested in the religious life of Jesus' day. The Sadducees were really in the line of the priestly development of later Old Testament history in their emphasis upon correct ceremonial, a kind of emphasis which made religion impossible for the common people even though, with their comparative wealth, they were able to meet these demands. The Pharisees were in the prophetic tradition, even though they had made the demand of the prophets for righteousness into a legal code, but they were interested in the Law's being followed by the people and so had by their various interpretations brought it within the understanding and to some extent within the possibility of observance.

Equally important in understanding Jesus is the political situation. The Jews were still a subject people but had not lost their hope of deliverance. There was a definite political party, the Zealots, who expected that this would come about by military revolution. The success of Judas the Hammerer was a recent evidence, along with other parts of Hebrew history, of the possibilities of this method. But as had happened previously, there was also a strong apocalyptic emphasis in accordance with which it was expected that the Messiah or Deliverer would come from Heaven and miraculously establish the New Age. That Jesus rejected the military method and was more in sympathy with the apocalyptic hope seems clear. But how far he held the apocalyptic emphasis of the early church, as found in certain New Testament interpretations, is not so evident. In any case, that he called men to repentance and to a life of "perfection" because the Kingdom of God—the New Age—was imminent, seems to be established.

Jesus also profoundly modified the Pharasaic emphasis in regard to righteousness. It was not to be a matter of burdensome legal requirements but rather a question of attitude and purpose and something to which God was very directly related in making it possible. Whether in his thought he was to be the inaugurator of the New Age or whether it was to be the "Man from Heaven" is not clear. The evidence would seem to show that Jesus did not think of himself as the Messiah, in the sense the Church came to think of him, but rather as pointing to what was to happen. But that he thought the New Age would be the reign of God in a distinctly different manner from that of the present age and that it would come by some form of crisis, there seems no doubt. That he did not think of it in the modern terms of bringing in the Kingdom of God seems evident. Further, it is necessary to place his ethical teachings, in regard to wealth for example, in this setting if they are to be understood. Thus it seems that it is necessary to use an historical approach and method, if Jesus is to be understood and if he is not to be interpreted so as to give authority to some modern conception, however justified it may seem to be.

An examination of the Synoptic Gospels makes evident that it is necessary to know the historical situation in order to understand them. Even these writings of the New Testament present diverse points of emphasis in regard to Jesus. In understanding these Gospels, it is necessary to recognize what was less evident or at least less emphasized in earlier criticism, that the Gospels are not biographies of Jesus in the ordinarily accepted sense of that term. It is true that there is no real biography which is not to some extent an interpretation of the character depicted, influenced by the point of view and the interest of the biographer. It is a portrait rather than a photograph. But one does not have to accept *in toto* the results claimed by the *Form-geschichte* school of New Testament criticism to realize that even in the Synoptic Gospels the interpretative element has been developed much further than in ordinary biography. They are all "church" documents, apologetic and missionary in character. They were written to deal with problems about Jesus faced in the early church and to set forth an interpretation of him, to defend Christianity against its opponents and to commend it to others.

Two problems are central in the earliest Gospels: the relation of Christianity to the Jewish religion and particularly to the Law, and the place of Jesus in the New Age which was believed by the primitive church to be imminent. The earliest Gospel, Mark, shows in its very structure the atmosphere of controversy. The first half of the Gospel, according to Grant, is not organized chronologically but rather around "a dozen or thirteen great controversies in which Jesus had engaged and in which the church, a generation later, was still engaged." [14] The defense is against Jewish attack, but the questions were also of interest to the Gentiles.

But this was not all. There were questions agitating the church in regard to the true leaders of the church, the prerogatives of the family of Jesus, the relation of the followers of John the Baptist to those of Christ, the marks of true discipleship, the hope of the Kingdom. All of these important issues which had arisen in the church are dealt with in the first part of the Gospel. But the most important question and that which occupies the last half

---

[14] From *The Growth of the Gospels* by Frederick C. Grant, p. 105. Copyright 1933. Reprinted by permission of The Abingdon Press. These were controversies over interpretations of the Jewish law and its binding character upon the Christian Church—eating with sinners, Sabbath observance, external requirements of the Law like fasting, etc.; the question of the source of Jesus' authority; the relation of Jesus to John the Baptist; the place of signs and wonders; and the relation to the Roman authority.

of the Gospel was that of Jesus' Messiahship. That the Messiah, the Son of God, as the early church thought Jesus to be, should have died a shameful death on the cross made a serious problem for the early Christians. Mark answers this question. Not only was he put to death because he was rejected by the Jewish leaders through their anger at Jesus as seen in the various controversies, but also and chiefly because he willed to die to give his life as a ransom and because it was the will of God that the Messiah should so die. Thus the conception of the Messiah as the "Suffering Servant" as foretold in phophecy is given form in Mark's Gospel.[15]

Matthew's Gospel grew out of the problem of the relation of Christians to the Jewish law, a problem which is evident in the record of the Acts. Are Christians under the Jewish law? Paul had made a radical break with the Law and had introduced his doctrine of freedom in the Spirit; but the Jerusalem party were conservative and wished to stay by the Law. The compromise associated with Peter became a more burning question when, through the scattering of the Jewish Christians after the Jewish revolt of A.D. 66 and particularly after the destruction of Jerusalem, there was no longer a center for temple worship. Matthew's Gospel, whether written in Palestine or at Antioch, as Streeter holds, reasserts the importance of the Law, though not in its Pharasaic form but in terms of what the writer considers to be Jesus' interpretations. It is in fact in defense of Peter's *via media*. The question of the return of Christ in the Parousia was also a crucial question. Matthew emphasizes the expectation that "the visible return of Christ will be within the lifetime of those who saw and heard him." He also modifies many of the passages which he took from Mark to give them more of an apocalyptic

[15] *Ibid.*, p. 108. See also MacKinnon, James, *The Gospel in the Early Church*, pp. 4–6.

emphasis. Here then is a Gospel dealing more particularly with the problem of Jewish Christians, but it grew directly out of the actual situations and its reaction against the liberalism of Paul in regard to the Law was an effort to solve part of this problem. Certainly its emphasis is not that of Paul.[16]

Luke's Gospel, and also the Acts, grew out of an entirely different situation from that of Mark or Matthew, and Christianity is interpreted in relation to the needs of that situation. Toward the close of the century, interest had developed in Christianity among the Roman aristocracy and some were secret or open followers. Streeter says that Flavius Clemens, the first cousin of the Emperor Domitian, whose sons had been designated by the emperor as heirs to the throne, was at least an inquirer, and that his wife, if not actually a baptized member, was at any rate an adherent of the Church.[17] Streeter uses this as one item of evidence of the situation facing the Christian church at Rome toward the close of the first century. For such a situation, the Gospels already available were too provincial in outlook and unsatisfactory in style. Further, despite this acceptance of Christianity within the Roman aristocracy, it had the reputation of being a Jewish religion and Nero had attempted to make anti-Roman criminals of the Christians. A new and more able defense of Christianity was needed which would place it in a world-wide setting. Thus we have the Gospel of Luke which, taken with Acts, emphasizes that Christianity is not a religion dangerous to Roman law and order.

More important for evidence of reinterpretation are two points of emphasis in Luke. Whereas Matthew's Gospel had only modi-

[16] See Streeter, Burnett H., *The Four Gospels,* pp. 500–527; Grant, Frederick C., *The Growth of the Gospels,* Chapter VII; Lake, Kirsopp and Silva, *An Introduction to the New Testament,* pp. 38–42.

[17] Streeter, Burnett H., *The Four Gospels,* p. 535. Streeter makes the interesting comment: "Had Domitian died a year before he did, it might have been, not Constantine, but Flavius Clemens, whose name would have gone down to history as the first Christian emperor." *Ibid.,* p. 536.

fied or supplemented the Law by Jesus' teachings, Luke substituted Jesus' teachings for the Law. This is the reason that this Gospel is the richest source for Jesus' teachings, though it can be defended that this substitution was a departure from Jesus' own emphasis. There is also a departure from Matthew's interpretation and a clearer exposition than in Mark that Jesus did not consider himself a Jewish Messiah, but a "World-saviour, the founder of a world religion."[18] Taken in connection with Acts, it is evident that Luke did not expect an immediate Parousia, even though he believed that the Lord would ultimately return, but that he thought of the Church "as a society inspired by the gift of the spirit sent from on high by the exalted Jesus."[19] This Gospel, written as some critics think with sources independent of those of Mark and Matthew and certainly with a larger historical sense, not only was of a type to commend Christianity to the group for whom it was written, but also it changed the interpretations of the Christian faith in important particulars because of Luke's attempt to meet the situation about which he was concerned.

It is, however, in the interpretations of Paul and of the Fourth Gospel that the differences in interpretation become most evident. Paul's interpretation is so different from that of the Synoptic Gospels, particularly Matthew and Mark, that critics for a time concluded that it had developed out of his own peculiar experience and was divorced not only from the faith of the primitive church, but also from the historical Jesus. That this conclusion is not justified has been made clear by the review of the evidence.[20] But it does not follow, as some hold, that because Paul's interpretations were related to and influenced by the Jesus of history,

[18] *Ibid.*, p. 537.

[19] Lake, Kirsopp and Silva, *An Introduction to the New Testament*, pp. 47–48.

[20] See Porter, Frank Chamberlin, *The Mind of Christ in Paul;* Hoskyns, Sir Edwyn, and Davey, Noel, *The Riddle of the New Testament.*

his interpretation is simply a fuller amplification of the faith which was already current in the primitive church.

Paul's religious experience and his later interpretations of the Christian faith show more clearly than those of any other New Testament characters the degree to which both grew out of personal situations and problems and formed for the individual a solution of those problems. Paul's struggle to keep the Law as a Pharisee and his sense of sin and defeat through his failures were the root of his experience. Seemingly in his opposition both to liberal Judaism and particularly to Christians who were liberal in their interpretation of the obligation of the Law, he had become even more rigid than most Pharisees. He was a Pharisee of the Pharisees. But he had been in contact with Christians and had seen the sort of experience that Christians seemed to have through their faith in Christ. It must be remembered also that he was raised and educated in Tarsus and that even though he was a strict Jew, he had come under many Hellenistic influences and was acquainted with Greek thought and outlook. While the climax of his struggle with his problem of sin and the Law came suddenly in the experience on the Damascus road, that experience grew out of a long and severe struggle. His own personal experience seems to have profoundly influenced his interpretations of Jesus Christ and of the Christian faith, even though those interpretations, even in their earliest formulations, were not developed quickly. They were formulated only after long reflection and probably with opportunities for consultations with Christians. Indeed, his was a growing religion, forged out in his work as a missionary and in his efforts to meet the problems in the churches.

Paul's interpretations seem to differ radically in several important regards from the current ones in the primitive church and from those of the Synoptics. He himself later insisted that they were a direct revelation. He had a conception of the sinfulness of man which was so different in degree that it was indeed almost a difference in kind. The corruption of man through sin seemed to him so complete that "the mind of the flesh is enmity against God, for it is not subject to the law of God, neither indeed can it be." [21] "I am carnal, sold under sin. In me, that is, in my flesh, dwelleth no good thing: for to will is present with me, but to do that which is good is not." [22] Therefore, Paul became convinced, out of his experience, that all human attempts to do the will of God in the Law were hopeless, only plunging man into a deeper sense of sin. This was the human problem for which there was no human answer.

McGiffert says that the difficulty Paul "had experienced in realizing his moral idea he explained, in the light of the common Hellenistic dualism of the age, as due to the possesson of human nature or flesh." [23] MacKinnon holds that it grew out of his Hebrew background and his extreme acceptance of the Old Testament teaching of demonic powers which had so taken possession of mankind that man's originally good nature had been fatally and completely vitiated and that his own "experience tended to confirm his inference from history and observation of the universal and innate dominion of sin." [24] Whatever the origin, his interpretation was radically different from the Old Testament and the Synoptic Jesus. The reality of sin and the need of repentance were recognized in these earlier interpretations; but there was no such extreme conception of the inability of man to do any good thing as is found in Paul. Paul's conception of the sinfulness of man, along with his repeated dualistic expression of the warfare of the flesh and the Spirit, has been widely influential in Christian

[21] Romans 8:7–8.
[22] Romans 7:14 ff.
[23] McGiffert, Arthur Cushman, *A History of Christian Thought*, Vol. I, p. 20.
[24] MacKinnon, James, *The Gospel in the Early Church*, pp. 57–65.

thought. It seems to be a source of the present neo-orthodox emphasis in regard to the sinfulness of man in opposition to conceptions of man which liberals hold are more true to the emphasis of Jesus.

Paul also introduced radically new features in the interpretation of Jesus Christ and his relation to the believer. The vision he had on the Damascus road he interpreted as that of the risen Christ who had come down from Heaven to assume flesh for man's redemption, but who had laid it off again in the Resurrection to take his place at the right hand of God. Thus, the risen and exalted Christ of the primitive tradition, who had been adopted by God for his divine work, becomes the transcendental Lord who was "in the form of God" before he became man, in whom dwelt the fullness of the Godhead bodily, and who is "the manifestation and the agent of God's will and purpose in creation and onwards in the history of the universe and man, till the final realisation of this purpose at the end of the ages." [25] On the basis of his conversion experience and influenced doubtless in his conceptions both by late Jewish apocalyptic thought and the Greek doctrine of the pre-existent Logos or Divine Word, he interpreted Jesus Christ in a way radically different from any thought of which we have evidence in Jesus' life and certainly far beyond the thought of the primitive church. His interpretation has not only been formative in Christianity but has also been the center of controversy and of heretical beliefs about the person of Christ down to the present time.

But equally important is Paul's conception of the redemptive work of Jesus Christ. He found the solution of his own moral problem under the Law and of his devastating sense of sin and guilt through his experience of the risen Lord on the Damascus road, and this experience he interprets in conceptions of redemp-

[25] *Ibid.*, p. 71.

tion and regeneration also distinctly his own. Since God for Paul was the sovereign ruler and since right and wrong were determined by his decree, some satisfaction for the rebellion of man against God seemed to him necessary. Therefore, he interpreted Christ's death in a juridical and propitiatory sense as making possible the justification of the sinner by acceptance of this atoning work by faith.

Even more important is the conception he introduced into Christian history as to the effect of this experience of Christ upon the individual sinner. By the acceptance of Christ through faith, Paul believed that the individual becomes possessed by the Spirit of Christ so that he is no longer under the domination of the flesh but of the Spirit. It is thus seen that his insistence on the complete emancipation of the Christian from the Law was due to no lack of ethical interest or sensitiveness. His doctrine of the freedom of the Christian grew out of his belief that the individual really possessed by the Spirit of Christ could be counted upon to act as a Christ-possessed person should act.[26] It is true that this doctrine caused difficulty because at times it became the justification of license, as in the Corinthian Church. Paul also emphasized conduct which was not consistent for a Christian. There is also in his letters, as Porter points out, considerable evidence of his use of the earthly life of Jesus as giving a guide to conduct.[27] "Be ye imitators of me, even as I also am of Christ." But it still seems true that he thought the source of conduct which to him was un-Christian arose because the individual was not really possessed by the Spirit of Christ. These examples from the thought of Paul make clear that Paul did far more than develop interpretations already held. He introduced into Christian think-

[26] McGiffert, Arthur Cushman, *A History of Christian Thought,* Vol. I, pp. 21–25.
[27] Porter, Frank Chamberlin, *The Mind of Christ in Paul.*

ing ideas which were not only different but distinctly his own.[28]

The Fourth Gospel seems to reflect the earnest search of a great soul for the solution of problems of Christian belief which were not only his own but were also those of many other Christians, even though he claims, as did Paul, that his thought was a revelation of the Spirit. The church in Ephesus and indeed in wider areas in the latter part of the century, as Streeter points out, faced a twofold problem in regard to the Christian faith.[29] On the one hand, it was threatened with Gnostic influences from outside and from within, and on the other hand, it had to meet the problem of a conservative Jewish party within the church and the opposition of Jews and also of the Baptist party. The one influence tended to make of Christ a spiritual being separate from and not even dependent upon the Jesus who lived in the flesh, and the other was in opposition to the conception of the divine nature of Christ which had developed under Paul's influence. Further, the Christian church still faced a serious problem in interpreting to the Greek world a religion of Jewish origin and with Jewish thought forms. Paul, the great missionary to the Gentiles, had only succeeded in divorcing the Christian religion from Jewish domination, but he had still retained many of the interpretations and thought forms of his Jewish background. John's Gospel is an attempt at the solution of this threefold problem. In it, Jesus Christ and his meaning and significance are interpreted for the first time in terms of Hellenistic thought and the establishment of Christianity as an independent religion is made complete. By casting what is really a devotional book or a theological treatise in biographical form, he was able to defend the humanity of Jesus,

[28] See also Hoskyns, Sir Edwin, and Davey, Noel, *The Riddle of the New Testament*, Chapter IX; Lake, Kirsopp, *Paul*; Deismann, Adolph, *Paul*; *A Study in Social and Religious History*.

[29] Streeter, Burnett H., *The Four Gospels*, p. 386.

while at the same time he was able, by the use of the Logos doctrine, to carry much further than Paul the interpretation of Jesus as divine, since he was the incarnate word of God. The Jesus of the Fourth Gospel is not simply the Christ, but the Son of God.

Another problem in the church of this period concerned the second coming of the Christ. It has already been indicated that in Matthew's Gospel this problem is met by a reassertion of the doctrine in its Jewish apocalyptic form. But the years had passed and the last of those who had been apostles of Jesus would soon have died. Yet Christ had not come. John's Gospel offered a solution of this problem which at the same time modified and perhaps enriched the doctrine of Paul as to the union of the believer with Christ. By changing the Parousia into the Paraclete, he interpreted the second coming in the spiritual sense of the coming of the Spirit, which had already happened, and gave Christians the basis for a sense of personal relationship to their divine Lord. Moreover, by his emphasis upon and interpretation of Baptism and the Lord's Supper, he not only gave the basis for successful opposition to current mystery religions by justifying the incorporation in the Christian church of sacramental practices with a distinctly Christian interpretation, but he also gave Scriptural basis for the whole sacramental system of the Catholic church. These have authority for Catholics for they accept the authorship as that of John the Disciple, who incorporated incidents in the life of Jesus which were omitted from the Synoptic Gospels. Therefore, the sacramental system for them is based on the authority of Jesus Christ himself. But the general recognition of the different and later authorship of the Gospel makes it evident that these interpretations of the Sacraments are not a part of the teaching of Jesus nor of the primitive tradition, but grew out of Hellenistic Christianity.

While the writer of the Fourth Gospel was probably acquainted with Mark's Gospel at least, Grant says that "something wholly new and different is presented in John, and it is offered not as a supplement, but as a *substitute* for the Marcan discourses or sayings." [30] While the influence of Paul's experience and thought is evident, again John made interpretations which go beyond and modify Paul's in important ways. "What we have in John, in other words, is an apologetic statement of Christian faith and practice in wholly new terms." [31] Grant says that there is little evidence for a continuous Palestinian-Ephesian type of historical tradition. While in outward form John's Gospel appears to be history, that is not what the author was attempting to write. It is not even commentary or amplification of the earlier accounts, such as would be found in Jewish Haggadah. Grant adds:

What "John" did, whoever he was, wherever he lived and wrote, was to give creative expression to a type of Christian faith and piety without which Europe might never have become even outwardly Christian. It is probably true that he is in large measure responsible for bringing into the church a one-sided and self-centered mysticism, for setting up an academic and superficial criterion of orthodoxy, for legitimizing a type of emotional piety diametrically opposed to that enjoined by our Lord—who had no patience with those who "said but did not." [32]

But it is still true that no one contributed more toward the evolution of Catholic Christianity than the writer of this new and revolutionary account of the life of Christ. [33]

It seems evident from this brief survey of New Testament writings that they are the record of the living experience of individuals and of the early church and that the interpretations therein contained represent efforts to make clear the meaning and sig-

[30] From *The Growth of the Gospels* by Frederick C. Grant, p. 202. Copyright 1933. Reprinted by permission of The Abingdon Press.
[31] *Ibid.*, p. 217.   [32] *Ibid.*, p. 218.   [33] *Ibid.*, p. 218.

nificance of those experiences. Moreover, they represent experiences and interpretations that came out of actual situations of bafflement or conflict either in the life of individuals or in the church, and represent solutions which were found for these problems. Since this is true, it would seem that they cannot be appreciated or understood except in relation to the actual situations out of which they emerged. They were inevitably and rightly influenced, not only by these experiences and situations, but by current ideologies and by rival points of view. While the interpreters often felt that the answers were direct divine revelation, it seems clear that the medium of that illumination was earnest reflection upon the problems and upon the experiences which individuals and the churches had realized in their relation to Jesus Christ. They represent that which should happen in the church today: efforts to find for themselves the meaning of the experience of Christ and to express the interpretations of the Christian faith which were true to their experience and which would have significance for the current situation.

This brief survey should also make clear why the claim that there is a single authoritative interpretation of the Christian faith in the New Testament, which is normative for today, seems unjustified. The insistence of Kraemer that different interpretations are only new thought forms to make the fundamental message understood, and that this message is not and must not be affected by current ideologies, seems untrue even of the New Testament interpretations. While all of these New Testament interpretations center in a conception of Jesus Christ which gives him distinctive significance not only in personal experience but as a revelation of religion, they vary so widely that they can be considered all of one piece only by Brunner's theory of progression in making the later interpretations normative. When the changes seem to be amendments not by amplification and clarification but by sub-

stitution, and when, throughout the records, there are evidences
of fundamental differences within the Christian communities and
between them on many important points, it seems that unity is
secured only by choice. That the theological interpreters have
settled this problem by choice of interpretations seems evident
from the preponderance of quotations from Pauline and Johannine sources and the small place they give to the Synoptic writings and to those of the type of James.

The issue in regard to the interpretation of the Bible is basic.
Barth and Brunner and those of like emphasis insist that only the
believer can truly interpret the Scriptures, and for them the
believer is one who accepts Jesus Christ and the Scripture records
as *they do*. In other words, they insist that the only study of the
Scriptures which can be authoritative is that which accepts in
advance their particular approach. Therefore, instead of coming to the Scriptures with open mind and heart, asking God to
illuminate their understanding, they really come with convictions
already formed and ask God to confirm those convictions through
the Scriptures. Brunner objects to Ritschl's and other similar attempts to make the Christian interpretations from the Scriptures
respectable in a scientific world; but he falls into the error of trying to make the Scriptures fit into his conceptions of revelation
and of Christianity. It must be recognized that the liberal theologians and religious educators have also been guilty of attempting to fit the Scriptures to their particular pattern.[34]

It must be admitted at once that no one can come to the Scriptures with a completely open mind. No one has reached the age
of accountability who has not had experiences and developed
viewpoints and convictions which influence his interpretation. If
he has been raised an Anglo-Catholic he will come to the Scriptures with a different set of convictions from the ones he would

[34] See Cadbury, Henry J., *The Peril of Modernizing Jesus.*

have if he had grown up as a Methodist or a Presbyterian. And if he has been raised in a strictly scientific atmosphere and one antagonistic to "revealed" religion, he will have a different set of predilections from an orthodox believer. It is not possible to divorce oneself from all his convictions and predilections nor is it necessary to do so in studying the Scripture records. But it is possible to be aware of these pre-judgments and to be critical of them rather than to seek to confirm them. But even more important, it is possible to recognize that God is not finally and authoritatively revealed in any single interpretation in the Scriptures known only to faith. It is possible also to recognize that conceptions of God are reached by men in their reverent search to find the meaning of the manifestations of God in nature and history as well as in their own experience. If this assumption is correct, there will inevitably be various interpretations, partly because of the differences between interpreters in their knowledge and in their personal needs and partly because of the diverse situations in connection with which the interpretations are made. However satisfying or helpful any interpretation may be to an individual or a group, it will inevitably be inadequate because of human limitations. No human being can fully discover or interpret the meaning of God. Nor does this point of view mean, for the person within the Christian tradition and in the Christian church, simply a general search for God in nature and history, important as this is. It is focused in Jesus Christ, his life and death and resurrection, and is interested not only in the records of what he said and did, but also in the interpretations of him recorded in the Scriptures and in the history of the church. But a radically different assumption from Brunner's would dominate this search. The assumption would be that there are within the Bible and within Christian history many diverse interpretations of Jesus Christ and of the Christian religion and that these are to be studied and compared with a view to coming to a personal experience and interpretation which is meaningful for our day. In such a search, it would be recognized that individuals or groups might, on conviction, decide not to be Christian because they felt themselves outside of the Christian Gospel. But no individual or group would be excluded who sincerely believed himself to be a Christian.

It is seen that the basic issue is not one of the centrality of the Scriptures to the Christian faith. It is in fact a basic difference as to how revelation becomes known. For the neo-orthodox interpreter it has become known through an act of God in Jesus Christ through which he has made himself known. But the revelation is veiled and its meaning is known only through the apostolic interpretations and these can be understood only through faith and the illumination of the Holy Spirit. Both the revelation and the interpretation are direct acts of God. The other conviction is that God is manifest supremely in Jesus Christ, but that nature and history are also manfestations of God who becomes known only through the experience and the reverent search of men. What Brunner and Kraemer call natural religion seems to represent the process of true religion wherever found.

On this latter assumption, an educational process is essential to the interpretation of the Christian faith. The religious educator with this viewpoint has not come to this conviction in order to justify his position as a religious educator. It is because of this conviction that he has adopted an educational approach and has become a religious educator, whether his position is that of minister, teacher, director of religious education, or missionary. But in acting on this conviction, he has to be sure that he does not fall into the error which has so often dominated supposedly educational approaches to the Scriptures, as well as those with an authoritarian emphasis; viz., of using an educational methodology to justify preconceived convictions. He will save himself from this error in proportion as the educational process is characterized by two things: first, it must be rooted in a personal or group problem regarding the Christian religion about which there is real concern. It must not be just an interesting intellectual search, but something which makes a fundamental difference to the personal or group experience. The second characteristic of the process is equally important. While the individual goes to the historical material with a formulated problem for which he wishes help in finding an answer, he must pay the price of a comparative study of these historical interpretations in their historical setting. It is not enough to look around for verses or passages in the Bible which may give him a clue. By this method he will inevitably find what in advance he wished to find. For a time he must divorce himself sufficiently from his own problem and situation to understand the situations in New Testament times or in a period of church history, to compare the problem with his own, and to note the differences and the likenesses. He must then make a comparative study of the answers to that problem as found in the New Testament or in history, and of the experiences on which these answers were based. Therefore, while historical study is motivated by a personal or group concern, it must not be biased by a preconceived answer.

Such a process would make it necessary for the church to take the question of Bible study much more seriously than it has in the past. It is necessary for the religious educator to make serious use of the results of historical criticism. This is but one manifestation of the problem which a life situation approach entails. It is necessary in an educational process in whatever realm that the work of the experts shall be used. Since in historical criticism of the Bible, as in many other fields, the experts disagree, it is necessary for the educator to choose between the experts, and either take one for his authority or come to working conclusions of his own on the basis of a comparative study of the expert data and interpretations. The latter seems the more desirable procedure.[35]

The relation of the expert to an educational process is one of the important and to a large extent unsolved problems of general and religious education. It arises partly because the experts, interested as they usually are only in the expert knowledge of their particular field and in their differences with other experts, so often fail to make their results available in a form which can be utilized in an educational process. As a result the educator has to carry on an unnecessary amount of reading and study to get at the data he needs. The educational process, for the religious educator, demands not only a knowledge of psychology, sociology, anthropology, as well as of education, but he ought to be at home in the Bible, church history, systematic theology, and Christian ethics. Small wonder that in the face of this demand many welcome a philosophy of religion and of education which makes of religious education merely an improved method for presenting an authoritative interpretation. Because of the difficulty of mastering the expert knowledge essential to an educational process, the religious educator has often been in danger of using a life situation approach to justify confining the educational process within the limitations of his own immediate knowledge or that of the children and youth to whom he is related. Thus, the educational process

[35] The utilization of an historical approach to the Biblical records by volunteer lay teachers in the Sunday School has been one of the main difficulties in a modern educational approach. As Streeter says succinctly, it would have been better for Sunday School teachers, though not for the historical accuracy of the records, if the effort in the early church to develop a single authoritative Gospel had succeeded. Presumably it should be the function of the minister of the church to help Sunday School teachers and other lay leaders to be able to take an historical approach to the Scriptures, since this is an area in which he is supposed to have been especially trained; but since the minister has usually thought of himself as a preacher and has failed to recognize his distinctly educational functions, he seldom carries out this responsibility.

ends where it begins, in the ignorance and prejudice of those participating in the process. The religious educator, concerned as he is with a religion with a long and rich history, cannot avoid, even if he would, the question of the relation of expert knowledge to the educational process.

Certain changes in the historical approach to the Bible are necessary. These have been made evident partly by the latest historical criticism and partly by the emphasis of neo-orthodox interpreters like Brunner. One is a recognition that to know what Jesus did and taught is not as easy a matter as was assumed in the earlier days of New Testament criticism. Then the tendency was to assume that in the Synoptic Gospels, there were biographies of Jesus Christ, written, it is true, from different viewpoints and for different purposes, but nevertheless, on the whole, accurate pictures of Jesus. Because of this assumption, the tendency was to center upon the Synoptic Gospels for a knowledge of the life of Christ because the Fourth Gospel and other New Testament writings were clearly interpretations of Jesus. Now it is recognized, as has already been discussed, that while this doctrinal and evangelistic purpose is more evident in the Fourth Gospel, it is nevertheless a controlling purpose in all of them. To discover what Jesus really did and taught is a more difficult matter and more dependent upon a knowledge of historical criticism than was thought in the days of the easy selection of the Synoptic Gospels as the true biographies.

The historical study of these Gospels, as well as of the other New Testament writings, is an even more difficult matter than was earlier assumed. Then in studying the Synoptics it was held necessary to know the background in the Old Testament and the current situation in Palestine at the time of Jesus' life in order to understand what he said and did, because while these were recognized as having more than current significance, he acted and spoke in a particular time and place. Now it is recognized that it is necessary also to know the situation both in the church and in the current scene at the time of the writing of the Gospels and something of the audience and purpose of the writer, in order to understand the particular points of emphasis which the writers make in regard to Jesus. The historical approach to these writings is not less but more important, if we are really to come to understand for ourselves Jesus Christ and his meaning and significance.

We should fully recognize the importance of the New Testament interpretations of Jesus Christ, and indeed of those in church history, for a full understanding of the meaning and significance of Jesus for today. There has been at times, in the efforts to get back to Jesus, a tendency to ignore the fact that the life and death and resurrection of Jesus were interpreted and their significance for those who were nearest to his earthly life recorded in the New Testament. The interpretations were looked upon as doctrines about Jesus and there has been at times a suspicion of the divisions of the church over doctrine. But there is now recognition that what are called doctrines are in fact interpretations of the meaning and significance of Jesus Christ, and it is robbing the present generation of the advantage of the great interpretations of the past and divorcing them from history to ask them to go solely to Jesus and to his life and teachings.

It is evident from the discussion in this chapter that those with an educational approach take their stand on the original Protestant emphasis of the right of each individual to interpret the Scriptures for himself and to come to his own understanding and experience of the Christian faith. They feel that the Reformers and Protestantism were untrue to this basic principle when they substituted an "authoritative" interpretation of the Bible for this right of private interpretation of the Bible; in other words, when they placed the pulpit rather than the Bible in the center of Protestant churches. In an educational approach the records and interpretations in the Scriptures are used in the development of one's own experience and beliefs. There is expectation that individuals and groups will find for themselves the meaning of the Christian faith and that in the process the Christian faith will be both reinterpreted and enriched.

CHAPTER VI

Human Knowledge and Religious Education

A QUESTION CLOSELY related to those already considered is the bearing of human knowledge upon an understanding and an interpretation of the Christian faith. Indeed, this question was involved in the discussion of an historical approach and an educational process in the interpretation of the Christian religion. But since the pertinence of scientific and historical data to the interpretation of Christianity is an important issue, it needs to be directly considered.

This issue was met in the Christian church during the first century of its existence. When Christianity ceased to be a Jewish religion and moved out into the Gentile world, it came into contact with ideologies different from those which had formed its Jewish background. Since it thus came in contact with Greek life, where speculation and various conflicting viewpoints existed in regard to all the questions about which Christianity was concerned, it had to make some adjustment to Hellenistic knowledge and thought. Within the New Testament records there is evidence of the two radically different methods by which Christianity has sought to adjust to new knowledge and conflicting viewpoints.

Paul attempted to solve the problem by what in later history was the Protestant Reformation answer to the problem. Paul's attitude is made clear in his discussion in the Corinthian letter where he draws the contrast between the wisdom of this world and the experience and revelation in Christ. This is set forth in the familiar passage in First Corinthians:

Christ did not send me to baptize but to preach the gospel.

And to preach it with no fine rhetoric, lest the cross of Christ should lose its power! Those who are doomed to perish find the story of the cross "sheer folly," but it means the power of God for those whom he saves. It is written,

I will destroy the wisdom of the sages,

I will confound the insight of the wise. Sage, scribe, critic of this world, *where are they* all? Has not God stultified the wisdom of the world? For when the world with all its wisdom failed to know God in his wisdom, God resolved to save believers by the "sheer folly" of the Christian message. Jews demand miracles and Greeks want wisdom, but our message is Christ the crucified—a stumbling-block to the Jews, "sheer folly" to the Gentiles, but for those who are called, whether Jews or Greeks, a Christ who is the power of God and the wisdom of God.

For the "foolishness" of God is wiser than men,

and the "weakness" of God is stronger than men.

Why, look at your own ranks, my brothers; not many wise men (that is, judged by human standards), not many leading men, not many of good birth, have been called! No,

God has chosen what is foolish in the world to shame

the wise;

God has chosen what is weak in the world to shame

what is strong;

God has chosen what is mean and despised in the world—

things which are not, to put down things that are;

that no person may boast in the sight of God. This is the God to whom you owe your being in Christ Jesus, whom God has made our "Wisdom," that is, our righteousness and consecration and redemption; so that, as it is written, *let him who boasts boast of the Lord.*[1]

There is in this passage, as Porter points out,[2] Paul's criticism

---

[1] I Corinthians 1:17–31 (Moffatt's translation).
[2] Porter, Frank Chamberlin, *The Mind of Christ in Paul,* p. 102.

of the Hellenizing tendency as well as a definition and defense of the simple gospel he had preached to them. He says that it had not been possible to come to a knowledge of God by the way of human wisdom, but this knowledge had been vouchsafed to the untutored and unlearned through the Gospel.

In Chapter 3, Paul discusses the adjustments he had to make in his message because they were "babes in Christ." Porter thinks that Paul's inference is that those who were trying to formulate and explain the Gospel in terms of the science and philosophy of the age—those who were developing Greek-Christian theologies—were only betraying their ignorance by their pretense of wisdom.[3] "Let no one deceive himself about this; whoever of you imagines he is wise with this world's wisdom must become a 'fool,' if he is really to be wise. For God ranks this world's wisdom as 'sheer folly.' It is written, *He seizes the wise in their craftiness,* and again, *The Lord knows the reasoning of the wise is futile.*"[4] Thus, it is seen that Paul in fact denies the pertinence of human knowledge and wisdom to the interpretation of the Gospel.

An example within the New Testament records of what in later history became the Roman Catholic approach to the problem is found in the Fourth Gospel. In the Johannine Gospel, as has already been pointed out,[5] there is a new interpretation of the Christian religion in which is incorporated not only Greek terminology but also Greek thought. It was an effort to make an interpretation which would be intelligible to the Greek mind. It was not by any means a perfect integration, and conflicts between the Paulino and Greek influences still persisted, as Ernest Scott points out,[6] just as Thomas Aquinas' effort to adjust Chris-

---

[3] *Ibid.,* p. 104.
[4] I Corinthians 3:18–20 (Moffatt's translation).
[5] See pp. 109–111.
[6] Scott, Ernest F., *The Fourth Gospel,* pp. 9–16.

tianity to Aristotelian thought is not without its difficulties. But it did represent an entirely different solution of the problem from that of Paul.

The Reformers adopted the Pauline solution of the problem whereas the Roman Catholic Church has followed the Johannine. "Origen and Aquinas were both pronounced intellectualists, who believed that divine revelation was finally harmonious with the best human knowledge; Luther and Calvin were pronounced anti-intellectualists, who perpetually insisted that the wisdom of man is foolishness with God." [7] In its attitude toward human knowledge, the modern religious education movement has, upon the whole, been in the Catholic rather than the Protestant tradition. On the other hand, the present neo-orthodox interpreters of the Christian faith tend, as has already been noted, to reassert the traditional Protestant position of the irrelevance or the subsidiary importance of human knowledge. Human views are important to the Christian leader because they enable him to bring the Christian Gospel into contact with human life. Christianity "should always carry on discussion with its rivals." But human knowledge seems to be considered unnecessary for understanding or correcting the historic interpretations in the Bible and in Christian history and for the reinterpretation of the Christian faith today.

That Karl Barth takes the distinctive Pauline and Reformation attitude toward natural knowledge is seen by the introduction to his Gifford Lectures. [8] As he states, the invitation to give these lectures placed him in a difficult position, since by the express direction of the will of Lord Gifford, these lectures are to have as their subject Natural Theology "in the widest sense of the term" but "without reference to or reliance upon any supposed special

[7] Horton, Walter, *Contemporary Continental Theology*, p. 228.
[8] Barth, Karl, *The Knowledge of God and the Service of God*, pp. 3–7.

exceptional or so-called miraculous revelation." In reply to the invitation, Barth reminded the Senatus of the University that he was "an avowed opponent of all natural theology." He comments: "I certainly see—with astonishment—that such a science as Lord Gifford had in mind does exist, but I do not see how it is possible for it to exist. I am convinced that so far as it has existed and still exists, it owes its existence to a radical error." He adds that as a Reformed theologian, even if his personal opinions inclined him to it, as they did not, he is "subject to an ordinance" which would keep him away from natural theology and which would prevent him from raising "so much as his little finger to support this undertaking in any positive way." [9] He solves the problem of carrying out the stipulations of the will by saying that he can serve its intentions indirectly by throwing natural theology into relief against "the dark *background* of a totally different theology." [10]

Emil Brunner has broken with the consistent attitude of Karl Barth and holds that there is a general revelation of God in nature, conscience, and history. But he makes this general revelation one of an entirely different sort and subsidiary to divine revelation and holds that the Scripture revelation is the sole norm of our knowledge of God.

The classic Protestant solution of the problem of science and religion is being reasserted at the present time in a new form. For example, Brunner says that the problem was not a real problem at all, but one which was created by misunderstandings on both sides. It grew out of the unwillingness of the Biblical interpreters to recognize that whatever takes place in time and space is the object of research and not of faith, and that Biblical scientific views, which were simply those of antiquity, must have the corrective of modern knowledge. But the problem also arose,

[9] *Ibid.*, pp. 5–6   [10] *Ibid.*, p. 6.

he says, because scientists assumed that knowledge of the genesis of anything explains its nature. In other words, they sought to make philosophic interpretations on the basis of their scientific knowledge. The essential nature of man and God's nature and will he holds to be the realm of religion; that is, of revelation and faith.[11] Following this analysis, he makes a sharp distinction between natural psychologies, which are scientific descriptions of man, and Biblical psychology, which is God's revelation about man, just as he distinguishes between the historical study of the Bible and the illumination which comes by faith. So Brunner attempts to solve the problem of the relation of human knowledge and divine revelation by dividing the field between them and giving full play for each in its own realm.

Some form of division of the field has been the most common method used in attempting to solve the problem of science and religion. It is one in which some scientists of religious faith have joined. For example, Newton, who was a religious man, said that his physical science gave him answers to some of the problems of the operation of the physical universe; but that there were other problems for which he had no answer and for these he had to turn to religion. A world-renowned physicist, Robert Andrews Millikan, took a similar position.

The world is of course "incurably religious." Why? Because everyone who reflects at all *must have* conceptions about the world which go beyond the field of science, that is, beyond the present range of intellectual knowledge. As soon as we get beyond that range we are in the field that belongs to religion, and no one knows better than the man who works in science how soon we get beyond the boundaries of the known.[12]

[11] Brunner, Emil, in *The Christian Understanding of Man*, An Oxford Conference Book, pp. 170–172. See also a paper in the same volume by T. E. Jessop on "The Scientific Account of Man."

[12] Millikan, Robert Andrews, *Evolution in Science and Religion*, p. 86.

This effort to place religious knowledge in the realm of the scientifically unknown made religion face an intolerable state of affairs and had to be abandoned, as it has been by the present-day neo-orthodox interpreters like Brunner. On this basis, one realm after another which man did not understand, in the sense that he had not yet discovered the orderly processes under which it operated, was considered the distinctive realm of religion, only later to be surrendered by religion because science had invaded it. For example, soon after Newton's time, those processes which he had posited a God to explain were brought under scientific description. With the advance from astronomy to physics, biology and physiology, and from these to psychology, sociology, and anthropology, one realm after another of the universe has been invaded by science and its processes described. One reason for the tenseness of the present situation is due to the fact that many are claiming for psychological science a realm which was supposed uniquely to belong to religion; viz., the development of character and the remaking of conduct. It is not a satisfactory solution to call a realm which has already been mastered, natural; and a realm which is still unexplored and is therefore mysterious, supernatural. This not only puts religious insights out of touch with advancing knowledge, but puts religion in unnecessary opposition to science.

A more commonly accepted division of the field between science and religion is one which has grown out of the Ritschlian theology and belongs to the Kant-Schleiermacher succession. Kant was favorable to the Newtonian science, but, at the same time, became keenly aware of its threat to the assumptions of historic religion. By restricting science to a strictly phenomenal world and by making the realm of morals and religion autonomous, with its own sanctions and methods of verification, he sought to give a free field to scientific advance without having its results in any way affect morals and religion. Following Kant, the efforts of this type to save morals and religion from the influence of an advancing science have been alike in these two fundamental particulars: first, they have maintained for religion a separate realm in which moral and religious values are secure; and, second, they have insisted upon there being for morals and religion, within this separate realm, some special organ of knowledge different from the methods of observation and experiment, reflection and interpretation, used in the empirical affairs of life and in experimental science. This solution proved fairly satisfactory as long as science was largely physical. But in the development of the sciences of psychology, sociology and anthropology, the supposedly autonomous realm of values was inevitably invaded and this solution has also proved unsatisfactory.

The radical division of the field between science and religion, between human knowledge and divine revelation, which is now being proposed by interpreters with a neo-orthodox emphasis, seems also to be unsatisfactory. Human knowledge does seem to be relevant to understanding and interpreting the Christian faith. It is often important to use scientific information and insights for understanding or even for modifying the interpretations of experiences recorded in the Bible. Indeed, the Biblical interpretations themselves were influenced by current human knowledge. For example, Paul's interpretation of his conversion experience was influenced by human ideas of his day regarding man. From the current ideologies, he had accepted a notion of a corruption of human beings so complete that man could of himself do no good thing. On the basis of this conception of man, he interpreted his conversion experience as in reality transforming this corrupt nature by the control of the Christ-spirit so that conduct would be Godlike. Even though Paul accepted current human ideas about man, this conception comes under what Brunner calls Biblical psychology and has been given the authority of divine revelation. It has been widely accepted in the church as has Paul's interpretation of the results of his conversion experience.

Present-day human knowledge which has come by way of psychological data regarding human nature and psychological study of the effect of the conversion experience upon conduct would seem to bring under question both the conception of human nature of Paul's time and the particular interpretation he made regarding the transformation of the individual by the conversion experience. That he was controlled by the Christ-spirit in the way he assumed and that his converts were thus transformed seem to be denied even by the evidence in the New Testament record. His conduct was not always Godlike and certainly on his own testimony his moral struggle continued. He himself had to deal with the failure of the Christians to show the "fruit of the Spirit." The same has been true of those who have professed conversion and the "second blessing" of sanctification. Sanctified people have not always been easy to live with. And yet on the authority of Biblical psychology, these interpretations both of human nature and of conversion were fastened upon the church.

There is no question about the genuineness of Paul's experience nor need there be any doubt of the aid it brought in the solution of the moral struggle which had proved so baffling to him. But if Paul's experience is to be understood, and particularly if it is to aid rather than hinder the development of Christian experience today, there is need to reinterpret it on the basis of our larger knowledge of human nature. Paul had been struggling to be moral by keeping the law. All such efforts turn individuals in on themselves destructively, and tend to increase the struggle and to end in defeat. Paul found in his conversion experience a new centering of his life in Christ, through which he ceased to struggle negatively with his sin, and used his tremendous energy positively in the Christian enterprise. In short, he found the solution of his problem in a center and purpose beyond himself. Such an interpretation of Paul's experience makes it more meaningful for today than the explanation Paul himself gives. Human knowledge would seem to be pertinent both to the understanding of Paul's experience as recorded in the Bible and to its significance for life today.

In their discussions of human nature and Christian experience, neo-orthodox theological interpreters make frequent references to the Biblical account of the Fall. None of them takes it as actual history. It is spoken of as "myth" or an ancient story with a true religious teaching. It is taken as revelation, and the traditional Biblical interpretation is followed that man was created in the image of God, that through the Fall he lost that image and became a sinner, and that his right relationship to God can be restored only through Jesus Christ, the Word of God made flesh. Brunner recognizes that this is contrary to the evolutionary theory of science, which he accepts for human affairs, and yet he defends it as a true account of man's spiritual origin, the source of his difficulties, and the way they may be met. But, here again, it would seem that the empirical data are pertinent. When they are not taken seriously in the interpretation of the Biblical accounts, which are built directly upon what seems to be a false cosmology and anthropology, there results less significant Christian conceptions than would be developed if based on a more accurate picture of man's history.

The miraculous elements in the Scriptures have been a source of much difficulty in Biblical interpretations. Particularly has this been true of Christ's healing ministry. It would seem possible to deal with miracles constructively only if the current conceptions in Biblical times of God's relation to the world are taken into account and if the larger knowledge of today is utilized. Many of those whom Jesus is recorded as healing were said to be possessed by demons and the cure was assigned to Jesus' power over demons. But this interpretation was based upon a false psychology of demon possession as the source of a conduct which we would today call neurotic and psychotic. The significance of Jesus' helpfulness to those who were possessed can better be understood in terms of our knowledge of mental hygiene and, by such a re-interpretation, the help of Jesus Christ is made available for people of today with personality difficulties.

The same can be said of God's providential direction and care. In the Bible, it is represented as the work of a God of direct action. Failing to bring to bear upon the Bible the aid of our larger knowledge, Christians have tended to alternate between asserting no direct concern of God in individual affairs because he is a God of orderly processes, and reasserting his direct intervention in individual life. But neither extreme gives the basis for the most significant interpretation of divine providence. It would seem that the majority of individuals will not be able to realize the sense of providence which they so much need unless the Biblical notions are reinterpreted in terms of our larger knowledge of the universe and of human life.

These illustrations could be multiplied. They are used to point out that since the Biblical interpretations were profoundly influenced by current conceptions, they cannot be understood except in relation to current ideologies. Since the ideologies were often inaccurate or inadequate, the interpretations were often warped. The only way the revelation in the Biblical experience can be made meaningful for life today would seem to be through a willingness to bring to an understanding of the Biblical interpretations the aid of larger knowledge so that the significant experiences there recorded may be meaningful for present life.

Another aspect of this question seems equally important, viz., the significance of present-day natural knowledge for one's conception of God. It is sometimes claimed that progressive religious educators, in seeking to work out their view of God from human experience, project their own ideas upon God and that, as a result, their God is a human creation. Their process is from the human to the divine rather than from the divine to the human. Such a criticism is a misrepresentation of the progressive religious educator's position and, what is more serious, misses the real issue. Whether God is transcendent or immanent or both transcendent and immanent, he is known only through his manifestations in this world and in human history. All other ideas of God are sheer speculation. Even the Barthians emphasize the fact that God can be known only as he revealed himself objectively in Jesus Christ in human history. But it is out of man's experience of the manifestations of God in human life and history that his ideas of God have developed. It is through human experience that ideas of God arise, but human experience of the divine. It is thus seen that the process is neither from the human to the divine nor from the divine to the human. The human and the divine are integrally inter-related in any revelation of God.

The real issue is: what are the manifestations of the divine? What is revelation of God? Specifically the question is how important for a knowledge of God are the manifestations in nature and history of whatever power is in or back of this universe. While the progressive religious educator would recognize the central place of Jesus Christ in our knowledge of God, he would give an important place to the continuous manifestations of God in nature and in human life. Scientific knowledge, instead of being irrelevant, furnishes him data of importance in coming to a knowledge of God. He believes that the revelations of God did not cease with the first century of the Christian era nor are they confined to the Christian religion.

The neo-orthodox interpreters, who have been quoted, not only make unique and final the revelation of God in Jesus Christ, but they give little or no weight to other manifestations. They have characterized as natural and therefore as irrelevant or unimportant for one's knowledge of God those powers and potentialities by which human beings live their lives and on which they depend. In the face of an advancing science, this refusal to recognize these natural manifestations as revelations of God has contributed to the devastating secularization of life which has thrown man back upon himself destructively. The recognition of the manifold manifestations of God in nature and in history makes every aspect of life sacred. There is no scientific advance which is not dependent upon given powers and potentialities of the universe as it impinges upon human life. These we have come to understand through science, in the sense that we know more about the conditions under which they are available, but every scientific discovery enhances rather than destroys their mystery and wonder.

The work of the physician offers an illustration. Medical science has come to recognize that all it can do is to remove the obstacles to the healing of the body. A wound is cleared of infection and closed against it, and the surgeon says that in so many days it will be healed. But what is this healing power upon which the surgeon depends? Interpreters of the Christian religion have tended to call the physician's work scientific and to pray to God to supplement his work by divine power. Would it not make for greater knowledge of God and a greater reverence in the presence of His mysterious manifestations in human life if this healing power were in fact recognized for what it is: one of the given resources of life which man has learned how to utilize but for which he is not responsible. In other words, it is one of the "natural" revelations of God. Truly the physician can subscribe to that which is written over the Presbyterian Hospital in New York City: "Of the Most High cometh healing." In the presence of a major operation, one ought really to take off his shoes because he is on holy ground, for there is manifested not only the possibilities of man, but also the wonder-working power of God.

The Bible speaks of God as love. But God as love is being challenged in the world today in perhaps as devastating a manner as in any recent period of history. God as love will never be really believed in by human beings until Christians cease talking of love as something which is bestowed upon evil human beings, and come to recognize and demonstrate by their lives how fundamental love is as a manifestation of God in human life. Whether love is more powerful than hate; in other words, whether God is stronger than the Devil, will never be known except as the way of love is really tried. Already, there seems to be sufficient empirical evidence to give one confidence that God is love.

An interesting illustration of a scientist's attempt to keep his Christian faith separate from modern knowledge is found in Eddington's Gifford lectures.[13] The greater part of this book is given to a fascinating account of the new physics. In the discussion of the last three chapters on the bearing of the new physics upon religion, he says that there is no bearing, because religion belongs to "regions of the human spirit untrammeled by a world of physics." [14] In his closing chapter, he gives a direct defense of mystical experience as the foundation of religious confidence, an experience which is evidently his own because of his Quaker heritage. But in his book, Eddington had shown that as "a con-

[13] Eddington, A. S., *The Nature of the Physical World.*
[14] *Ibid.*, p. 322.

sequence of the quantum theory physics is no longer pledged to a scheme of deterministic law;" indeed, that "determinism has dropped out altogether" and in its place is an attitude "definitely hostile to determinism." [15] It would seem that his world of physics is not so irrelevant to one's interpretations of religion as Eddington claims.

It is because of considerations such as have been reviewed that the religious educator is convinced of the pertinence of human knowledge to the educational process by which the Christian faith is interpreted by any individual or any generation. The issue as to the use of extra-Biblical material in religious education is an important one. Unless a truly religious interpretation is given to the knowledge youth are getting in the physical and social sciences, in history, and in other aspects of their education, some of the most significant opportunities for religious education are missed. Natural knowledge is of help in understanding the experiences of the Bible and in revising the interpretations where they have been influenced by inadequate or false conceptions of man, of nature or of God's relation to human life. It is important for the enrichment of the Christian faith through the manifestations of God which have become known through the larger knowledge of man, of nature, and of the universe.

The discussion thus far has been concerned with the contribution human knowledge may make to the processes of religious education. But it is important to recognize the validity of the criticisms of certain uses of human knowledge in relation to morals and religion. The extreme division of the field between science and religion, which is being advocated at present, is in part a protest against certain unwarranted developments in the relation of science and religion. One of these developments has been a tendency to equate scientific knowledge and religious in-

[15] *Ibid.*, p. 294.

terpretations and thus to make science and religion one. In a scientific age such as ours, there has been and is great confidence in the findings of science. These findings seem to represent the most accurate knowledge available about physical and human nature and about the way this universe operates as it impinges upon human life in the world. But scientists have not only presented their findings, but they have also—and rightly—made interpretations of the meaning of their findings for human life and for the management of human affairs. Scientific findings, except as they are interpreted as to their meaning, are useless, and the scientist should be better able to make these interpretations than the layman.

Some scientists have done more than make interpretations of their findings. They have drawn conclusions as to the nature of the universe or of human beings and as to the meaning and purpose of life. In other words, they have tended to be philosophers as well as scientists and to draw conclusions as to the ultimate questions with which philosophy and religion must deal. Such philosophic interpretations would have represented a desirable contribution to our common thinking had it not been that the scientists have often identified their scientific findings and their philosophic interpretations. In other words, they have held that their philosophy is proved by their science. Because they found that in this universe physical law seems to reign and mathematical accuracy seems to be found, some of them have said that the universe is mechanistic and has no place for God and no regard for human life and human aspirations and needs. Because certain psychologists found orderly processes in the development of human characteristics they concluded that man also is mechanistic, with no soul, simply a mechanism at the mercy of the forces of his environment.

The difficulty here has arisen from two sources. One has been the failure to make a distinction between scientific data and the philosophic interpretations based upon these data. While the data must be taken into account in making the philosophic interpretations, they do not prove them. On the same data, different people will make different interpretations as to the nature of things or as to the significance of human life. In attempting to identify the data and the philosophic interpretations, they have fallen into the same error as the people who have attempted to identify the life of Christ with one interpretation of that life, and thus both groups have tended to become dogmatic about their interpretations. The second source of the difficulty has been the failure of the scientists to recognize the limited and partial character of their knowledge. The very need for accuracy in scientific research means that any particular scientist works in a very limited area. But he tends to generalize for all of human life and for all of the universe on the basis of his partial findings. It is not without point, therefore, that the great philosophers have been at home in more than one realm of human knowledge. It is just because of the partial character of the knowledge of any scientist or indeed of any philosopher that the limitation upon philosophical interpretations must be recognized. The more inclusive the knowledge, the more likely is there to be a true philosophy, but the interpretations are never proved by the data. Therefore, science can never become the authority for religion.

The other unwarranted development in the relation of science and religion is the one in which religion, in any historic meaning of that term, is denied altogether. This is the point of view of those who would use scientific method and scientific knowledge for the management of affairs in this world and would waive all ultimate questions as either irrelevant to the human scene or as unsolvable. Since intelligent human effort through the use of scientific methods has brought the present attainments and seems unlimited in its possibilities, they believe that it is better to cease speculating about the cosmos and the future and give attention to exploring the possibilities of the here and now in the human scene. They hold that man has learned enough already about physical nature and social relationships so that he is no longer at the mercy of these happenings which seemed to primitive man beyond his control, and that he is already reasonably well able to protect himself against the precarious elements of nature and to manage affairs in his world. Since the scientific approach to life has already so much to its credit, it would be better, they think, to extend the area of scientific knowledge rather than spend time speculating on theological questions. Instead of making science the authority for religion, people of this point of view would substitute science for religion.

Recognizing the distinct contribution which has come through focusing attention upon human responsibility and possibility, it is still true that in this point of view there is failure to recognize two pertinent considerations. One is that, in this confidence that through scientific procedures man can manage things in his world, there are basic assumptions as to what man can count on in the universe as it impinges upon this world. Science does not create any of the forces or resources upon which the scientific management of life depends. It discovers and utilizes them. Man is able to manage things in his world only in proportion as he discovers what the forces with which he deals are like and what the resources are upon which he can depend. For example, in the confident belief of many of this persuasion that human life could be so managed that everybody would have enough to eat or that disease would be increasingly controlled, they are making far-reaching assumptions as to the nature of things and have in fact entered the area of ultimate questions.

A second consideration arises from the fact that individuals of this viewpoint not only have assumptions as to what can be counted on in nature, but also in regard to what can be counted on in human relationships. Because man could manage things so that everybody would have enough to eat, it does not follow that he will. Even in the presence of the possibility of enough for all, individuals are in need because human beings either are not able or are not willing to manage human affairs coöperatively to that end. They still compete disastrously with each other for the good things in actuality and possibility, and live in an economy of scarcity instead of one of abundance. Therefore, when individuals of this persuasion believe not only that man can but that he will manage things so that there is enough for all, they are making far-reaching assumptions as to what can be counted on in man as well as in nature.

The difficulty, then, does not grow out of a lack of basic assumptions. Both a metaphysic and an ethic are fundamentally implicit. It arises because these basic assumptions are not made explicit. As a result, they cannot be examined and criticized nor can they be made the conscious basis for human endeavor. Sometimes, leaders in religious education have focused upon method and have not made explicit the basic assumptions on which their confidence in the educational process is based. In so far as this has characterized religious education, it is subject to the same criticisms. In every use of method, fundamental assumptions on which it is grounded are involved. Those assumptions should be made explicit in order that they may be examined and criticized and in order that the full possibilities of the educational process may be realized.

CHAPTER VII

Religious Education and the Human Predicament

THE THEORY of religious education, as formulated by the Bower Committee, emphasizes growth in the Christian life in and through the experience of individuals and groups, and particularly through choices which are made in meeting life's situations. It places the emphasis upon nurture. On the other hand, the neo-orthodox interpreters are in fact challenging the possibility of nurture in the Christian life. They are reasserting the diagnosis of the human problem as due to sin and are insisting that sin represents a kind and degree of corruption of human nature which an educational process is unable and unsuited to meet. Sin can be dealt with only by an act of God. An educational approach, from the viewpoint of these interpreters, is based both upon a false appraisal of human nature and upon a false diagnosis of the human problem. An experience-centered religious education, the purpose of which is to help individuals and groups meet the situations of life and, in the process, develop Christian character and experience, is declared to be inadequate and indeed unsuited to the very purpose for which it is advocated.

The sobering fact about this challenge to religious education and other human efforts to solve the problems of individual and group living is that it comes from those who have sincerely and earnestly tried these methods. Under the influence of the historical criticism of the Bible and the developments and viewpoints of a scientific age, they had become "liberals" in theology. They had shared in the confidence in scientific methods and rational disciplines which originated in the Period of the Enlightenment and they had come to a more optimistic appraisal of man and his capacities than characterized traditional orthodoxy. However, all this was in the optimistic days before the War of 1914-18. The disillusionment of the post-war period and the tragic failure of human hopes for a better world made inevitable and necessary a realistic facing of the human problem and a basic reconsideration of man's capacities to solve it by human effort.

The issue does not concern what might be called the "intellectual" capacities of man. These theological interpreters recognize scientific achievements, whether in Biblical criticism or in the physical and social sciences. They are not repeating the obscurantism regarding human knowledge against which the Age of Reason was a justified protest. Nor does the issue concern man's native capacity to take responsibility in his world. Human capacity and responsibility for managing individual life as well as corporate relationships in this world are recognized. The focus of the human problem, according to these interpreters, is in man's relation to God. Modern religious education has gone astray because it depends upon human psychology and sociology instead of on divine revelation for an understanding of the human problem. What is necessary is a Biblical or a Christian psychology.[1] While natural psychologists should be encouraged in their own realm, it is only Biblical or Christian psychology which can give the view of man which makes clear and at the same time offers the remedy for the contradictions which all scientific psychologies reveal. "This knowledge is not the self-knowledge of man, but the knowledge of himself given to man by the Word and gift of God, the knowledge that comes from faith." Because

[1] Brunner, Emil, "The Christian Understanding of Man" in the Oxford Conference book of the same title, pp. 141–153; *God and Man*, Chapter IV.

it is knowledge "in the light of the Eternal God, this knowledge has the fundamental character at which scientific knowledge aims." [2] It is thus seen that neo-orthodox interpreters, like Barth and Brunner, take distinctly a theological approach in their diagnosis of the human predicament and in their doctrine of man. Indeed, Barth says explicitly in his Gifford lectures that if there was a special Reformed anthropology or doctrine of man, it could in fact consist only in the doctrine of sin.[3]

The human predicament, according to these interpreters, is due to sin; and sin is man's rebellion against the sovereignty of God. Following the Scottish Confession, which he used as the basis of his lectures, Karl Barth says that man and woman are "in the position of 'conspyring against the Soveraigne Majestie of God'—and in sixteenth-century Scotland, a place where there was no lack of conspiracy, men understood with exceptional clarity what that word meant." [4] Emil Brunner puts the matter in similar terms of personal relationship. He says that sin is different from evil which is a philosophical conception and represents only opposition to the norm or to the idea. Sin which is a religious conception is personal. It is like the "bold self-assertion of the son's will above that of the father." It is an "attack on God's honor," it is "rebellion against the Lord." [5]

Man was created in the image of God and it was intended that his existence should be in the love of God and in responsible relationship to God.[6] Man was endowed with capacities which made the bold self-assertion of his freedom possible but, created in God's image, he belonged to God and owed him both profound

---

[2] Brunner, Emil, *God and Man*, p. 151. See also Barth, Karl, *The Knowledge of God and the Service of God*, pp. 48–54.

[3] Barth, Karl, *The Knowledge of God and the Service of God*, p. 46.

[4] *Ibid.*, pp. 49–50.

[5] Brunner, Emil, *The Mediator*, pp. 444, 462.

[6] Brunner, Emil, *Man in Revolt*, p. 104. This reference is from Chapter V, "The Origin: The Imago Dei," in which there is discussion of this viewpoint.

gratitude and complete allegiance. But instead of gratitude and allegiance, man has sought to set up his own authority in place of God's. "Not content with his own human glory," he "grasps at God's glory, in order himself to be like God." Men "have set themselves up as the lords of their life, as if they were Gods." [7] As a result, "the original fellowship with God is broken" and man is cut off from and in opposition to God.

This condition is not an individual matter, but it is something which is now characteristic of all mankind. Through the Fall (which is not something which can be localized in the world of time and space but which is a revelation to faith that we have fallen away from our origin),[8] man has come to be in a state of opposition to his divine destiny.[9] There is such an alienation of man's nature from God that he can no longer do the will of God, indeed he does not even wish to do it.[10] Sin as guilt means that this is the condition of mankind in a wrong position with reference to God. In guilt, we see the perversion of human nature "as something which has actually taken place, which can never be undone; we are made to feel that this is an irrevocable, inescapable fact."

It is not that we as human beings are "far away from God, . . . that God has to come a long way to reach us; it is not merely the fact that we belong to a different order of being, that we are finite, which separates us from God. This would be a merely negative separation, a mere sense of incom-

[7] Barth, Karl, *The Knowledge of God and the Service of God*, pp. 47, 50. "Sin is defiance, arrogance, the desire to be equal with God. . . . And this is the very origin of sin: the assertion of human independence over against God, the declaration of the rights of man's freedom as independent of God's will. . . . Man's arrogance consists in believing that he can look after himself better than God can, that he knows what is good for him better than his Creator." Brunner, Emil, *Man in Revolt*, pp. 129–132.

[8] Brunner, Emil, *The Christian Understanding of Man*, p. 163.

[9] *Ibid.*, p. 153; *Man in Revolt*, p. 114.

[10] *Ibid.*, p. 164. See also *Man in Revolt*, pp. 116–118, 135–139.

pleteness. The truth is rather that between us and God there is an actual obstacle, which blocks the way like a great boulder, an obstacle so great that we cannot push it out of the way by our own efforts. This obstacle is sin, or, rather, guilt." [11] This is the source of the human predicament, according to these interpreters of the Christian faith. Man's sense of responsibility is ambiguous and confused because true responsibility is responsibility to God.[12] This condition of man manifests itself in baffling human phenomena: "in anxiety, in longing, in doubt, in despair, in a bad conscience." It shows itself in irresponsibility and in the elements of inhumanity in human existence.[13]

There is nothing that man can of himself do to meet this situation, for God cannot, being the Sovereign God, forgive easily as a human being might, saying he will forgive and forget. "God cannot permit His honour to be attacked; for His honour is His Godhead, His sovereign majesty. God would cease to be God, if He could permit His honour to be attacked. . . . It is the very nature of the Holy God that He should be supreme, that His sovereignty should be absolute and unquestioned." [14] Further, order in the universe as well as in the moral realm is dependent upon the personal will of God, expressed in the Law, and, therefore, "all order in the world depends upon the inviolability of His honour; upon the certitude that those who rebel against Him will be punished." [15] But this punishment is "not an educative, paternal punishment, but the punishment meted out by a master, the punishment of a sovereign upon a rebellious subject. God becomes the royal Judge, who utters the condemnation of the prisoner at the bar." Apart from ideas of this kind, impossible as

[11] Brunner, Emil, *The Mediator*, p. 443. See also *Man in Revolt*, pp. 133–135.
[12] Brunner, Emil, in *The Christian Understanding of Man*, pp. 162–163.
[13] *Ibid.*, pp. 166–167. See also, *Man in Revolt*, pp. 181–187, 195–204.
[14] Brunner, Emil, *The Mediator*, pp. 444, 461.
[15] *Ibid.*, pp. 444–445.

they seem to the modern mind, "the Holiness of God means little or nothing to us." [16]

A debt must be paid. Man cannot pay. Guilt costs. Man cannot pay the price. But God, in his great condescension and infinite mercy and as an expression of his love for man, has offered the way of reconciliation. Forgiveness has been made possible but in such a way that in the very act of throwing the bridge over the abyss, the depth and breadth of the gulf becomes still more evident. In the very act of removing the great boulder which blocks the path, its weight becomes still more evident. This is what the New Testament means by reconciliation through the Cross of Jesus Christ. This is the event in which God makes known his holiness and his love simultaneously, in one event and in an absolute manner. We can, however, perceive its full significance as a real act of forgiveness only if we see that it is far more than a symbol, however impressive—one symbol among others—that it is *the* act of revelation, which as an actual event constitutes the basis of our faith in forgiveness. God's forgiveness is possible only if there is a Mediator, and a Mediator commensurate with the crime of rebellion against God. Such a Mediator has been offered in the person of God's son. [17]

Brunner insists that it is the fact "that God comes to man and that man does not go to God; . . . that God makes reconciliation and not man" which constitutes the difference between the Gospel and all other religions and philosophies. "All religion, in the final analysis, bases salvation on an activity of man, either on his cognition, his cult, or his mystical meditations." All religion and philosophy, as Luther emphasized, "seek righteousness by works, by human self-assertion" and man thinks he can help himself in this way. But the Gospel denies the possibility of every human approach to God, even by the path of religion. "When

[16] *Ibid.*, p. 464. [17] *Ibid.*, pp. 449–450.

man no longer relies upon what is his, when he no longer stands or walks on his feet, but clings to the hand which is stretched out to him from beyond; that is, when the basis of his life is only what God offers him in his Word—then he truly lives by faith in God." This, says Brunner, is what Paul means by justification by faith alone. "For God is God only when he is the sole helper; when as the Bible says, he is not forced to give his glory to another, when without competitors he is the foundation of salvation. Where salvation is divided between God and man, man appears as co-partner and as equal with God. As in Stoic philosophy and in all religions, he is a fellow-God. God is not Lord, not sovereign, but a partner; but this is mocking God." [18]

Brunner's conception of God and man's relation to him seems to be like the situation of a son who has inherited from his parents a superior endowment and who has rich resources provided for him for the exercise of his native endowment in his growth to his own maturity. But the word of the father in this home is law and is not to be questioned. Any assertion by the son of his own will against that of his father or any exercise by the son of his growing ability for freedom is considered by the father as an infringement of his sovereign rights as head of the home and as rebellion against himself.[19] Punishment in such a home is not educative, but is that meted out by a master to annihilate rebellion, for such a father cannot tolerate any infringement upon his authority as father. To do so would seem to endanger the very law and order of the home. As long as the son continues in his rebellion against the will of the father, his relationship with his father is cut off and a seemingly impassable gulf, an irremovable

[18] Brunner, Emil, *The Theology of Crisis,* pp. 61–62.

[19] Brunner himself uses this simile of a father. Sin is like the "bold self-assertion of the son's will above that of the father." Brunner, Emil, *The Mediator,* p. 462. "Sin in its developed form is this presumption of the son who rebels against the father." Brunner, Emil, *Man in Revolt,* p. 130.

barrier, exists between him and his father. He is no longer a child in the home but an orphan and an outsider and he manifests anxiety and uncertainty. Under these circumstances, being reconciled to the father and being reinstated in the home is not in the son's power. Restoration can come only from the father and as his gift. But this type of father insists that reconciliation is possible only upon the son's renunciation of his rebellion and upon his willingness to yield in complete submission to the father's will. In other words, it depends upon the son's decision to repent of his rebellion and to throw himself upon the mercy of the father, and on the father's expression of his love in forgiveness and in restoring the son to his relationship to himself and to his home. When this restoration is granted, the son's anxiety is removed and he has a sense of confidence and assurance. But to continue as a member of the home in relation to his father, the son must be willing to have no will of his own but to yield in complete submission to his father and to receive everything as the gift from his father.

There are fathers who require this kind of submission, even from sons who are nearing adulthood. But any son who has such a father is in a difficult plight. If the God of the universe, who has endowed man with capacities for initiative and choice and responsibility and has placed him in a world with rich opportunities, considers the self-assertion of man in finding his way in the world rebellion against his sovereign will, which must be punished and annihilated, and insists that man can of himself do nothing but must submit completely to his will and accept reconciliation as his loving gift, then mankind seems to be in the plight of the son described. This does not seem a caricature of the theological position of Brunner and of those like him.

The review of this type of doctrine of God, from which is derived the doctrine of man, shows how complete is the denial of any such educational process as progressive religious educators propose. In the discussion of religious education and the interpretatation of the Christian faith,[20] it became clear that these interpreters believe that man *cannot* discover the meaning of religion by any such process. God can be known only as he reveals himself. But it is evident from the review of this chapter that the challenge to religious education is not based solely or chiefly on man's inability to find his way to God. Any such effort as human education is sinful. It is but a manifestation of man's sinful condition, cut off from God because of his rebellion against the divine sovereignty of God. Inevitably, in Brunner's viewpoint, it will lead to all the contradictions which inhere in that lost condition. Moreover, God does not wish any such reassertion of man's rebellion. What he wishes, and this alone will solve the human problem, is the acceptance of his loving offer of reconciliation through the expiatory work of Christ. Nor does he wish, even after an individual's reconciliation has been granted by God because of his act of decision through faith, any human effort such as religious education assumes. Even though God has granted man reconciliation, he is still as a human being a sinner, caught in the lost state of mankind through the Fall, and he must depend solely on God from whom alone comes help. Any idea that man could have partnership with God in any such human process as religious education is mockery of God. Thus, an educational process, which is based on reverent search to find and to do the will of God in human life and in which it is expected that human beings can actually feel themselves in comradeship with God, is attacked as man's presumption and sin. However much human beings will have to use educational and other human processes in finding their way in a sinful world, religious education can only be the proclamation of God's revealed Word on the

[20] See Chapter IV.

acceptance of which, through faith, man's salvation and eternal destiny depend. The issue between religious education and theological interpretations of this type is therefore a basic one regarding the conception of God and God's relation to mankind.

It is evident that this type of interpretation of God is in terms of the kind of absolute rule of a sovereign with which, as Barth says, Reformation Scotland was familiar and which Reformation Germany knew full well. Luther himself was protected from the consequences of the judgment upon him for heresy by the sponsorship of a ruler of this type. In such an arrangement, the personal will of the sovereign is law and opposition to that will is rebellion which must be annihilated. He cannot tolerate any infringement of his majesty. At times, as in the case of Luther's prince, Elector Frederick, autocratic rule was combined with manifestations of love and justice, but it was the personal will of the sovereign none the less.

Brunner says that there was no fundamental question of this conception of God's sovereignty until the time of the Enlightenment and argues that it is a manifestation of man's sinful self-assertion which, from his viewpoint, has characterized liberal Christianity during all of the modern period. But that there was no fundamental question is not surprising, for this conception of the relation of man to the divine authority of God was consistent with the practice in human relationships, whether it was that of subject to his sovereign, pupil to teacher, or child to parent. The will of the one in authority was supreme and any questioning of that authority or rebellion against it was considered sin in Brunner's sense of the term and was to be eliminated. But it is not surprising also that "democratic" man will not accept that kind of authority in human form and that he reacts against any such conception of God. It was against this sort of authority in the school that Pestalozzi revolted and that the modern education movement has protested. It was in protest against this type of autocratic rule that peoples dethroned their kings and insisted upon the rights of the people. It is against this type of authority in parents that the Child Study and Mental Hygiene movements are in protest. It is impossible for many to believe that what is reprehensible in rulers, teachers, and parents can be defended in God.

Nor does it seem necessary to believe that this God is the only one revealed in the Biblical writings. It is true that such a view of God and man is found in the Scriptures and in its most consistent and extreme form in the writings of Paul. As has already been indicated,[21] Paul carried over into his Christian interpretations the view of God which he had as a Pharisee of the Pharisees. God for him was not only the supreme sovereign of the universe, who had the right, as the Calvinists also held, to elect men to damnation for his glory, but he was also personally and directly the author of right and wrong. It seems to be the God of Paul whom Brunner is presenting to us. But it is not the God of much of the Old Testament, where man was considered able to follow the law of God and had the support of God in his endeavors. It is not the God of the great prophets. For them God comes in judgment upon all injustice and unrighteousness, which is a manifestation of failure to trust in God and to follow his Law, but he also is ready to accept true repentance, and man can count on God if he will but follow him. The great passage in Micah, so often quoted, seems strange in the atmosphere of Brunner's interpretation:

Wherewith shall I come before the Lord, and bow myself before the high God? shall I come before him with burnt-offerings, with calves a year old? will the Lord be pleased with thousands of rams, or with ten thousands of rivers of oil? shall I give my firstborn for my trans-

[21] See Chapter IV.

gression, the fruit of my body for the sin of my soul? He hath showed thee, O man, what is good; and what doth the Lord require of thee, but to do justly, and to love mercy, and to walk humbly with thy God? [22]

Nor does the God of Barth and Brunner seem to be the God of the Jesus of the Synoptic records. It is true that Jesus recognized fully the Father's will and purpose and that he demanded a righteousness which was beyond that and of a different kind from the righteousness of the Scribes and Pharisees. But his condemnation was for those who seemed to him to be exploiting the people in the name of religion, who bound heavy burdens upon the weak and needy. It was not a condemnation upon men as men. His sympathy with and understanding of sinners and their response to his confidence in them seem directly in contrast to the judicial system set forth in the theology of Brunner. Even according to the Johannine interpretation, he said to the woman taken in adultery: "Neither do I condemn thee; go and sin no more." There is no thought of modernizing Jesus and implying that in his use of "Father" he had in mind what this term has come to mean for a modern psychologist, but nevertheless the Father of Jesus Christ does not seem to be the kind of Sovereign God set forth in this type of theology.

Brunner says that a democratic conception of religion and of God was symptomatic of the assertion of man's freedom and rights and of the greater confidence in man's capacities, which has characterized the modern age. In this he is right. But the reassertion of God's absolute and sovereign reign and of man's complete futility is equally symptomatic of current events. Despite all efforts to divorce the Christian religion from human influences, they are unmistakable in present religious interpretations. There is no question but that man's increased use of his freedom

[22] Micah 6:6–8.

as seen not only in attempts at democratic forms of life but also in his scientific discoveries and inventions has involved him in tragic difficulties. As a result, in all areas of life fundamental queries are being raised as to man's capacity to exercise his freedom, and authority is being reasserted as the solution of the problem. The difficulties encountered in a "democratically" conducted home have led many parents to feel that the only way out is the reassertion of the personal and authoritative will of the parents. The problems in progressive education have resulted in reactions toward a more authoritative form of school. Particularly in the political realm has democracy been fundamentally challenged. It is not surprising in the presence of this fundamental distrust of man's capacity that those who have tried the way of freedom and have encountered its difficulties in tragic forms should diagnose the human predicament as due to man's assertion of his will against the sovereign will of God and should hold that the only solution is for man to give up his attempts to find his own way and yield completely to the sovereign and loving reign of God.

Were it possible for mankind to live under the direct rule of an all-wise and all-loving God in the way that a child in a home or a pupil in a school or even a subject in an autocratic state can live under the personal and direct will of the one in authority, there would be something to be said for this in view of the present tragic situation. This is the positive argument for all autocratic or oligarchic exercise of authority. It centers responsibility in those who are confessedly more able to take it than the rank and file of people. It certainly would seem a great boon to any individual or group or nation if it were possible, as some believe, to have the immediate and direct guidance of an all-wise God in all human decisions and affairs, even though the fundamental difficulties later to be discussed would make many question its desirability. But there is no evidence of a reign of God in human life of this sort. The difficulty with an interpretation such as Brunner's is that man's reconciliation to God has to do only with his eternal destiny, while in this world he still has to find his way as a sinner. But the effect is even more undesirable, for in human affairs in a sinful world divine authority is mediated, according to the doctrine of the Orders, through human instrumentalities and institutions. Therefore, the basis is given in the very theology itself for an authoritative home, school, and state. What we have actually had and will have again, if this theology is accepted, is not the direct reign of God but the authority of parents, teachers, ministers, and rulers which is identified with the will of God. The personal will of God becomes identified with the will of man.

That this doctrine has been practically applied, the history of Protestantism shows full well. There have not only been the authoritative interpretations of the Christian faith but also authoritative interpretations of the will of God in human affairs. From the Geneva republic through the rules of the Methodist Episcopal Church down to the last parent who has used God to enforce his will, this has been the record. The will of God in the home is the parent's will. Authoritative religious education uses God in this way to sanction its interpretations of religion and of morals. Every human right and every scientific advance have been opposed as rebellion against God. What a struggle the human race has gone through to free itself from the divine right of kings. How often some scientific advance or some new practice in human relations has been opposed on the authority of God. A sovereign God inevitably becomes associated with sovereign men. The denial of the right of the individual to assert himself before God is usually accompanied by a denial of his rights before the authority of men. Human initiative and responsibility are fundamentally threatened because in practice the individual is made to feel that when he questions the authority of parents and teachers and ministers he is in fact questioning the authority of God. That this is a real danger is seen in the very dogmatism with which these theological interpreters assert that all the great and good Christians who differ from them are refusing to yield to God's revealed Word. There seems in this theology to be no adequate basis for a fundamental critique of authority.

The issue is made very clear in the conception of punishment. There is an insistence at present that punishment is that which Brunner denies, "an educative, paternal punishment," and is not that which he affirms, "the punishment meted out by a master, the punishment of a sovereign inflicted on a rebellious subject." [23] Formerly, wrong-doing in a home or a school was doing anything which the parents or teachers forbade. The attention of the child was focused, not on his conduct and its consequences, but upon the parent or teacher and his attitude. Such punishment is non-educative because, as a result of the experience, the child has learned nothing fundamental about right or wrong. He has learned only that you had better do what the parent or teacher says. Therefore, punishment becomes just one more method of binding the child more firmly to the will of the adult and hindering his growth to maturity. The emphasis has now shifted from the personal will of parents or teachers to punishment which is the consequence of the conduct. This is often mediated through parents and teachers and is never perfectly administered; but for the adult and the child together to look at the consequences of the action fundamentally shifts the focus of attention. Further, in such punishment, the child is not cut off from the parent but the parent is associated with him, as he inevitably must be, in the consequences to the individual or to the home or the school of what has happened. Such punishment is educative because out

[23] Brunner, Emil, *The Mediator*, p. 464.

of it children learn that conduct has consequences which they cannot avoid, life being what it is, and they learn also something of what is right and what is wrong in the true method of judging action by its effects. Parents' and teachers' restraint is then put in its true light, not as an effort to make the child conform to their will, but as evidences of their concern out of their larger experience that children shall not suffer unnecessarily in trial-and-error learning.

God's punishment seems to be of this educative type rather than the punishment meted out by a master or a sovereign. God has not furnished mankind even the personal care and restraint which parents give their children. He has left man to learn, not only by asserting himself in the world, but by having to suffer the consequences of his action. Even when man's refusal to learn from his experience reaches the colossal proportions of a world war in which civilization is endangered, God does not intervene. That he shares with mankind in a Father's yearning, even as parents yearn for their children, is seen in the fact that Jesus Christ, who was the supreme manifestation of God, suffered with mankind to the extent of the Cross. There is no lack of seriousness in God's punishment any more than there is in the punishment from consequences which a child suffers. "Whatsoever a man soweth, that shall he also reap." But it is educative punishment, because it is only by the fact that there are consequences of action that there can be any growth for the individual or for the race.

The argument in defense of the autocratic reign of God is no different in type from that which is made for a return to an authoritative rule in home or school or in the political realm. There is no question but that law and order are more easily maintained in a home or a school or a state where the parent's or teacher's or ruler's word is law and has to be unquestioningly obeyed on penalty of severe punishment. There are also elements of efficiency in such a regime which the slower process of democratic life does not have. This is one reason that in times of national emergency, the rights of the people are so seriously sacrificed. All exercise of freedom contains a possible threat to law and order. But those who believe in a democratic organization of home or school or the political order have taken that risk because they believe that it is the only way that the rights of the individual can in the long run be safeguarded or that he will really grow in true freedom and responsibility or indeed that true authority can be established. It would seem as if the God of the universe had taken that risk in endowing man with the capacities which made his rebellion against absolute authority possible, and that he expected man to exercise rather than surrender his freedom.

The exercise of freedom is that on which growth depends. A child grows to maturity by trying out his own will. Often this takes the form of defying the will of the parent or of boasting of what he can do as compared with those bigger than himself. Many parents look upon any form of self-assertion of this sort as rebellion against themselves, just as Brunner says it is rebellion against God. If instead of recognizing it as a symptom of the growth of the child, the parent takes it as defiance of his personal will and attempts to annihilate these signs of independence, the effects upon the growth of the child to his own maturity are harmful, if not disastrous. If he yields to the parents' will in complete submission, he starts on the road of complete subservience to authority wherever he finds it and never becomes a mature person in his own right. "Yes" individuals of this type have not only been robbed of their God-given rights, but make any kind of democratic form of life difficult. If, on the other hand, the child carries through his opposition to the parent's will and insists on his own growing independence, he not only cuts himself off from that relationship to parents and others more mature than himself which is an important factor in growth, but his ego-assertion is exaggerated and he adds one more to that type of egoistic individual who makes his own will ultimate. Self-assertion has to be both restrained and encouraged—restrained when it will bring disaster to the individual, but always encouraged when it is simply a symptom of reaching toward maturity. A wise parent, however, never misinterprets the issue as one of defiance of himself personally. Only autocratic parents are in fact rebelled against by their children, and any parent who faces genuine rebellion in his children needs to examine his own attitudes and conduct rather than to attempt to subdue that rebellion. He will often find that he is the source of the difficulty.

It would seem that what is true of the growth of the individual to maturity has also been true of mankind. Whatever human progress has been made—and how much is a debatable question —has come from bold self-assertion of men and women in their world. They have learned whatever they know of the laws of nature and of human life and they have grown to whatever ability they have to manage their own affairs by the method by which each child grows to maturity. God has not made his natural laws or his will in the moral realm plain. Man has had to discover everything by the slow process of experience and experiment. The codes of the Old Testament show unmistakable evidences of this empirical origin, even though they are assigned the authority of the direct revelation of God. Monogamy has come to be widely recognized as the consequence of experience and experiment. Any degree of recognition of the rights of others and of conditions under which people can live together has come by this slow route. In view of these facts, which could be multiplied indefinitely, it seems that the attempt to interpret the self-assertion of man as sinful and as an evidence of his rebellion against God is to carry over into religion the same sort of interpretation that parents often make of this conduct in children. Not all self-assertion is sin. Some types of self-assertion are the conditions of growth.

Sin on the part of a son does not consist in his assertion of his own will nor in his growing assumption of responsibility. The son's attitude is sin if he assumes that all he is and has accomplished has come entirely of himself and if he fails to recognize the degree to which all that he has been able to accomplish has been dependent both upon the native endowment with which he was born and the rich resources which have been provided for him as he has been given the opportunity to use both in his own growth. Self-assertion also is sin if through it the individual misuses his native endowment and his social heritage. Sin against God is that type of self-assertion in which the individual fails to recognize the degree to which all that he is or has become is dependent upon his native endowment as a human being, something for which he is not responsible and which was given to him; and the extent to which not only life itself, but everything which he has been able to attain personally and corporately is dependent upon the resources of this universe as they impinge upon the world, resources which he did not and could not create. This is the kind of sin which is manifested by the individual who wins first honors in school and feels that it is solely due to his own particular efforts, whereas he was able to attain these honors as compared with others who applied themselves with equal energy only because of his native endowment for which he was in no way responsible. Human beings manifest sin also when they fail to recognize how small are their attainments as compared with the limitless possibilities in human life and in the universe, and when irresponsibly they misuse the opportunities which are theirs.

That sin of these types is a peculiar danger in man because of his distinctive human capacities, no one doubts; but to assume that all human effort is of this sort, even that of profoundly religious people, seems as one-sided as to designate all human effort as good. It seems to make sin something which lacks moral meaning. Further, the cure of self-centered assertion and sinful pride does not seem to be the attempt to "annihilate man before God," but the kind of Christian experience which a true educational process helps to develop in which the perspective and outlook of the ego-centered individual is fundamentally changed. True humility of human beings, which the Christian religion enjoins and which the Christian experience helps to produce, is that which comes from the recognition that in God we live and move and have our being. But this does not involve consigning man to a state of servile submission to God nor does it deny the possibilities of comradeship with him.

The very essence of an educational process is comradeship between the more mature and the less mature in the enterprises of life where there are goals beyond the private welfare of individuals in which that welfare is involved. Comradeship with God in life's affairs seems to be the possibility which the Christian religion offers. This does not mean equality, as Brunner assumes. The parent or teacher who attempts to make himself like one of the children or who assumes that the children have reached his degree of maturity denies the very comradeship which the educational process provides. Such a relationship means that the older and the younger, the more mature and the less mature together will face the situations of life, the immature taking initiative and responsibility and the more mature furnishing protection and guidance and making resources available out of the larger experience. Certainly Christians should have the right to look forward to comradeship with God in the educational process and in life itself. In such comradeship in meeting the situations of life in this world, human beings would be expected to take initiative, to make decisions, to take responsibility, but all the time in relation to a God whose resources they utilize and dependence upon whom they gladly recognize. In such comradeship God becomes a living reality and at the same time man grows in true humility as he recognizes the degree to which he is actually dependent upon God.

CHAPTER VIII

Religious Education and Sin and Guilt

A CONCEPTION of God and of his relationship to human life which results in calling all human self-assertion rebellion against God and therefore sinful was criticized in the preceding chapter. But the very attempt to diagnose the human problem in terms of sin and guilt needs examination, particularly when these concepts are identified with one particular form of attitude and conduct.

The complete identification of sin and guilt with man's rebellion against the sovereignty of God can be understood only in relation to the tradition out of which it has come. It is not without significance that those who are reaffirming this doctrine of sin and guilt in this particular and extreme form are of German Lutheran or Reformed (Calvinistic) background. They are not only in the Reformation tradition, where this was the distinctive emphasis, but they also belong to a culture where the issue of the relation to authority in home, church, or state is the crucial one. Since Paul Tillich, also of this same religious and cultural heritage, has published a description of his experience, it is perhaps fair to use it as an illustration of what is meant. He says that "it was only in severe struggles that it was possible for me to break through to the affirmation of mental and moral autonomy." The source of his difficulties in coming to his own maturity and independence, he places in the kind of authority which his father represented. "My father's authority, which was at once personal and intellectual, and which because of his position in the Church, coincided for me with the religious authority of revelation, made every manifestation of autonomous thinking a piece of religious daring." He says that his critique of this authority involved a sense of guilt. He adds this comment: "The immemorial experience of mankind, that new knowledge can be won only through breaking a taboo, that all autonomous thinking is accompanied by a consciousness of guilt, has been a fundamental experience of my own life." [1] He emphasizes that anyone who has won his autonomy through having "broken determinedly with the taboos of the most sacred authorities cannot subject himself to a new heteronomy, whether religious or political." He includes in the heteronomy of religion the authority of a church, like the Roman Catholic, as well as that of "Barthian Supranaturalism." [2]

This quotation is significant because it shows how central in the German Protestant manifestation of the problem is the question of relation to authority, and also because it emphasizes that guilt is always associated with efforts to rebel against authority, human or divine. It is interesting to note that the late Otto Rank, one of the former associates of Freud, himself a German, has also based his diagnosis of the human problem on relation to authority. For him, growth to maturity always means the use of the counter-will of the child against the will of the parent and it is always accompanied by guilt. In other words, it is rebellion against the authority of the parent which is always necessary if the child is to attain any autonomy and maturity of his own. He tends to interpret all relationships—parent-child, teacher-pupil, and the like, and even those between human beings of different levels of maturity and ability—in these terms. He also is interpreting the problem of mankind from the slant of his own German experience with authority. The Barthian and neo-Barthian

[1] Tillich, Paul, *The Interpretation of History*, pp. 22–23.
[2] *Ibid.*, pp. 24, 26.

emphasis regarding sin seems distinctly related to an authoritative background.

In distinction to the emphasis of Barth and Brunner upon sin as rebellion against the sovereign authority and reign of God, it is interesting to note that a prominent emphasis in this country has been upon sin in its moral aspects. This emphasis also shows plainly the influence of human situations. It was brought to this country by German Pietists who came to the Middle Colonies in the eighteenth century, and also by way of the Wesleyan revival in England in the evangelistic tours of George Whitefield in this country and in the influence of other Methodists who came to America. It was from his religious experience under the influence of the Moravians that John Wesley got his message, but it was at the corruption in England in the first half of the eighteenth century that the message was aimed. It was brought to the "England of the slave-trader, the kidnapper and the smuggler; the England of trading justices, South Sea Bubbles and commercial cupidity; the England of gin-shops, sodden ignorance and incredible child neglect; the England of bestial sports, and gambling and parading wantonness . . . the England of corrupt politics and soulless religion." [3] The message was not centered on God and man's rebellion against him, but upon man and his depravity and corruption and his inability to be moral without God's saving help through Christ. It was in this emphasis distinctly Pauline as compared even with Luther, because it was ethical in its emphasis and because it stressed the transformation of the nature of the individual. Wesley "was more concerned in escape from sin and the attainment of holiness than in escape from divine wrath and the attainment of peace with God." [4] The emphasis was upon regeneration and sanctification rather than reconciliation. It is

[3] Bready, J. Wesley, *England before and after Wesley*, p. 189.
[4] McGiffert, Arthur Cushman, *Protestant Thought before Kant*, p. 166.

true that pride was considered the chief barrier to man's conversion, but this was interpreted as a sense of confidence in his ability to live the moral life and his unwillingness to recognize the total corruption of his nature rather than self-assertive rebellion against God. It was this ethical emphasis which was responsible for the far-reaching influence of the Wesley revival, not only upon the vitalization of religion but upon individual morality and social practices in England.[5]

This moral accent with reference to sin has been in evidence in America ever since the great awakenings in this country contemporary with the Wesley revival. It was not only the "dullness of religion" but the licentiousness and the lewd practices in Northampton which aroused Jonathan Edwards and led him to preach the wrath of God.[6] The revival awakening in the Middle Colonies was distinctly moral in its tone, though the need of saving power was also asserted. The second great awakening on the frontier was focused on the corrupt conditions in this newly settled territory. It is interesting to note that both Calvinists and Arminians led in these revival efforts.

The point of attack of a generation ago in this country was largely on sex as sin, although drunkenness was also a serious problem and was the chief center of concern in the rescue missions. The study of adolescent conversions by Edwin D. Starbuck, published in 1899,[7] revealed that the great proportion of such conversions took place in relation to a conviction of sin and a sense of guilt around the sexual feelings and around problems of this period in a young person's life. Normal sexual desire was branded by both Roman Catholics and Protestants as sinful, and sexual relations, except for the conception of children, were designated as sin. The data from this period reveals the degree to

---

[5] See *ibid.*, Chapters XVIII–XXII.
[6] Sweet, William Warren, *The Story of Religion in America*, p. 187.
[7] Starbuck, Edwin D., *The Psychology of Religion*.

which the normal sexual feelings of adolescence and the love expressions of sex within marriage were interpreted as sin and, as a result, brought to religious people serious struggles with sin and guilt. The so-called "clean-up" meeting, in which the focus was upon sexual sins, was a regular part of most student conferences of this period; but the severe struggle of most of the students was not in relation to irregular sexual relations, but around the sexual desires of adolescence and around practices such as masturbation. Theater-going and dancing were also opposed by many of the Christian groups because of the sex element. The emphasis of the Billy Sunday revivals was on "Quit your meanness," but meanness was interpreted chiefly in terms of sex, drunkenness, and similar practices.

The list of sins given by Paul in Galatians might be classified into two groups. There are sins of the appetite—fornication, uncleanness, lasciviousness, drunkenness, revellings; and those of the will—enmities, strife, jealousies, wraths, factions, divisions, parties, envying. It seems fair to say that in the period just described, the emphasis in the interpretation of sin was distinctly on sins of the appetite, while at the present time it is predominantly on sins of the will or the ego. This discussion would seem to show that the interpretation of sin has varied and that the particular interpretation shows distinctly the influence of the cultural situation. Further, the causes of a sense of guilt have varied, for guilt is not inevitably connected with one particular type of behavior or attitude, but is related to that which is disapproved. All of these types of emphasis have been alike, it is true, in their insistence upon man's inability to solve his problem without the saving power of God through Christ, but they have differed so much that it is not possible to speak of man's predicament as due to sin and to assume that this is a term which always has the same meaning.

In the United States a careful and discriminating attitude is necessary in considering the emphasis of a Barth or a Brunner. The religious educator will not meet the moral and religious problems of American youth if he attempts to read into much of the American scene the diagnosis of the problem which grows out of a German Lutheran and particularly a Reformed background. The sense of sin and guilt in coming to one's own independence and maturity is found only where there has been strict and autocratic authority. The child who has had the relationships to his parents, and even to religion, of most American children, will not understand when he reaches adolescence what Tillich is talking about in his sense of guilt over his rebellion against his father and against God in the interests of his own autonomy. The child who has been encouraged to do his own thinking and has been granted or has won for himself growing autonomy in the family and other relationships from childhood on into adolescence will not have a struggle with sin and guilt as rebellion against authority. Not all new knowledge, either for the individual or the race, is won by breaking a taboo, important as is this fact where the taboos exist. It has been the glory of the scientific attitude, even despite difficulties, that it has removed in many areas the taboos upon new knowledge and has substituted just the opposite.

The problem for thousands of American youth is that they have had too little rather than too much authority. Their parents are confused and baffled by the present situation in the world and they have left their children to find their way without the security and the guidance which relationship with parents and home and other adults should give as the basis for a true autonomy. As a result, they are in danger of being as badly lost as their parents. They are the ones who, instead of seeking autonomy against the authority (heteronomy) of adults, are looking for some anchorage, some authority in which they can trust. It is not freedom which has never been fought for that leads youth to be willing to yield to a new bondage, as Tillich concludes on the basis of his experience.[8] It is rather the lack of early security from the kind of authority which makes freedom possible that accounts for the yearning of youth, not for a new bondage, but for some sort of bondage which they have never had. American leaders in religion and education must be sure that they do not, under the influence of European interpretations of sin and guilt, make a false diagnosis of the problem of American youth.

The danger facing religious education is that those who have found difficulties in the nurture of children and youth because of superficial and false elements in an educational approach, will give up responsibility for a true educational process, will fall back upon attempts to re-establish the authority of another day, and will reinforce it by authoritative interpretations of religion. For youth, the danger is that, not having found true freedom and responsibility, they will fall back upon authoritative direction, either of the state or of the church. In any case, it will be adult authority. Therefore, it is necessary that the criticisms of liberalism in religion and in religious education should be taken seriously and utilized for necessary reconstructions in the educative process, but it is important that these criticisms should not lead liberals in religion and in religious education to a general retreat. The educative process, at its best, recognizes man's limitation and finiteness and gives the medium for the kind of authority on the part of adults which will enable children and youth to take increasing responsibility. Further, it will be necessary to interpret the criticisms of liberalism in terms of the American situation, particularly in the free rather than the authoritative churches and for those who have lost all religious authority and sense of rela-

[8] Tillich, Paul, *The Interpretation of History*, p. 24.

tionship to organized religion. The latter are the real problem for religious education.

The emphasis of certain theological interpreters in this country is a more accurate diagnosis of the characteristic form which sin takes in America than is the interpretation of a Barth or a Brunner. They do not emphasize rebellion against authority and particularly against a kind of authority which has not been characteristic of American life. Instead of this, they interpret sin as man's over-reaching himself in the use of his freedom, thus attempting to make himself the center of his life and, therefore, like God. Robert Calhoun emphasizes the "disposition of every infant, every adult, every social group (including the organized churches and sects), and every culture to affirm its own wants and wills as ultimate." [9] Reinhold Niebuhr says that practically men "always mix the finite with the eternal and claim for themselves, their nation, their culture, or their class the center of existence. . . . Thus, the moral urge to establish order in life is mixed with the ambition to make one's self the center of that order." He thinks that man is destined "to make absolute claims for his partial and finite values. He tries, in short, to make himself God." [10] It is egoism, he says, which is sin and the source of the human predicament. He states explicitly that human egoism is sin, "however natural and inevitable it may be, and its sinfulness is proved by its social consequences. . . . The social injustice and conflicts of human history . . . spring from those virtuous attitudes of natural man in which natural sympathy is inevitably compounded with natural egoism." [11]

The ego-striving of which these interpreters complain has taken on characteristics peculiar to the American scene. The ef-

[9] Calhoun, Robert L., "The Dilemma of Humanitarian Modernism" in *The Christian Understanding of Man*, p. 77.

[10] Niebuhr, Reinhold, *An Interpretation of Christian Ethics*, p. 85.

[11] *Ibid.*, pp. 114–115.

fect of our seemingly endless frontier upon the American character has been repeatedly emphasized. More than in any country of the Old World, there has been opportunity for initiative and success. Success psychology has dominated our education and corrupted our religion. Both our education and our religion have tended to be not only self-centered, but also superficial, for they were influenced by the problems of agricultural and industrial expansion and not by the deeper problems of human living. These problems seemed unimportant in a land of unlimited opportunity where anybody might be President. We were "rugged individualists." Competition did not seem serious in a land where there were more than enough jobs to go around and opportunities for all. It was a spur to endeavor and added zest to the game of life. There was less need of God and religion because of the feeling of self-sufficiency. If God were recognized, it was in the assumption that our prosperity was evidence of the blessing of God and of the fact that America was his chosen land. The War of 1914–18 touched us but lightly and we seemed remote from the tragedies of the post-war period. In the 1920's we thought we could go on increasing our prosperity indefinitely. And then came the crash. Small wonder that a people who had built their security on rugged individualism and personal success should find themselves baffled and frustrated when they found they could no longer trust what had been the basis of their lives.

However true a characterization this may be of the sin of the dominant American type, it does not take into account the situation of those whose problem is exactly the opposite. It looks at the problem from the perspective of the aggressive, self-assertive, successful go-getters and forgets the large minority who are the victims of this competitive situation and whose problem is sensitiveness, fear, inability to call one's life his own, defeat. To try to generalize on the basis of the aggressive group and to say that not only is excessive egoism wrong, but that egoism is always destructive and that "it is the driving force of sin" [12] is to forget those who are not able to muster enough egoism even to maintain themselves in this self-assertive world. It seems as one-sided to interpret sin solely in terms of what Jung calls the "extroverts" as it is for Henry C. Link to interpret it entirely in terms of the opposite, the "introverts." Link insists in his *Return to Religion* that it is the "introverts" who are selfish and sinful, but that the "extroverts" are the righteous people. A gospel which emphasizes God's condemnation of all human striving and the certain defeat of all human endeavor is harmful rather than helpful to those individuals whose over-burdening sense of sin and guilt is associated with their inability to assert themselves in any effective way and linked up with their defeat in the face of the ordinary responsibilities of life. They need the gospel of a God who has understanding of man's problem and who supports human endeavor.

It must be said also, in Niebuhr's own terminology, that egoism is not always so unmistakably wrong, and affirmation of the life of others rather than one's own is not always so unmistakably right as seems to be assumed. Sacrificing the self for the sake of others can become sin when it so dominates the individual that his or her ego rights are unduly sacrificed, as is best evidenced by its consequences upon the life of children who have had exaggerated self-sacrifice from their mothers. The swing from excessive ego-striving to a willingness to submit destructively to human or divine authority and control is the danger when man gives up legitimate confidence in himself. True responsibility is neither excessively ego-striving nor love-sacrificing, but an integration of these opposites in true responsibility.

The danger of a general emphasis upon sin and guilt is that it

[12] Niebuhr, Reinhold, *An Interpretation of Christian Ethics,* p. 87.

will turn the individual in on himself destructively. This is particularly true since that about which the individual feels guilty has such a definite social reference. Feelings of sin and guilt are not of much service except as they lead the individual to do something positive about the situation. A sense of guilt out of proportion to the seriousness of the offense, which is so frequently the result when all sin is equated as equally serious in the sight of God, tends to result in personal recriminations but no positive action. There is often failure to see that an exaggerated sense of sin and guilt is as ego-centered as is excessive pride and self-assertion. The latter is ego-centeredness in times of success; the former in times of defeat and failure. Nor does offering the individual a God who will turn his wrath to forgiveness, if the individual will but submit to him, relieve the difficulty. It is recognized that when children's attention is focused upon the attitude of their parents to themselves as children so that they have a sense of guilt in relation to the parents and have to depend upon their forgiveness for the relief of the guilt, they are still thinking of the attitude of their parents to *themselves* and are turned in on themselves destructively. That it is the supreme authority of the universe who grants the forgiveness does not change the situation, but rather accentuates it. The problem is solved only when the attention is turned from the self to the situation of which the individual is a part and he is led to do something positive about it, that he ceases to be destructively self-centered and finds the real solution of the problem. This involves a different kind of relationship with God and a different kind of religious experience from that which is often emphasized by those who stress sin and guilt in relation to all human efforts.

A recognition of the varied points of emphasis regarding sin, and of the individual and cultural factors in relation to sin, should lead to a more careful and discriminating analysis than is usually made by those who diagnose the human problem as due to something basically wrong which they call sin. Waiving the question as to whether all the manifestations which look like sinful conduct should be called sin, no one can question that there is a basic difference between conduct which grows out of ignorance and human limitation or out of circumstances over which the individual has no control, and the conscious and deliberate choosing of the wrong which characterizes some acts. It would seem that the use of the generic term "sin" is incorrect and that, instead, it is necessary to talk about sins. There are different kinds of sin. It is equally necessary to be more careful and discriminating in statements about the cure of sin. There is not one blanket answer to sin, called "Saving Grace." Different kinds of sin need different types of "Saving Grace." What might be the corrective or might furnish healing for one type of sin, might only aggravate another type. It is an over-simplification and a misinterpretation of the human problem to assign it to something called Sin, and it is equally unfortunate to offer religion in some general scheme called Grace.

It is against this over-simplification that John Bennett protests.[13] He says that there is vagueness and over-simplification in the diagnosis of the particular social evils which we face and a tendency to reduce all evil to one root—sin, which, since it can be used to explain everything, really explains nothing in particular. He feels that the term "demonic" is in danger of becoming such a catch-all. He says he wishes to press for more precise thinking, first, because different forms of sin require different forms of cure; and, second, because he objects to the dominance of pessimistic interpretations of human nature. He then describes five types of experience which need to be taken into account.[14] The

[13] Bennett, John, "The Causes of Social Evil" in *Christian Faith and the Common Life,* an Oxford Conference Book, pp. 175-176.
[14] *Ibid.,* pp. 177-182.

first form, he says, is of an entirely different kind from the others. It represents "the attitude of religious humility which makes the best men unable to give themselves credit for moral or spiritual achievements, which makes them regard themselves as part of the world's wrongness, which creates a sense of unworthiness which is not necessarily related to any particular evil for which they are morally reponsible." While this form of consciousness of sin has the danger of becoming pathological, as in Bunyan and Kierkegaard, it keeps our highest standards and achievements under judgment and is thus a growing point of the soul and of society and the pre-condition of all high religion. As to treatment, Bennett says this is a psychological problem and when it becomes too acute, demands provision for relief, religious or psychological.

The second and third forms of experience which Bennett describes, he says involve no personal moral responsibility. The second is found in "the choices of men who are limited by an external situation which is beyond their control and which forces them to make tragic compromise with evil." He cites as an illustration the way in which whole populations are drugged by propaganda and blinded by censorship. The third form which he gives is closely related to the second. It is manifested in "the choices of men who are living in the presence of far better possibilities than those which they choose to realize, but who are blinded by unavoidable ignorance which has for them external causes." The second form of sin he thinks can be dealt with only by large-scale change of social conditions and the third can be cured only by enlightenment.

The fourth type he cites differs from the third in that the individual is blinded in his choices "by ignorance which is primarily the result of inertia, selfishness, moral insensitivity." Therefore moral responsibility is involved because it is ignorance which is due to the individual's neglect. The fifth kind, according to Bennett, is the only one in which moral responsibility is clear and he feels there is much to be said for the argument of F. R. Tenant in *The Concept of Sin* for limiting the idea of sin to such deliberate choice. It represents those who in the presence of far better possibilities, "deliberately and with full knowledge violate the standards of conduct which they know to be binding upon them." In the fourth and particularly in the fifth type of conduct, a reorientation of the personal life is necessary.

Bennett also makes a careful analysis of the objective and subjective factors which have to be taken into account in diagnosing the sources of social evil. He feels that since so-called sin is extremely varied according to his five-fold classification, and since various subjective and objective factors are involved, a multiple attack upon social evil is necessary. Such an analysis of the problem of sin, he thinks, does make it possible to be more fair to people and to avoid blanket condemnations. It enables us to recognize "the permanent limitations in human nature" which make it impossible to realize a human utopia, and at the same time "to do justice to the stubbornness of evil in the human situation without blinding ourselves to the good in human nature." [15]

Those who take the approach of mental hygiene follow this discriminating method in the diagnosis and appraisal of human conduct. They emphasize the variety both of the manifestations and of the sources of undesirable conduct together with the necessity of suiting treatment to the causes rather than to the manifestations of such behavior. This latter is necessary because the same sort of behavior may be due to very different causes. For example, what looks like ego-striving and selfish pride may be really a cover for extreme sensitiveness and fear. The viewpoint of mental hygiene leads to a distinction between sin, in any responsible sense of the term, and personality sickness. This distinction does not minimize the seriousness of the human problem,

[15] *Ibid.*, pp. 194–195.

but only recognizes that many individuals who look like sinners are really the victims of circumstances beyond their control and are not responsible sinners.

Religious educators and other religious leaders should make this more careful diagnosis of the problem of sin. They should recognize that however much conduct may look like sin, it is often the manifestation of a sick, rather than a sinful, personality. Often the individual's seemingly sinful conduct is the result of conditions which were faced in early childhood, before there was opportunity for personal choice, and is socially caused by the mishandling of parents or by unfortunate home and environmental conditions. He is the victim of circumstances which were too difficult or too easy. His conduct represents the efforts of the individual to meet the situation. However undesirable such conduct may seem, it is of positive significance for him and may represent his way of protecting himself or of maintaining himself in the face of difficult conditions. Therefore, any effort to rob him of his ways of meeting life is bound to be resisted, for without it he is left helpless.

Under the condemnation of religious leaders, these sick persons often put up a brave front of defense which seems to confirm the diagnosis of sinful self-assertion, but underneath they have felt repentant over and over again for conduct they seem unable to change. Even the spoiled individuals who attempt to make all life adjust to them are the victims of those who have spoiled them, and are only made more self-centered by condemnation. The individual with sick personality does not need condemnation which may accentuate his difficulties; he needs the offer of positive help from someone who has genuine understanding of his problem. It is necessary also to recognize the variety of sources of difficulty, for only then can one be sure that the right type of help is being given. What might help a person with one kind of difficulty might hurt another with a different sort of problem.

There are sinners in every community, individuals who with mature responsibility have faced the alternatives, have rejected God and his will in the world, and have given their lives to the exploitation of others for their own ends. Sin is, to a certain extent, within the experience of all. But many of those with personality difficulties which manifest themselves in what looks like sinful conduct are the victims of our un-Christian social order, and the sin, if there be sin, is more largely that of their forbears or of a ruthless competitive society than of themselves. This distinction is already recognized in juvenile delinquency and some day will be more largely a part of the criminal procedure with adult offenders. We have punished the offender when often he is the victim of circumstances for which he is not responsible and over which he has no control. The real offenders are seldom brought into court.

It is necessary to suit what is done in the educative process to the character of the difficulty. The responsible sinners will need to be called to repentance and society must protect itself against them. The irresponsible sinners may at times need hospitalization for the protection of society as well as for their own welfare. But the treatment will be different. This distinction is recognized in the interpretation of Jesus Christ in the Gospels. His treatment of needy individuals was full of understanding sympathy. His condemnation was for those who exploited or who in self-righteousness failed to recognize true humility and responsibility. Compare his treatment of the Pharisees with that of the woman taken in adultery.

It will thus be seen that a much more careful analysis of the problems of individuals and a larger recognition of the variety of manifestations of so-called sinful action are important. Particularly is it necessary to make a distinction between sickness and sin; that is, between that sinful conduct for which the individual is responsible and that which has grown out of circumstances beyond his control. Instead of focusing attention upon the individual wrong-doer, there should be more sense of social responsibility and a larger consciousness of social sin. This gives the basis for a realistic religious education which recognizes fully the limitations of human beings and the seriousness of the human problem, but, at the same time, renders it possible to make a positive attack upon the problem through the educative process, the kind of an attack which will lead to a mature Christian experience in which there is "responsible existence."

CHAPTER IX

Human Nature and Religious Education

THE NEO-ORTHODOX INTERPRETERS, as has been evident in the discussion of the preceding two chapters, diagnose the human predicament in distinctly theological terms. They challenge an educational approach and method in meeting the human problem on theological grounds. But there are those who find the source of the human predicament in human nature, using that term in its psychological meaning. They base their doubt as to the possibilities of education on undesirable tendencies in human nature. When it is proposed that something might be done through an educational process to mitigate the ruthless competition of the present social order or to eliminate war between classes and races and nations, they reply that this is impracticable. "Human nature being what it is," the argument runs, "we can never expect to get rid of ruthless competition or devastating war. Man is born to compete with his fellows and to fight against them."

Certain theological interpreters in this country have supported their pessimistic, or realistic, diagnosis of the human problem by similar conceptions of human nature. For example, Reinhold Niebuhr has based his insistence that tragic conflict in human life is inevitable, not only on his analyses of the collective life of mankind in the past and present, but also on his descriptions of human nature. He says that education and other movements of liberal type are doomed to failure because they are based on too optimistic an appraisal of human nature. "The real basis for all the errors of liberalism is its erroneous estimate of human nature. The wise men of our day cannot gauge the actions of our strong men because they do not understand the tragic facts of human nature. They do not know to what degree the impulses of life are able to defy the canons of reason and the dictates of conscience."[1] It is in the egoistic impulses that Niebuhr locates the main source of the human problem. These are the ones which are able to defy both reason and conscience.[2] "In analyzing the limits of reason in morality it is important to begin by recognising that the force of egoistic impulse is much more powerful than any but the most astute psychological analysts and the most rigorous devotees of introspection realize."[3] Reason may be used "not only to justify egotism prematurely but actually to give it a force which it does not possess in non-rational nature."[4] Rather than being employed to "check and restrain impulse," reason may be used more easily "to justify impulse and to invent instruments for its efficacious expression."[5]

An examination of Niebuhr's writings shows that he has followed the commonly accepted conception of human beings as born with certain more or less well-defined impulses which are curbed and restrained or organized and directed by mind or reason.[6] He seems to think of these natural impulses as instincts.

[1] Niebuhr, Reinhold, *Reflections on the End of an Era*, p. 48.
[2] This is his emphasis in his earlier writings. In his latest books he has somewhat shifted his emphasis. See p. 201–204.
[3] Niebuhr, Reinhold, *Moral Man and Immoral Society*, p. 40.
[4] *Ibid.*, p. 41.
[5] Niebuhr, Reinhold, *Reflections on the End of an Era*, p. 16.
[6] It must be admitted that to determine what is Niebuhr's conception of human nature (in the more exact psychological sense of the term) is not easy. Since he is avowedly doing a "mythological" type of writing and is not holding himself to a precise scientific use of terms, he does not use the terms "nature," "impulse," "spirit," and the like with consistency of meaning. One has to attempt in each case to discover in what sense the term is being used in order not to reach false conclusions in regard to his thought. Further, one can never be sure how far he is using psychological conceptions for homiletic purposes in illustration of

He does not commit himself as between the orthodox instinct theory of original nature, as set forth by William James and amplified and modified by Edward L. Thorndike and William McDougall, in which these impulses are considered to be "discrete and underived," and a modified theory of instincts according to which "they are sharply defined only after they are socially conditioned." [7] But he does give to these inborn impulses the propulsive and directive power of instinct. While he recognizes the organic inter-relationship of various types of inborn energy, nevertheless he insists that every type of energy "maintains its own discrete existence" and "seeks to preserve and perpetuate itself and to gain fulfillment within terms of its unique genius." [8] Examples are the self-preservative energy which seeks the maintenance of the life of the individual and the sex energy which seeks the perpetuity of his kind. [9] This inborn human energy, he says, does not differ in its propulsive and direct power from that of the whole world of nature. It differs only in the degree to which reason directs the energy. [10] He also makes the distinction between natural impulses before and after they have been disciplined by reason. [11] He holds that the imperialistic forces of life are not "pure nature" but "natural impulses" organized and directed by mind. [12]

---

his thought, and how far these psychological interpretations represent his own convictions and are used in support of his thought. But with all these difficulties, there does seem to be in these early writings a well-defined picture of human nature which he uses to support his conclusions. This conception has been accepted by many who have been influenced by his pessimistic, or as he would call it, realistic diagnosis of the human problem. It is also a conception widely held and one which should be examined.

[7] Niebuhr, Reinhold, *Moral Man and Immoral Society*, p. 26.

[8] *Ibid.*, p. 25.

[9] *Ibid.*, p. 26.

[10] *Ibid.*, p. 25.

[11] Niebuhr, Reinhold, *An Interpretation of Christian Ethics*, p. 93.

[12] Niebuhr, Reinhold, *Reflections on the End of an Era*, p. 9.

Natural impulses, in Niebuhr's conception, are of two kinds: selfish or egoistic and unselfish or social.[13] The self-preservative instinct or the will-to-live is an example of the former. As examples of social impulses, he says that "whatever the theory of instincts which we may adopt, . . . it is obvious that man not only shares a gregarious impulse with the lower creatures but that a specific impulse of pity bids him fly to aid of stricken members of his community."[14] Other examples are "a mother's concern for her child or the emotion of pity for the distress of another."[15]

Niebuhr's thought as to the dual character of natural impulses is seen in his discussion of the paradoxical relation of "nature" and "spirit." These, he says, are "mythological" conceptions rather than exact scientific terms. "Nature" is used to designate the phenomenon in human life which has already been described. Instead of reason's being used to curb egoistic impulses, it is utilized to rationalize them and to give them greater effectiveness. "Nature" then represents egoistic impulses "directed and organized by mind." "Spirit" is used to designate both the "force which impels men to affirm the life of another rather than their own life" and also "the impulse to subject the individual or social ego to the universal."[16] In "spirit" reason not only carries the natural altruistic impulses beyond the limits set by nature,[17] but also contributes the basis for a sense of justice, which is so important for creating harmony between man and man and which is the product of the mind and not dependent upon natural social impulses.[18] The tragic human predicament, which "liberal" education fails to understand and with which it is unable to cope

[13] Niebuhr, Reinhold, *Moral Man and Immoral Society*, p. 25.
[14] *Ibid.*, p. 26.
[15] Niebuhr, Reinhold, *An Interpretation of Christian Ethics*, p. 93.
[16] Niebuhr, Reinhold, *Reflections on the End of an Era*, p 9.
[17] "Nature" and "natural" are seemingly used here in the ordinary psychological sense.
[18] Niebuhr, Reinhold, *Moral Man and Immoral Society*, p. 29.

successfully, is due, according to Niebuhr, to the strength of "nature" as compared with "spirit," particularly in the collective life of mankind. "When the impulses of self-preservation are mixed with reason and a form of life grows more self-conscious the will-to-live develops into the will-to-power." [19] The strength of this will-to-power is due to the fact that it is so inextricably bound up with self-preservation itself. This is seen particularly in collective life where classes and nations tend inevitably to become power groups in order to protect themselves and to maintain their life.

There is no question but that Niebuhr's general conception of human nature has been the prevailing one in modern education of the "liberal" type and was even followed by leaders in religious education in their first attempts to formulate a social theory. For example, George Albert Coe in his *A Social Theory of Religious Education,* published in 1917, attempted to fit such a theory into the mould of the current instinct conceptions of original nature. In his discussion of human nature in this book, he follows Edward L. Thorndike and William McDougall in saying that man is born with instincts, and by instincts he means "any readiness to act in a specific way in a particular sort of situation without having learned to do so." He is in accord with Niebuhr's classification of impulses as selfish and unselfish, when he says they are antisocial and social. Part of the function of education, according to Coe's discussion in this book, is to suppress the antisocial instincts and thus take measures to stop the socially destructive tendencies at their source in human nature. But it is also the business of education to foster and train the socially constructive instincts. He says that the parental instinct has unique social significance and it is upon this that he particularly centers his hope for a social and democratic form of education.[20] Thus he

---

[19] Niebuhr, Reinhold, *Reflections on the End of an Era,* p. 8.
[20] Coe, George Albert, *A Social Theory of Religious Education,* Chapter X.

follows the general assumptions about human nature found in Niebuhr's exposition, but differs from him in his conviction regarding the strength and possibility of the social instincts.

It is interesting also to note that the more realistic psychology which has developed in this recent period has not brought any fundamental critique of this general conception of human nature. It has been of the same type as Niebuhr's emphasis in asserting the strength and dominance of the more primitive urges and their control over the conscious life as represented in reason and intelligence. The very term "rationalization" was coined by these psychologists. This more realistic psychology was inaugurated by the work of Freud and arose entirely independently of education from the work of those who were dealing, not with the respectably intellectual group, but with those for whom life was tragic. Freud and his associates delved into the "unconscious" and uncovered in this sub-rational realm of the personality hates and jealousies and other undesirable deep-seated attitudes which Freud held were influencing and even shaping conscious life. He interpreted his data and diagnosed the human problem in a manner somewhat similar to that of Niebuhr, even though he emphasized sexuality rather than the will-to-live as the formative impulse. The basis of his conception of the human problem is found in his notion of the Id, the deep-seated stuff of human nature made up of primitive urges or drives predominantly sexual in the broad sense in which he uses the term. The Freudians expect that the *libido* or energy of the Id will manifest itself in well-defined patterns. They expect that every child will have curiosity and secretiveness or shame about the sexual organs and those of excretion; that there will be evidences of the Oedipus or Electra complex in the relations of parents and children in all families; that all persons of the female sex will suffer to a greater or less degree with the Castration complex; and that narcissistic tendencies in children will be universal.

According to Freud, the primitive urges of the Id are built into the Ego or personality through the discipline of the Super-ego, which represents the demands of civilization upon the Id brought to bear through man's mind and which is roughly comparable to what is known as conscience. The problem for the Ego or human personality grows out of the fact that man is caught between the imperious pressures of the Id for the expression of primitive urges and the restraints upon such expression which are imposed through the Super-ego. Were men allowed to express these primitive impulses, there would be little more conflict among human beings than among the animals. This is evidenced by the fact that neuroses are not found among primitive groups where the control of the Super-ego is more nearly on the level of the primitive urges. Neurosis is distinctly a symptom of civilization. In civilization, the urges of the Id are either restrained or given expression in more appropriate manner through what he calls sublimation. But the human problem is never solved. Although the primitive impulses of the Id are to some extent curbed or sublimated through the control and discipline of the Super-ego, it is always an unsatisfactory compromise with civilization. Education based on the Freudian psychology is the development of controls by bringing the demands of civilization to bear upon the personality through the development of the Super-ego or conscience. But conscience has all the limitations, in face of the imperious demands of the Id, which Niebuhr emphasizes.

It is in a fundamental examination of these conceptions of human nature that social scientists and educators have been engaged and it is out of this work that there has developed a radically different conception from that set forth by those who hold views of the type of Niebuhr or Freud. The first fundamental challenge was directed toward the idea that human beings are born with instincts or impulses of discrete and more or less defined character, which pre-determine or at least influence the type of conduct. The conviction that man has developed his anti-social individual and collective ways of behaving because he has the roots of such conduct in inborn tendencies or patterns was perhaps the natural conclusion to reach on the basis of the strength and persistence of this behavior. Since psychologists, like Thorndike, had done their earlier research in animal psychology and had found an instinctive basis of behavior in animals, they inferred that human nature was of the same sort, but differed from the animals in the number and variety of instincts and the consequent versatility of man, and also in the degree to which these instincts could be restrained and directed because of the human mind. The study made through the social sciences, widely separated geographically and from very different approaches, has led to a definite trend away from an instinct theory and to an emphasis upon the difference between human beings and animals in connection with inborn impulses which tend to take particular forms. The emphasis is upon the extent to which patterns of behavior have been developed by mankind in his experience and are learned by the young. Observation of infants in the first hours and days of life by John B. Watson and others in the United States revealed only the most limited unlearned responses. The experiments with the conditioned reflex by Pavlov and his associates in Russia and by psychologists in the United States showed the ease with which fear and other responses could be developed and then eliminated, and yet these were responses that in the case of the human young were held to be due to inborn instinct and to be inevitable. Freud and his associates were able to trace the origin of feelings and attitudes to the experiences of the individual in early childhood and in the family relationships and, despite their interpretation of the basis of these in the Id, carried on their therapeutic work on the assumption that these had been learned in unfortunate experience and could be released in the imaginative experience of the analytic process. The work of the analytical psychiatrists with adults and of the social psychiatrists in dealing with juvenile delinquency, family problems and the like, showed that undesirable ways of behaving and even criminal conduct yielded in a manner which would hardly be possible were they manifestations of inborn and inevitable tendencies. The sociologists have shown to what degree the mores and the morals of the family and of other forms of corporate life are influential in determining individual attitudes and conduct.

The researches of the anthropologists are particularly pertinent because they have studied primitive tribes where there is complete social control of the influences which affect the young. For example, Margaret Mead studied three tribes in the same general area of New Guinea.[21] In two of the tribes studied, the general assumptions about human nature and conduct which have been reviewed in this chapter were completely reversed, while in the third tribe they showed themselves in accentuated form. She found that the mountain-dwelling Arapesh had developed a type of life in which gentleness and coöperation predominated and where the satisfactions were found in service to the welfare of the tribe. The men as well as the women had characteristics which in our civilization are called feminine. The ego-asserting individual, who would make a success in our civilization, was in a difficult position and was the maladjusted person. Individual differences were as marked among children as in this country, but the range was different. The most active Arapesh child was far less aggressive than a normally active American child. These characteristics of the Arapesh could not be accounted for on the basis of inborn

[21] Mead, Margaret, *Sex and Temperament.*

physical differences, for their plain-dwelling neighbors, like the Arapesh in physical characteristics and language, were a warlike tribe. The characteristics seemed to be due to the patterns of life which the tribe had established and to the education of children in this pattern through their experience in the tribe.

In contrast with the Arapesh, Margaret Mead found another tribe, the Mundugumor, who carried aggressiveness and fighting beyond that which we know in the West. The men of this tribe found their greatest satisfaction in fighting and in the competitive acquisition of women. The fighting endangered the whole life as a tribe because it went on between relatives and in all parts of their life. In contrast with both of these, she describes a third tribe, the Tchambuli, in which the characteristic rôle of men and women in our society was reversed. While the tribe was patrilinear in organization and the men were nominally the owners of their homes, the heads of their families, and even the owners of their wives, the actual initiative and power was in the hands of the women. The women carried on the business and the men did the shopping for the women and represented them in marketing their products. The women also chose their husbands, so it was the man and not the woman who was in danger of not being chosen. Aside from their service to their wives, the men gave their time to various sorts or artistic pursuits—dancing, carving, plaiting, painting, etc.—and also put on entertainments for the women. The conclusions from her study not only emphasize the social origin of personality characteristics but also show that the characteristics of men and women are not inborn but socially produced. This conclusion is particularly interesting because she undertook the study with the assumption that there were inborn differences in characteristics as between men and women and the purpose of her study was to define these differences more exactly.

The most searching criticism of the interpretation of human nature and of the human problem of the Freudian psychology has been made by a woman who is herself a practicing psychoanalyst of the Freudian school, Dr. Karen Horney, of New York City. While recognizing the indebtedness of those who deal with personality difficulties to the revolutionary insight of Freud, which has changed the whole course of treatment of neurotic and psychotic difficulties and has influenced social work, education and criminology, she holds that his insight in regard to the origin of personality difficulties in early experiences and as to the possibilities of therapy is not dependent upon the particular interpretation of human nature he made, but is in fact hindered by it. Her criticism of Freud is that he has made an individualistic and biological interpretation of the human problem which does not do justice to the sociological factors. She shows how patterns of conduct, which an orthodox Freudian expects to find in every person, have been developed in the particular circumstances and social experience of the individual.[22]

In an earlier book,[23] Horney holds that the neurotic personality of our time is peculiarly the product of our competitive society, the kind of society which Niebuhr describes. Instead of the individual having two kinds of impulses, egoistic and social, he has two types of needs and problems: ego or individual and love or relationship. Each person has the problem of maintaining and developing his personality and at the same time having relationships with others. When both of these needs have a chance for development in organic inter-relationship, when the personality is respected and relationship with others can be maintained, there is then an opportunity for the healthy growth of personality in a constructive self-other inter-relationship. From her point of view,

[22] Horney, Karen, *New Ways in Psychoanalysis.*
[23] Horney, Karen, *The Neurotic Personality of Our Time.*

neuroses in our time are caused because in our individualistic and competitive society, the two sets of needs and possibilities are placed in unnecessary conflict. The individual has to compete for his ego development and satisfaction with the very individuals with whom he needs to be in relationship to satisfy his love needs and even to maintain his own life. As a result, there is disastrous conflict. Neurosis is, therefore, social in its origin and can be prevented only by a reconstruction of the social situation out of which it grows. Incidentally, it might be remarked that this diagnosis could be applied to our neurotic society. For example, labor has to compete disastrously with owners for the maintenance of its ego needs, but it is competing with the very group with which it needs to be in organic relationship for any maintenance of the corporate life of industry.

The late Otto Rank, one of the former close associates of Freud, carried this social emphasis into psychology itself. He insists that there is no warrant for generalizing regarding all human beings from particular experience in a particular time and set of circumstances in the world. In a very true sense he holds it to be true that there is no such thing as human psychology as such; that is, there is no description possible of man or of human behavior in general. All realistic psychologies are to a large degree cultural psychologies. From this point of view, he holds that Freudian psychology is a true description of upper middle-class bourgeois individuals of the Victorian period, and particularly a true description of these persons in Roman Catholic Vienna; but it does not fit the person who has not come under those influences. On the other hand, Alfred Adler was a Socialist and was identified with the suppressed classes and his psychology is a true description of individuals or groups who are handicapped or discriminated against and who are seeking to overcome their inferior status. Thus from his point of view, it is not possible to understand man as man,[24] but only men and groups in relation to circumstances or culture.

Gordon W. Allport, Associate Professor of Psychology in Harvard University, makes a somewhat similar emphasis in his latest book.[25] He says that psychologists, in so far as they have attempted to make psychology an exact science, have followed scientific presuppositions and procedures which are not useful in the study of human beings. They have assumed that the individual is only an instance or example of a universal principle. Therefore, they have first attempted to abstract elements in personality, then they have studied the manifestation of each particular segment in many individual cases, and have attempted to arrive at a generalization or law which applies to all individuals. Even differential psychology, he says, "does not deal with the particular at all, but rather with variations in the general." The result of such a procedure from his viewpoint is often to bring conclusions which are of no practical value because there is no such thing as "generalized mind." In the psychological field, he says, "there are only single, concrete minds, each one of which presents problems peculiar to itself. In ordinary life we deal with our acquaintances, not by applying abstract laws, but by studying their individual natures." His criticism of Freudian and other forms of analytical psychology is at this point. Like general psychology, they are preoccupied with the search for universal causes; the "design is traced upon the patient, and then *mirabile dictu*—is discovered to exist there." He emphasizes a much more "personalistic" type of psychology.

It is on the basis of data and considerations such as have been reviewed that the conclusion is reached that it is a false picture of

[24] This summary is based on an academic lecture, given by Otto Rank at Union Theological Seminary.

[25] Allport, Gordon W., *Personality, a Psychological Interpretation*, Chapter I.

human nature to think of it as consisting of more or less well-defined egoistic or selfish and social or unselfish tendencies, which are curbed and restrained or organized and directed by reason. Particularly does the emphasis upon the strength and the evil character of the egoistic tendencies seem untrue. Such emphasis upon the predominance and power of the evil tendencies is as one-sided as former optimistic appraisals of man as by nature good. The fact is there are no such well-defined inborn tendencies in man, either evil or good. Original nature is a-moral in the sense that there is nothing in the nature with which an individual is born which predetermines whether he will be a saint or a devil. Whether the "divine" or the "demonic" possibilities are developed depends upon what happens to that original nature in the experiences of life. The individual's personality is of social origin. It is developed in the learning which takes place in incidental life experience and in that more formal experience in home and school and church which is called education. By this is not meant that human nature is moulded like clay by its environment. Human beings respond to these environmental influences, sometimes by submission, at other times by rebellion. They have the possibility also of doing something about the environment or of acting in ways contrary to it. But this emphasis does mean that certain conditions in the family, community, national or international life of a time, certain conditions indeed in a church, tend to bring out the "demonic" and make it difficult for the "divine" while other conditions foster the "divine" and give it a chance to be developed. A thorough-going recognition of the social origin of the self is necessary in any realistic appraisal of the human problem, and a social approach is essential, if education is to be of positive help.

Man is distinguished from the animals by the degree that he has to learn everything, and also by the extent that his characteristics are determined in this learning through experience and the more directed experience called education. The equipment with which the individual is born is an important factor in that learning. Each infant has a certain physical body, a certain physique, with which he must negotiate life. Whether he has a sound body, a good vegetative system, good eyes and ears is important in his development. He is born also with a cerebro-spinal nervous system with its center in the brain. This determines the level of his intelligence, though not how much that intelligence will be developed. He is born with the basis of what Gordon Allport calls temperament; such things as speed of reaction, glandular set-up which affect the basic metabolism, and the like. The range and limit of possibilities are determined by this equipment. He can do only what it is possible for a human being to do. Further, individuals differ in the soundness of the physical body, in the quality of brain, and in speed-reactions and glandular set-up. Thus, there is the basis in original nature for feelings of inadequacy and inferiority and for the attitudes of jealousy and rivalry. But there is nothing in the raw material with which a person is born which predetermines what personality characteristics the individual will have. Often an individual with a poor equipment makes a finer adjustment to life and its responsibilities than one with a superior native endowment.

The basis of developing this original equipment into the personality is activity of all sorts. The organism is set to function. The tension which develops in the muscular set-up itself after rest presses for activity. This is evident in the brief time that a little child or even an adult can remain entirely quiet. Internal pressures of hunger, of the eliminatory organs, and later in connection with the sexual set-up, make the organism restless and stimulate it to do something; but what is done is a matter of learning. That the inborn energy of the organism has definite forms or some purpose it is trying to achieve seems to be denied by the data. The internal pressure from hunger manifests itself in the baby in random motions of arms and legs, squirming, and crying—certainly not methods of getting food. The baby does not know that he is hungry. He is just uncomfortable from the internal pressure. When food is supplied, the pressure is released, but what is eaten, how it is eaten, when it is eaten, is first determined by the parents and slowly built into the habits of the child. Even connecting the internal pressure with hunger is learned. Not only the method of satisfaction but the significance of the pressures themselves is thus the result of learning. This is evidenced in the little child, who is just learning toilet controls and is not free like the infant to release the eliminatory pressure. Often he is very restless without knowing the reason. When it is suggested that he go to the toilet, he follows the advice and the pressure is released. By this method of identifying the source, he learns toilet controls. It is out of the large uncoördinated random motions and squirmings of the little baby that through activity little by little the more precise coördinations and differentiations are made; and it is out of the original repertory of unintelligible "goos" and "awes" that little by little speaking is built. Maturation is a factor in this learning. Both brain and body grow. But while maturation increases the possibility of learning, it does not determine what is learned. Possibly walking is an exception to this general conclusion, although this is a moot issue.

When the child reaches the place where he can get around himself, his learning takes place through his own activity in finding his way in his physical environment and in his relationship with others. But this environment, in turn, furnishes its own stimuli, in part through the controls and demands which are placed upon him and in part by the very interest which is aroused in that with which he comes into contact. As the child moves from the more complete control and protection of infancy into wider areas of activities, life on the routine basis is no longer completely possible. Choices have to be made and he must take added responsibility for what he does. But while the capacity to choose is found in the original equipment, the ability to choose is developed in experience, as are other skills.

Of all the inborn energy, that of sex would seem as if it ought to carry its own propulsion to definitely defined ends. Niebuhr assumes that this is true. He says that nature endows man "with a sex impulse which seeks the perpetuity of his kind with the same degree of energy with which he seeks the preservation of his own life." [26] But the sex impulse does not carry through to the certain sexual intercourse and the procreation of children that it does in animal life. It is true that the internal pressures of sex make for restlessness and activity. But frequently the release is found in sex experience with the self in masturbatory practices and the individual lives permanently at an ego-centered level of sex. Often again because of the circumstances of life, it is expressed in homo-sexual relations. What are in fact homo-sexual marriages are not uncommon, and however much they may release sex pressure, they are hardly useful for the perpetuation of the race. Promiscuity is common. It has taken mankind centuries to learn that marriage with a mate who is loved is the most satisfactory expression of sex, and yet monogamy is instinctive in certain animals and birds. Further, the pressure of sex is often not recognized as such at all, as in the case of adolescent boys who sublimate it through crime without recognizing the origin of their activity, or of women who are everlastingly busy managing other people's affairs because of their unsatisfied sex pressures. Even sex does not follow in mankind the predetermined course which is found in other parts of nature.

[26] Niebuhr, Reinhold, *Moral Man and Immoral Society*, p. 26.

Emphasis is frequently placed upon the power of the cravings and desires, the likes and dislikes, the loves and the hates of men and women and it is often assumed that these are found in the person independent of his experience. Robert L. Calhoun says: "The trouble with man is centered in his feelings and desires, far down beyond the range of conscious thought and will. A man is as he *loves*."[27] *Why* he desires or loves as he does may be out of the range of an individual's conscious thought, but *what* he desires has been influenced if not indeed been determined by his experience. All the way from his tastes in food to his love for music or art, and the kind of music or art he loves, experience and learning have been operative. Nowhere is it more in evidence than in the way individual success, and particularly surpassing others and being first, is prized. This has been held before the young by parents. Particularly has this been the case in school and college where the appeal for such education was success.

Without question the original equipment of the individual is a factor in determining what he loves and desires. A person with a sensitive ear and a certain kind of glandular set-up will respond more readily to music than one without that equipment. Certain speed of reaction and ease with which coördinations are formed, in which individuals differ because of inborn equipment, may influence one's love for pursuits in which these are important. But these factors are not of the purposive and propulsive nature that is assumed in purposes and desires.

It has been assumed that falling in love was one aspect of life above all others in which learning did not enter. You just fell in love, that was all there was to it. But the experience and learning elements in determining what kind of person an individual will fall in love with have become evident when we have been willing to analyze this supreme experience. All through early

[27] Calhoun, Robert L., *What Is Man?*, p. 69.

life there are many influences upon children and youth which are forming their ideal of a mate. One's wishes and desires, his loves and his hates, his interests and his aversions are learned.

It is true that these desires and aversions which have been built up under the pressure of experience come to have their own propulsive power. On what Gordon Allport calls the principle of "functional autonomy" these operate long after the circumstances that brought them into being are over. As an example, he gives the standard of good workmanship, which was built up in some people in the days of hand-work when excellent craftsmanship brought them approval and economic advantage, but which persists in a machine age, even when it is a disadvantage.[28] Many things which individuals have learned to do because of the pressure of circumstances have come to have their own drive even after the necessity is past. But these are not the drives of original nature but of a "second nature"—to use Professor Calhoun's term —which has been built through experience and learning.

It must be evident that the common assumption that the source of the human predicament lies in anti-social impulses in man is erroneous. The emphasis upon the predominance and power of so-called evil tendencies in man is as one-sided as former optimistic appraisals of man as being by nature good. The fact is, as John Bennett says, that through the new appreciation of the pessimistic interpretations of human nature which have been an important strain in the Christian tradition, we are "being led from a dogmatic optimism which was founded on theories of progress and human perfectibility, for which there is insufficient empirical evidence, to a dogmatic pessimism which is founded on theological theories of man, for which there is also insufficient empirical evidence." [29] The empirical evidence seems to show

[28] Allport, Gordon W., *Personality, a Psychological Interpretation*, Chapter VII.
[29] Bennett, John, "The Causes of Social Evil," in *Christian Faith and the Common Life*, an Oxford Conference Book, p. 176.

that there is nothing in human nature with a predetermining influence that the individual will be a saint or a devil; but there are resident within that nature possibilities which will never be exhausted in any lifetime of either or both, and possibilities which are unknown in the animal world. Man can carry the ruthless struggle for existence to excess in the utilization of his mind for the development of instruments of power which are never known in the animal world, or he can substitute for the competitive struggle for existence a degree of coöperative relationships in home and community and nation or even in the world which infinitely transcend Kropotkin's description of mutual aid in animal life. He can devise methods of egoistic self-assertion, both individual and collective, of diabolical strength, or he can voluntarily sacrifice his own life for the sake of others. He can go to the depths of debauchery in eating and drinking unknown to the animals or he can make these a social and aesthetic event of a kind which animals never know. He can use his sexual relations for extremes of cruelty and exploitation of others that is never a part of the animal sexual urge, or he can carry his sexual expressions far beyond the necessities of reproduction and make them the supreme expression of regard and love for his mate. A realistic appraisal of human nature will place no exclusive emphasis upon either the "demonic" or the "divine" tendencies, but will recognize the exhaustless possibilities of both. But this by no means infers the perfectibility of man because he is always within the finite limitations of human beings.

CHAPTER X

A Social Strategy of Religious Education

THE CONCLUSION reached in the preceding chapter is that there is nothing in the original nature of man which makes it inevitable that he should be in his present predicament in his social relationships. The fact is, however, that the description of society, which Niebuhr and other similar interpreters make, is an accurate one. For some reason, even though man did not need to develop a devastating type of competitive social order, he has actually succeeded in building this sort of society. Further, the spread of education and the growth of intelligence do not seem to have solved the problem.

Niebuhr thinks that liberal educators follow the faith of the Enlightenment in trusting the removal of ignorance and the development of intelligence for solving the human problem. "The faith of the Enlightenment is still the creed of the educators of our day and is shared more or less by philosophers, psychologists, and social scientists. The sorry plight of our civilisation has qualified it only in the slightest degree. The traditions and superstitions, which seemed to the eighteenth century to be the very root of injustice, have been eliminated, without checking the constant growth of social injustice. Yet the men of learning persist in their hope that more intelligence will solve the problem. They may view present realities quite realistically; but they cling to their hope that an adequate pedagogical technique will finally produce the 'socialized man' and thus solve the problems of society." [1]

[1] Niebuhr, Reinhold, *Moral Man and Immoral Society,* p. 24.

Rational individualism and liberalism assume "that the moral possibilities which the reason of an individual is able to envisage are immediately capable of realization in history, provided only that a little more education purify the reason of others to the degree of purity it feels itself to have attained." [2]

Niebuhr is quite ready to admit what can be accomplished through reason or intelligence and therefore recognizes that education has certain possibilities and can show worthwhile achievements. Indeed, he is critical of those religious interpreters who hold these achievements in contempt. Education, he says, "can no doubt solve many problems of society." [3] Ideally reason should be able to prevent and reduce social conflict "by relating interest to interest and will to will in ever widening circles of social harmony." [4] But despite Niebuhr's recognition of the possibilities of reason and therefore of education which in his conception has as its function the development of intelligence, he is fundamentally critical of trust in reason for the solution of the human problem because of its decided limitations. These are due in part to man's finiteness. "No man will ever be so intelligent as to see the needs of others as vividly as he recognizes his own, or to be as quick in his aid to remote as to immediately revealed necessities." It is difficult if not impossible for even "an astute social pedagogy to increase the range of human sympathy." [5] Further, while reason is able to project "goals more inclusive, and socially more acceptable, than those which natural impulse prompts," [6] and even to envisage "possibilities of order, unity, and harmony above and beyond the contingent and arbitrary realities of its physical existence," it is nevertheless the "prisoner of the partial perspectives of a limited

[2] Niebuhr, Reinhold, *Reflections on the End of an Era*, p. 116.
[3] Niebuhr, Reinhold, *Moral Man and Immoral Society*, p. 24.
[4] Niebuhr, Reinhold, *Reflections on the End of an Era*, p. 5.
[5] Niebuhr, Reinhold, *Moral Man and Immoral Society*, p. 28.
[6] *Ibid.*, p. 35.

time and place" and is "not capable (because of its finiteness) of incarnating, all the higher values which it discerns; nor even of adequately defining, the unconditioned good which it dimly apprehends as the ground and goal of all its contingent values." [7]

The limitation of human reason is not, however, the main factor in Niebuhr's doubt as to its potency and therefore in his criticism of an education which trusts in the development of intelligence. Rather, it is the power of impulse. "The dominance of reason over impulse is much more tentative than modern culture realizes." [8] He criticizes what he says is the conception of the modern empiricist that human history is the "gradual triumph of mind over impulse," and that there is "historical progress toward an ethical goal" involving "a gradual cumulation of individual triumphs of reason over nature until the whole of nature is subdued." [9] Not only is it true that "mind is the servant of impulse before it becomes its master," but also that "the first effect of mind upon impulse is to make man more deadly in his lusts than the brute." [10] Rather than being employed to "check and restrain impulse," reason may be used more easily "to justify impulse and to invent instruments for its efficacious expression." [11]

It is true that reason can, to a certain degree, mitigate the struggle and do something toward the introduction of harmony. But this is more effective in personal face-to-face relations than it can ever be in collective life, because of the lack of personal contact between conflicting power groups and because the issues become badly confused through the very use of intelligence in propaganda and other methods of forming the minds of individuals in the group. Reason not only seems powerless in the pres-

[7] Niebuhr, Reinhold, *An Interpretation of Christian Ethics*, p. 66.
[8] Niebuhr, Reinhold, *Reflections on the End of an Era*, p. 5.
[9] *Ibid.*, p. 123.
[10] *Ibid.*, p. 17.
[11] *Ibid.*, p. 16.

ence of strongly organized collective life, but it also tends to be utilized for strengthening and extending power and for rationalizing its use. Any realistic understanding of human beings and of the facts of the situation shows, he says, that power groups have never listened to reason and persuasion, no matter how effectively presented. Persuasion has pricked the conscience at times, it is true, but it has never been sufficiently effective to lead those in power to change their course of action.[12]

In view of this situation, he believes that it must be recognized that if there is to be any fundamental change in the situation, it will come only through the conflict of power groups. When the underprivileged become strong enough to contest the reign of the powerful, the crisis of conflict comes and a different order may be established. But the new order will be subject to the same egoistic impulses and the will-to-live as have the regimes which it supplants. Therefore, the conviction of Marxians that the victory of the proletariat will end the class struggle is just as great an illusion as that of liberal Christians that change can come about by gradual and peaceful methods.

In his later writings, Niebuhr changes his diagnosis of the human predicament and places the source of the human problem in what he calls "spirit." He uses the term, however, in a different sense from his earlier writings. It is no longer the social impulses as organized and extended by reason, but is now that which gives man his freedom as compared with the animals. In other words, it is man's capacity to think and remember and imagine, to utilize his past experience and project plans for the future, which is designated as "spirit." Man is not bound by the limitations of nature as are the animals, but through intelligence is able to transcend them. He says that "it is human freedom, . . . created by the

---

[12] See *ibid.*, Chapter III, for testimony from history as to the ineffectiveness of the persuasions of the wise men with the mighty men.

transcendence of reason over impulse which makes sin possible." [13]
He indicates that according to the prophetic conception with which
he seems to identify himself, "moral evil lies at the juncture of
nature and spirit. The reality of moral guilt is asserted because the
forces and impulses of nature never move by absolute necessity,
but under and in the freedom of the spirit." [14]

The source of man's difficulty, according to this diagnosis, lies
in the very possibilities to transcend nature which his intelligence
makes possible. Standing as he does at the juncture of spirit and
nature, of freedom and necessity, he has finite limitations and perspectives because he is still a part of nature, but he refuses to admit
his finiteness and his limitation because of the transcendence which
reason makes possible. Man has to face the insecurity of a contingent world, but he tries to transcend that insecurity. All men
suffer from insecurity because of the precarious and unpredictable
character of human existence. Their undue self-assertion and their
efforts at dominance, individually and collectively, are a compen-
sation for the feeling of inferiority which they do not wish to
admit. This, according to Niebuhr, is the root of injustice.

This possibility of the transcendence of spirit over nature betrays
man into his imperial ambitions. By reason of the fact that he is
involved in natural processes but is able to transcend them, he is
always tempted to claim greater finality for his achievements than
they deserve. "Ideally men seek to subject their arbitrary and contingent existence under the dominion of absolute reality. But
practically they always mix the finite with the eternal and claim
for themselves, their nation, their culture, or their class the center
of existence. . . . Thus, the moral urge to establish order in life
is mixed with the ambition to make oneself the center of that
order; and devotion to every transcendent value is corrupted by

[13] Niebuhr, Reinhold, *An Interpretation of Christian Ethics*, p. 91.
[14] *Ibid.*, p. 84.

the effort to insert the interests of the self into that value." He adds that "man is destined, both by the imperfection of his knowledge and by his desire to overcome his finiteness to make absolute claims for his partial and finite values." [15] Pride, jealousy, envy, and the like are thus, according to Niebuhr's later view, sins of the "spirit." Human pride is "greatest when it is based upon the solid achievements of human life" but achievements which are "never great enough to justify its pretensions." [16] These pretensions would not be possible if man "did not have capacities for self-transcendence which permitted him to see his finite existence under the perspective of its eternal essence. But it would also be impossible if man's finiteness did not betray him into a corruption of the highest values. . . . Thus, evil in its most developed form is always a good which imagines itself, or pretends to be, better than it is." [17]

Man is thus, according to Niebuhr, in the curious but tragic predicament that his reason has made him a moral being, capable of choice, so that he cannot live the instinctive life of the animal in natural harmony and without conflict, and yet his reason plays him false because it leads him into self-centered efforts to deny his limitations and to make his will ultimate. These are the sources of individual pride and of social conflict. He becomes an egotistical, self-centered individual who competes disastrously with his fellows, whether individuals or racial, economic, and national groups. Able because of his intelligence to solve the problems of

[15] *Ibid.,* pp. 84–85.
[16] Niebuhr, Reinhold, *Beyond Tragedy,* pp. 29–30. "Thus man builds towers of the spirit from which he may survey larger horizons than those of his class, race and nation. This is a necessary human enterprise. But it is also inevitable that these towers should be Towers of Babel, that they should pretend to reach higher than their real height. . . . The higher the tower is built to escape unnecessary limitations of the human imagination, the more certain it will be to defy necessary and inevitable limitations. Thus sin corrupts the highest as well as the lowest achievements of human life." *Ibid.,* p. 29.
[17] Niebuhr, Reinhold, *An Interpretation of Christian Ethics,* pp. 86–87.

production and make enough available for all, he is unable to utilize these productive capacities because he cannot solve his problems of selfishness and pride. Able to use science for the amelioration of human life, he finds science itself used in the development of instruments of destruction by which he seeks to protect himself against his fellows or to make his will dominant over them.

The basis for Niebuhr's distrust in education as a solution of the human problem is evident from this review of his thought. Education, according to Niebuhr, is centered on the removal of ignorance and the development of intelligence. There is no question but that this has been the conception of "liberal" educators. This idea of education would seem to have been warranted on the basis of either of Niebuhr's diagnoses of the human problem. If the function of reason is to restrain and control or to organize and direct impulses, it would seem to follow that the better trained is the individual's mind and the more he is furnished with useful information, the better will he be able to use his mind in accomplishing this task. If man's freedom as compared with the animals is due to his ability to transcend nature because of his superior mental equipment, it would seem that the more his intelligence is developed, the greater will be his freedom. But the hopes which originated with the Enlightenment have not been realized. The spread and development of intelligence through education has not solved the problem. Indeed in some regards the growth of intelligence has increased the seriousness of the human predicament because intelligence has often been used for greater dominance and more deadly competition than in primitive life.

The difficulty would seem to lie not in man's intelligence but in the strategy which has been employed in its use. Religion's educators with a social viewpoint would be as critical as is Niebuhr of the type of education he describes, and it is in efforts to develop religious education of a fundamentally different kind that they are engaged. There has been a two-fold difficulty in "liberal" education. In the first place it has been over-intellectual. There has been almost exclusive attention to the training of the mind and little or no attention has been given to the emotions. It has been assumed that by the development of intelligence through education the basic impulses and emotions of mankind could be controlled and directed. There has been failure to recognize the psycho-physical unity of the organism and the degree to which both intellect and emotion are integrally inter-related in every human decision and human act. While the superior equipment of the mind makes choice possible, those choices which are of any importance involve the whole organism and are charged with emotion at every stage. They involve important concerns of the personality either in relation to security or to the satisfaction of personal needs and they are related to vital purposes or goals beyond the individual. A human problem is never solely an intellectual affair and thinking about it is always emotional as well as intellectual. It is not only that the concern of the individual which would lead him to think at all is emotional, but all decisions involve values in which emotion is important. Man's intelligence as compared with the animals, on which his freedom and moral responsibility are based, is not an affair of the intellect solely. The entire organism is involved through the close inter-relation of all its parts in the integrative set-up of the human body. Therefore an education which has been centered on intellectual training was bound to be ineffective because the more the intellect was developed out of relation to the emotions, the greater was the likelihood of conflict and disharmony within the personality.

The second difficulty is equally serious. It has been an individualistic education. It sought to solve the human problem by increasing man's individual ability. It was founded on a *laissez-faire* philosophy, that by developing persons with individual initiative the problems of society would be solved. Such an education does not fit man to live in a society where his life is integrally bound up with that of his fellows. It increases his self-assertion and his ability to compete with his fellows, but it does not prepare him to live coöperatively in a social group. Under these circumstances, reason becomes the servant rather than the master of the will-to-power and the growth of intelligence results in the organization of life on the basis of competition between individuals and groups and furnishes more deadly instruments than in primitive society for this competitive struggle. The more man frees himself from the limitations of nature by the growth of his intelligence, the greater is likely to be his arrogance in assuming that he is in fact the arbiter of his own life. The more he is able to achieve, the greater is the temptation to exploit his less fortunate fellows and to seize power for himself. Thus education of this type has tended to accentuate rather than to solve the human problem.

The difficulty with this type of education is that it is based upon a negative and individualistic strategy. Review has already been made of Niebuhr's earlier emphasis upon the inadequacy of reason to restrain and control the egoistic or selfish impulses of man in their individual expression and particularly in their collective manifestation. But this "restraining" and "controlling" function seems to be prominent in his earlier thought. Such a negative strategy in the use of reason might be considered inevitable on the basis of a conception of human nature as composed of selfish and unselfish impulses which are to be restrained and controlled or organized and directed by reason. But it does not seem at all necessary in the conception of human nature and the functioning of the human organism already outlined. In view of what we think we have learned about human personality, it seems poor strategy and one usually doomed to defeat. Even where the restraint and control succeed temporarily, there is no real solution of the problem. The conflict continues. Reason is a poor policeman. So also are will and conscience. The ineffectiveness and the undesirable results in attempting to handle imperious sex desire by control of the will is recognized. Of the three—reason, will and conscience—conscience is usually the most effective because in its negative rôle of restraint, it usually has been socially conditioned and therefore represents the public opinion of the group or the community. Therefore, it is armed with the weapons of public disapproval and of possible punishment.

The difficulty with this strategy is the fact that the individual uses his intelligence in attempts to persuade himself to give up one desire in favor of another conflicting desire; or to give up something he wants to somebody else. For example, he is asking himself to give up some of his desire for success and recognition so that his desire to be thoughtful for others will have a better chance. At best, he is turned in on himself in undesirable fashion in a never-ending debate as to just how much he should give up and just how much he should retain; at worst, one side or the other wins, but the loser is dissatisfied and persists in calling it not settled.

The same thing happens in his attempts to adjust his own rights and demands to the rights and demands of others. What he faces is not a conflict between individual desires and social demands, but a conflicting set of demands upon him as an individual, those of his own self-interest and those of the interests of others. It becomes in fact a conflict between egos. But the same process goes on. It is manifested often in making up a budget or in spending money. How much shall he deny himself in order that his sense of obligation to others may be met; how much shall he restrain his sense of obligation to others in order to have what he wants for himself. Efforts to adjudicate the conflicts which arise between children in a family on this basis of giving up something to little brother or sister never solve the problem. The negative method of using reason to restrain individual wants within the personality, or one's own wants as compared with others, is poor strategy. It does not seem to be much improved when it is the restraint of individual wants which conflict with those of the community, because it is still on the negative basis.

The conflict between power groups which Niebuhr envisages as the fate of mankind, is based upon the same strategy. The "have nots" organize to wrest rights or privileges from the "haves" or rival collective groupings compete with each other for the necessities or the luxuries of life. Under these circumstances, the efforts to restrain imperious desires of one group by reason and intelligence are ineffective. The same strategy is followed in attempting to get one group to restrain its demands in the interests of a rival group, be it race or class or nation. To expect one grouping to give up something to a rival in the competitive struggle is a false strategy. It involves, as Niebuhr emphasizes, a never-ending struggle between rival groupings, with now one and now another in the ascendency.

It would seem that a positive attack should be made upon the problem instead of a negative one. The most worthwhile organization of personality and that which best realizes the possibility of the psycho-physical unity of the organism is in purposes beyond one's self which the individual has made his own. It is perfectly true, as Niebuhr emphasizes, that such an organization of personality can be made around limited and ego-centered purposes: personal success, possession, or power. He holds, on the basis of his earlier conception of human nature, that reason tries to set up social goals which go against rationally-organized egoistic impulses and therefore that the limited egoistic goals are bound to win. If the so-called social goal is one which is simply pitted against an immediate egoistic goal, that may be true, particularly in our competitive society. But it is the business of education to make a social instead of an individualistic approach and to attack the problem by using intelligence in such social arrangements as make possible goals in which both the self and others are included. Take the family as an illustration. It is possible to conduct a family so that the parents are continuously attempting to adjudicate conflicts between the children. But it is also possible to go a long way toward a type of family life in which the attention of parents and children is focused upon the welfare of the family and upon those enterprises both of play and work in which all the family is recognized and needed and in which the welfare of each member, as well as of the family as a social unit, is involved.

The same can be said of a school. The average school room is made up of thirty or so individual egos with a teacher who attempts to use reason and will in controlling the individual egos and in adjudicating the differences between them. It has no real corporate life. The egos of the pupils are pitted against the reason and will of the teacher. But it is possible to organize a school class around enterprises in which both teacher and pupils are involved, in which individuals are respected and have chances proportionate to their ability and yet in which the welfare of the class as a whole is the controlling factor.

The shift in the kind of activities and enterprises in school or church where this viewpoint is adopted is illustrative. The older notion was to have individualistic activities, or group activities which were competitive to keep up the interest. In this type of program will is pitted against will, and desire against desire, and whoever is in charge is the referee or the policeman. Group enterprises to which all may contribute and in which all are needed, shift the attention from individual assertion to group success. The individual receives his proper recognition but he receives it in reference to a goal in which all are involved.

It has been pointed out that part of the difficulty in Europe has grown out of the arrangement in which it was expected that the excessive national desires of independent, self-determining states and the conflicts between them were to be adjudicated and restrained by a super-reason and will in the form of a League of Nations. Increasingly it is being recognized that efforts of individual nations to protect themselves against other nations by increasing their own strength offers no hope for the future. This has led only to war and to exploitation of weaker nations by the powerful. Nor does there seem to be hope in a League of Nations which is set up to curb and control by a super-reason. The only possible method by which small nations can escape domination or absorption by the powerful would seem to lie in some such federal organization as is found in the United States of America, where the autonomy of the individual units is guaranteed and where their own lives are so integrally bound up with the federal expression of their common life that conflicts between the individual states are minimized and the attention is turned to the corporate welfare upon which the individual welfare depends. It would seem that a similar analysis is applicable to industrial conflicts and other large group relationships.

It is evident that the strategy of a social form of religious education is not to train the reason and develop the intelligence in order to curb egoistic desires and strengthen social impulses. It is rather to utilize the intelligence in organizing the life of the family, the school, and the church, and indeed the larger group relationships of industry, nation and international relations, increasingly on a truly corporate basis. Religious education of this type would attack the problem of the ego-centered individual on a social basis. If the present conception of the social nature of the self is correct, no one will be able to organize his individual life around a social rather than an individualistic and ego-centered purpose by saying: "Go to now, I will have a social purpose." Nor can education develop the "socialized man" of whom Niebuhr speaks in any individualistic form of education, such as has predominated and still persists. Since individuals learn in and through their social experience and are influenced in their individual attitudes and purposes by those which prevail in the society of which they are a part, whether that society be a home, a school, a church, or the larger social relationships, it is not possible to have a social center for the organization of the self unless the group relations of which they are a part are organized on this basis. Progress in the solution of the problems of individuals is integrally bound up with the reconstruction of the life of which they are a part.

Such a strategy will not eliminate the problem of the discipline of individuals, but it will give it a different focus. Pressure brought to bear upon an individual to make him give up conduct which is harmful to the life of the group, in which all the others feel themselves intimately involved, is far different from the effort of a parent or teacher to make a child conform to his will or to restrain a child from undue assertion of himself against others in the group. And pressure upon a recalcitrant nation in a federal organization of nations would be far different from the efforts of the League of Nations to restrain the will-to-live and the consequent will-to-power of a recalcitrant independent state.

A social strategy of education is important if the Christian religion is to form both an incentive for and a critique of human endeavor. Some theological interpreters place the perfection of an absolute God over against human effort and achievement. Thus it becomes a divine judgment upon all human effort with the resulting sense of sin and guilt. This emphasis is useful in preventing pride but it does not furnish a guide and incentive for human endeavor. Even where the relevance of the "impossible ethical ideal" of Christianity is recognized, as in the case of Niebuhr, he places it in such extreme contrast with human possibilities of realization that this same element of judgment becomes predominant. He would have man "seek after an impossible victory" and "adjust himself to an inevitable defeat." [18] But for an individual to strain "after those final possibilities of life which transcend the human" and thus to seek to surpass the "mediocre realities of social life" [19] amid which he has to live, results in devastating conflict within the individual between the ideals he holds and the life he has to live. Unless the "final possibilities" are translated into intermediate goals which give some indication of the possibilities of human endeavor and unless these goals are social, involving both one's self and others, the contribution of the Christian religion to the solution of the human problem is not fully realized.

Where the intelligence of individuals is enlisted in coöperative endeavor for the realization of social goals, which are the human approximation of the Kingdom of God, "final possibilities of life" become both the incentive and the critique of every human endeavor. Further the individual is turned from individual striving to coöperative effort. Instead of being involved in devastating individual conflict, his energies are used positively in social endeavor. Prophetic religion under these circumstances becomes a positive experience because each attainment is judged both in its progress toward and its distance from more ultimate goals. By this is not meant that the Kingdom of God can be fully realized in the human scene. But it does involve the translation of the ideals of the Kingdom into goals which are pertinent to human life. There is then incentive for endeavor, but undue pride in any

---

[18] Niebuhr, Reinhold, *Reflections on the End of an Era*, p. 14. See also Chapter XV.

[19] *Ibid.*, p. 116.

attainment is minimized. Instead of striving being attended with a sense of defeat, both earnest endeavor and basic criticism of results are integrally inter-related. In such a process the possibilities of religious experience are best realized.[20] A social and experience-centered religious education represents a process for this type of human endeavor.

A social strategy in education and in the wider social relationships seems particularly important in view of the very provisions in the human organism for what has been called the instinct of self-preservation. Self-preservation is not an instinct in the sense that there is a well-defined impulse of this sort. But human beings do have, in common with the animals, an emergency apparatus, the function of which is to enable them to meet situations where their lives are endangered. In sub-human life, that animal survives which can run fast enough to get away from its enemy, or if cornered, can fight successfully against its foe. Consequently it has happened in the economy of nature that what is called the autonomic nervous system in man—the part of the nervous system which controls the vegetative functioning of the body—is set up to meet the sudden emergency of danger to the life of the animal. This system is divided into two parts, the cranial-sacral and the sympathetic. These two work in opposition and under ordinary conditions, along with the glands of internal secretion (the endocrines), maintain the normal balance of the functioning of heart, lungs, digestion, and elimination, and the general balance of the body. But in the presence of sudden danger, the sympathetic nervous system automatically takes control to aid in extraordinary effort in getting away from threatened danger or to help in successful combat, if cornered. The heart beat is speeded up, breathing increases, digestion and elimination which are not needed in

[20] For discussion of the relation of religious experience to such a process, see Chapter XIII.

the immediate emergency are slowed up, and adrenalin is thrown into the blood which resuscitates muscle as much as something like two hours of rest and also helps in the formation of blood clots in case of wounds. What is even more important from the viewpoint of this discussion, the rational control of the brain tends to be cut off. In the presence of physical danger in nature, flight must be immediate and automatic, if the animal is to be saved. In primitive life also there is not time to stop and reason about a threatened danger. Nature has thus provided for self-preservation under animal and primitive conditions by an apparatus which automatically works in helping to get out of the danger.

The problem which civilized man faces arises because this emergency apparatus is set for physical flight or combat and ordinarily is not needed in circumstances where safety depends upon "keeping one's head" or is ensured by the social arrangements of society. But it tends to operate in the presence of the more refined or organized threats of our modern life, even though the danger usually is not wild animals or physical death, but dangerous social or business competitors, rival classes or nations, and the like. It operates, in other words, where the threat is to the security or success of the individual or the group. It is this apparatus which propaganda seeks to throw into drive by showing the danger to which the individual, the class or the nation, is exposed from its enemies. Fear in the presence of danger and the corresponding drive to get out of that danger or to fight against it is the irrational element in the will-to-live, as it is organized into the will-to-power in self-protection.

Viewed psychologically, the difficulty with Niebuhr's proposal to solve the human problem by organizing power groups of those who are suffering injustice in order to threaten and wrest control from other power groups is that he proposes to solve the problem in a way which inevitably accentuates it. However necessary this may seem under present conditions, to accept it as the permanent answer to the problem is in fact to condemn mankind to devastating conflicts. There is abundant evidence that the threat which one group brings to another, however just the cause may be, tends to arouse irrational behavior in the threatened group through the operation of the emergency apparatus of the autonomic nervous system. Whatever the issue, whether between individuals, classes, races, or nations, this is what tends to happen. The irrational character of the conflict is increased under modern conditions by the use of propaganda. Each contending group pictures the other as dangerous—radicals, imperialists, or the like. Such a method not only consigns mankind to the solution of his problems on the primitive level of combat, even though the instruments used are those of civilization, but it also tends to make collective life even more irrational than on the primitive level because of the powerful instruments of propaganda for arousing fear and hate.

The basic difficulty with the acceptance of this method as inevitable is that in it there is failure to recognize the distinctive capacities of man as compared with the animal. The emergency apparatus tends to go into drive and irrational behavior to take place in the presence of a dangerous threat of any form; but the organism functions normally and intelligence has a chance to operate when there is reasonable guarantee of security and success. There are two ways open for man to guarantee this security. One is for him, either individually or collectively, to arm himself so thoroughly that he feels safe in the presence of danger. This defense apparatus is not confined to physical weapons. It includes financial reserves, intellectual resources, social solidarity, and the like. The other method open to man is to set up those social arrangements by which security is maintained through the character of the group or inter-group life. The degree of security now possessed by individuals or groups has come more by the second than by the first method. Indeed there seems little hope of solving the problem by efforts to increase the "armament" of individuals or groups, as is seen in the results where it is being tried in economic, racial, or international relations. There seems nothing in human nature, even in its collective manifestations, to make impossible substituting a social and coöperative attack upon the problems for the competitive method of strengthening rival power groups. Indeed, there is abundant evidence that this is a distinctively human possibility and that the progress we have made in eliminating the continuous threat to security and the consequent danger of irrationally devastating behavior has come by building up social arrangements which guarantee security to individuals and groups small and large. The use of human intelligence in a social and corporate attack upon the problem rather than prostituting intelligence to the rivalry of power groups should be the goal of realistic educators with a social passion.

Even in the midst of the threats which will be found in those areas of life which are not as yet organized on a social basis, it is possible to utilize and foster the distinctive characteristics of human beings as compared with the animals. The animal seems to be completely at the mercy of its emergency apparatus, but man is not. Since in civilized life, "keeping one's head" is a better way to meet danger than to run or fight irrationally, it would seem important to place the emphasis upon this distinctive human possibility. What is meant can be illustrated by the danger of traffic in a crowded city. The individual who is unaccustomed to this congested and dangerous condition tends to have the emergency apparatus go into drive. Irrationally such a person rushes across the street or attempts to run from the danger. But an experienced person learns to "keep his head" and negotiate the traffic in an intelligent manner. There is ample evidence of the possibility of man's meeting the emergency on a rational rather than on an irrational basis. For example, there is increasing evidence that in the midst of the confusion of propaganda he can learn to keep his head. Biddle found in his experiments with children that he could by education both reduce their gullibility to propaganda and increase their skepticism and resistance in relation to it.[21] The Institute for Propaganda Analysis is an enterprise among adults with the same purpose. The creation of irrational fear by propaganda methods is dependent upon control of what comes to the group or nation, and in a world of short-wave radios and other methods of communication, this becomes increasingly difficult. Since man can learn to "keep his head" in the presence of danger, it would seem a better approach to the problem to attempt to utilize these distinctive human possibilities than to appeal to fear and prejudice in the interests of one's class or nation. Certainly it should be a goal for the attainment of which all the resources of education should be enlisted.

The recognition of the social nature and of the psycho-physical unity of the self, which is the basis of the present experience-centered theory of general and religious education, does not minimize the seriousness of the human problem. It does, however, change the focus of attack. It is not centered upon efforts to increase the intelligence of individuals so that they will be better able to control and direct impulse or will develop greater freedom from the limitations of nature. Rather, the strategy is that of enlisting individuals in coöperative endeavor in negotiating and doing something about the social situations of which they are a part. It involves a fundamentally different conception of the educational process from that which Niebuhr assumes liberal educators hold. There is no evidence in Niebuhr's writings that he has taken this newer view of education into consideration. His

[21] Biddle, William W., *Propaganda and Education.*

attacks are upon an education of which progressive religious educators would be as drastically critical as he. His occasional references to Dewey show no recognition of Dewey's social theory of education, and while they are useful in pointing out weaknesses in his conceptions, they become almost a caricature of his complete thought. Without question, there are weaknesses and inadequacies in the newer education, and the searching critique of a Niebuhr would be very useful; but his criticisms of education as it has been are of no help, save possibly in confirming the disillusionment already felt in regard to the "liberal" education of the past. They give no positive help in the reconstructive process which is now in progress.

CHAPTER XI

Religious Education and Christlike Character

A RECOGNITION of the social nature of the self makes evident the importance of a social theory of education, but it increases rather than decreases the problem of religious education. If confidence could be placed in the instruction of individuals apart from the experiences of life, and particularly if such a procedure could have as its result the acceptance of the saving work of Christ by which the individual's attitude and conduct are transformed, the task of religious education would be compassable and comparatively simple. But if religious education must be concerned with the life situations of individuals and with their social experience, then it becomes involved in all the complications and difficulties of our current life.

If children learn in and through their social experience, they are exposed to accumulated evil as well as accumulated good as these are brought to bear upon them in the standards and practices of current society. The social heritage makes it possible for every child to start life with the advantage of the accumulated positive achievements of the race, but it also weights him down with the evil. Robert L. Calhoun has succinctly stated this influence of the social heritage in its negative aspects. He holds that "instead of rising steadily from the animal nature from which he set out," man as a morally responsible being "has mired himself in a 'second nature' of individual habits and social customs that hobbles him at every step." This is not something which is outside of him, like a physical object, but "because he is through and through a social being, it is within him as well as outside." This forms what Calhoun calls a "pervasive 'second nature' of acquired depravity," which corrupts and influences him at every point. "Though still free to think, plan, and choose as other animals are not, he cannot of himself choose as he ought." As a result, his efforts result in perennial failure.[1]

J. W. D. Smith emphasizes the problem facing religious education because of the secular character of community life. He says that "the subtle forces of community life shape the mind and character of its members far more powerfully than verbal teaching can do. Children growing up in a community unconsciously absorb its traditions, and the prevailing values and beliefs of the community mould their life and conduct." Recognizing that every individual belongs to several communities and that these different groupings will often be at variance with each other, he holds that "there are certain features common to any one age which permeate the thought and life of every community comprising it." The common feature at present he says is the secular character of life. This is "the root cause of the present crisis in Christian education." Even though children are receiving Christian education in the church, they "belong to other communities and are subject to other influences. Provision for religious teaching is quite inadequate, therefore, unless there is clear recognition of the nature and extent of those deeper influences to which everyone is subject." [2]

Any attempt to minimize the seriousness of this problem tends to lead to the sentimental trust in religious education which its critics deplore. By no stretch of the imagination can our present

---

[1] Calhoun, Robert L., *What is Man?*, pp. 69–70.
[2] Smith, J. W. D., "The Crisis in Christian Education" in *Church, Community, and State in Relation to Education*, an Oxford Conference Book, p. 124.

social order be called Christian and yet it is into this society that children are born. They learn in and through their experiences in this society to follow the practices and to accept the standards of that order. By the age of six, children have been conditioned to the practices and ideology of contemporary society. But this society in many and tragic ways denies in its practices two fundamental tenets of the Christian religion—the supreme worth of the individual and the dominant importance of love or good will in the relationships of life. It has widespread and ruthless discriminations on the basis of race, religion, class, and economic status, quite without reference to individual worth; and it is dominated by ruthless competition and devastating struggle between individuals and groups in social, economic, and international relationships. A degree of justice has been attained which curbs the practices of a more primitive society, and certain rules have been etasblished for the competitive struggle which ameliorate it to a certain extent; but the basic ideology of our society is un-Christian.

Being born into our present competitive, predatory society, the human young learn from their elders the conduct patterns necessary to protect themselves and to get along in this kind of world. In proportion as community, business, municipal, and national life is conducted on the present un-Christian basis, will the children who grow up under these influences develop un-Christian characteristic in order to make a success in life, no matter how much the churches may attempt to win individuals to a different sort of life. Respect for the individual in our society has been prostituted to rugged individualism under which attention is focused upon individual success and the welfare of one individual is set over against the welfare of others. In short, we have asked people to develop the Christian virtues of respect for personality and interest in the common welfare in a society where success and even the right to enough to live on have been dependent upon the opposite characteristics.

The problem is accentuated by the fact that it is difficult to find smaller and more intimate groupings within the social order which are dominated by the Christian ideals. Children are not born into society in general, but into homes, and their experience is in play, school, and other groups. But unfortunately these groups, as J. W. D. Smith points out, also are to a large extent dominated by the current practices and standards. While we have universal education, that education is open, particularly on the higher levels, only to those who can qualify. In our educational system the more able do not help the less able, but compete with them for the prizes of grades, promotion, graduation, honors, and the like. The school system itself often discriminates on the basis of race, while its social and athletic life is filled with the competitive spirit.

Nor have the churches themselves been able to embody the Christian ideals which they profess. They are very human societies, dominated to a large degree by the practices and standards of the society of which they are a part. Church members, accustomed to life on a competitive basis, bring into their church relationships the attitudes and techniques they have developed in other aspects of life—the rivalries and jealousies, the efforts to win at the expense of others, the tendencies to seek personal reward and recognition. These are found in church school classes and young people's societies as well as in the adult congregation. Indeed, membership, attendance, and participation are often promoted by utilizing competition for personal reward and recognition. Pins and rewards are given for Sunday School membership and attendance; individuals are enlisted in responsibilities by playing upon their desire for recognition; and there are membership, attendance, and subscription contests in various aspects of the churches' work. Nor are the ministers freed from this situation. They compete with other ministers within their own communion for promotion and with rival churches for membership and attendance. We would like to think that homes are more dominated by the Christian spirit of concern for the individual and good will in the relationships between individuals than other aspects of life; but here also it must be admitted that the attitudes and practices of the current society are found to a large extent. Many homes seem small and intimate replicas of the social order.

These examples could be multiplied to include descriptions of play groups, social affairs, community life, national and international relations. The ideology of a competitive society dominates small and more intimate groupings as well as the relationships between races, the practices in industry and business, and the relations between nations. Under these conditions, the more children and young people learn in and through experience, the more will they develop individual attitudes and practices which are basically non-Christian if not indeed anti-Christian. They become like the society in which they have their experiences.

Nor has the experience of the "new birth" had too encouraging results, judged by the record of the use of this approach. It is true that there have been notable changes in conduct and that in their intimate, face-to-face relationships individuals have shown more of the Christian spirit of concern for others and goodwill in their relationships with them. Charitable and other services have grown out of this new spirit and attitude. But these changed individuals still have had to participate in economic, political, and other aspects of the common life, and have found it difficult, if not impossible, to carry on their affairs with a fundamentally different ideology from that which prevailed in these relationships.

An examination of conversion experiences also shows the degree to which the changes, which some denominations assumed to be a complete transformation of the individual, have been conditioned and limited by the current conscience of the community. While, from the viewpoint of Protestantism, conversion has involved a sense of sin and guilt in relation to God, the feeling of sin as would be expected has usually been related to some specific human attitude or problem. Sexual practices and feelings were found by Starbuck to be dominant in adolescent conversions, as has already been noted. Life work decisions have often been the center of the conversion struggle. Drinking, gambling, swearing, and other practices which were deemed immoral have often been the focus. But it is interesting and sobering to note that these have usually been practices or attitudes concerning which there was already concern or condemnation in the current mores or at least in a large section of the community. In other words, conversion has usually taken place at the level of the current conscience of the community and has changed individuals so that they lived up to the highest current standards more completely. It has usually not involved any fundamental reconstruction of life in opposition to and beyond the best of the current ideology. It has been limited by the current attitudes and practices, as have the efforts to change individuals in and through their social experience.

Nor has the conversion process produced the complete transformation of the individual which it has planned. There has been a difference in the degree of change, depending upon the character of the problem. If the problem was of central significance, the experience changed the direction of life even though it did not change practice in all regards. A life work decision as the center of conversion has often resulted in a more fundamental change in the individual's attitude and conduct than one centered around swearing or smoking, for example. But an examination of what happens would seem to indicate that instead of effecting a complete transformation of the nature of the individual, on the basis of which he could be counted upon to act as a Christian in all the relationships of life, the divine work has usually been confined to the area of life in relation to which there was a sense of sin and guilt.

There needs to be some factor in the religious educational process which will lift human life above its present standards and attainments. Otherwise, both education and religion leave individuals as good or as bad as the present level of society. An examination of history would seem to indicate that this result has taken place only when the current standards and practices themselves were criticized and changed and when individuals and groups came to see the inadequacy of things as they were as compared with things as they might and ought to be. Sometimes, this fundamental criticism has been felt to be the condemnation and revelation of God, as was true of the eighth century prophets with their "thus saith the Lord" as the basis of their drastic criticism of current life. Sometimes it has come from the vision of a social reformer who claimed no divine sanctions, as when Marx made fundamental criticisms of our present economic arrangements. Sometimes there has been a combination of the two, as in the Abolitionist movement whose leaders founded their agitation for the freeing of the slaves on human as well as divine grounds. Whatever the individual or group considered the source of its dissatisfaction, something vital has happened when there has been a basic dissatisfaction with life as it is and earnest concern for its reconstruction.

Evidently, the fear, so often evidenced, of making children and young people critically minded, and the emphasis upon education as a method of training them in the accepted adult beliefs and practices, are in part responsible for the failure of religious education in the past to result in fundamental improvement of individual and corporate life. If the Christian ideology is not employed in basic criticism of life as it is, religious education tends to become the sanctification of current decencies.

If religious education is to be thus basically reconstructive, several important changes in present practice are necessary. In religious education, as in general education, attention has been focused upon children. Religious educators have said that adults already have their character formed and nothing much can be done with them, whereas children are still plastic and there is the possibility of influencing them through the educational process. Therefore, they have counted on educating the coming generation to be more Christian than the present one. But adults and the more mature set the circumstances in which children and the immature have their experiences. The immature have to adjust to the conditions which adults maintain; and by the time they are themselves old and mature enough to assume responsibility, they have so completely adopted the practices of their elders that they tend to perpetuate for their own children the type of life to which they have become habituated. It would seem that in religious education more attention must be given to adults in order that children may have a different environment in which to grow up. This is the practice of child psychologists and child guidance clinics. Recognizing the source of the difficulties of children in the home, they center their treatment for little children upon the parents in order that children may have a different kind of home condition. It would seem as if the religious education of adults were the strategic educational problem.

If religious education is to be thus basically reconstructive, there must be a shift from efforts to help individuals as individuals to the enlistment of individuals in the reconstruction of the life of which they are a part. The fundamental relationship between individual character and social conditions must be recognized.

Attempts to educate individuals so that they will be able to stand up against the prevailing practices of families, schools, communities, economic life, and social relationships can, in the very nature of the case, succeed only with the more rugged and able, and even with these, not without personality scars. There are emotional problems involved when the individual, because of his refusal to conform, feels he is not accepted in the group to which he needs to belong, be it the family or other social group. Serious personality difficulties often develop in the individual whose personal standards are in conflict with those of the group. One illustration is the problem of young people, who have accepted standards of parents or of the church which prevent them from participating in the "worldly amusements" of their school and other social groups. The attempt of an individual as an individual to change the group practices, which has often been suggested as the solution, requires still greater courage and ability and is usually unsuccessful.

Whatever may be the personal attitudes and standards, the individual has to live in social relationships. If he is to live in groups, he has in spite of himself to make some adjustment to the group mores. It is true that it is possible to develop in individuals a sensitivity of conscience which gives them feelings of sin and guilt when they participate in practices which are contrary to their Christian standards. This prevents a sense of complacency in the presence of un-Christian conduct, but it is not very useful if it is confined to a confession of sin and does not substitute positive action for negative practice. Further, it brings to sensitive souls a kind of devastating struggle which often reaches a pathological state.

It is evident from this discussion that the problem of Christlike character cannot be solved on an individualistic basis. Individuals find it difficult, if not impossible, to maintain attitudes and practices contrary to those of the group to which they are intimately related, and often it is impossible for an individual to secure the remaking of the group practice. For success, the individual must join with others in coöperative endeavor for the reconstruction of the group practice and ideology. But the recognition of this social approach does not solve the problem for Christians. In many of their group relationships, and particularly in the wider areas of economic and political aspects of life, Christians are a minority and often seem powerless to secure any such fundamental reconstructive process. What then is possible?

Certainly it would seem that the place to begin with such a process is in those aspects of life for which Christians are more directly responsible and over which they have control. The family is one such group. Probably it is the most important one as well, for, in the family experience, the basic attitudes and practices of children are first formed. Horace Bushnell's emphasis upon Christian nurture through the life of the family was a prophetic insight which is only now receiving the attention it deserved. The Christian education of adults for parenthood and for family responsibility is possibly the church's present, most strategic opportunity. Further, the family is of prime importance in relation to the emotional problems of the individual. When there is anchorage and security in the fellowship of the family group, the individual is able to weather many disastrous conditions in the wider life he has to negotiate. Christian educators will not only need to enlist but to help children and parents in the rebuilding of family life.

The church should furnish a fellowship which is being continuously remade by its members. J. W. D. Smith points out that Christian education is likely to be effective "if the community life of the church is strongly marked and the loyalty of its members well developed," and that its influence may be "profound in spite of contrary influences from other sources."[3] But he recognizes that the church lacks this educational influence today because it does not have such a "community life" which is distinctive as compared with the larger community of which the church is a part. There are two related causes for this situation in the churches. First, the church has tended to become an institution which provided things for individuals: worship, education, entertainment, and the like. As a result, it has largely lost the sense of solidarity found in the fellowship of a group, the members of which are banded together in their loyalty to the Christian ideals and practices. Individuals come to the church to get something, not to unite with others in fellowship around their common loyalties. Public worship is not corporate worship in the sense of the realization of a common fellowship in the presence of God, but rather the collective worship of individuals who come for individual help. The introduction of the project method into the church and the enlistment of children and young people in projects or enterprises has not corrected this situation. They have not been enlisted in coöperative effort for the remaking of their life together in the church. Too often the projects have been activities of individuals, carried on in the group for individual recognition or reward or, when they have been group enterprises, they have been focused on something for the group alone which would bring reward to the individual members. Further, these and other activities have been planned and made available by a few in the church for the benefit of the others. The rank and file of the members, old and young, have had no genuine sense of participation in the common life of the church.

The second and related cause of this situation is the fact that with the attention focused on things which are done or provided for those who come, little attention has been given to the stand-

[3] *Ibid.*, p. 124.

ards and practices of the church as church and of its various groups as groups. The members of the church have not been enlisted in the fundamental criticism of their own life together and in the effort to make the church in fact a Christian fellowship. It is a tragic evidence of this situation that it is only when the church is persecuted that it tends to recognize the distinctiveness of the quality of its life. "The early Christian church witnessed to a faith and life radically distinct from the life around it, and it nurtured men and women who 'turned the world upside down.'"[4] The church will become one of the groupings whch is influential in Christian education only as the reconstructive processes of education are brought to bear upon its own life and it becomes increasingly a Christian fellowship.

There are other minority group fellowships which can be developed within our semi-Christian or anti-Christian social order. Christian coöperatives give an opportunity for Christian fellowship in the criticism and remaking of current economic practice. Inter-racial fellowships are possible. Jacques Maritain, a French Roman Catholic theologian, according to Horton,[5] believes that this should be the present Christian strategy for the remaking of the social order. He feels that the present order is so close to liquidation that there is not much that can be done about it and that Christians during this period should form a "network of centers of Christian life" dotting our decaying civilization like cells of a new type of social organization. Each of these centers should try to penetrate its environment, by political and social action, but he believes that if this should fail, "the spiritual influence of such centers of Christian life, working by the 'poor' but powerful means of moral contagion, cannot fail to be used of God for the building of the new age. When the old order at last col-

[4] *Ibid.,* p. 125.
[5] Horton, Walter, *Contemporary Continental Theology,* pp. 60–62.

lapses, these Christian *foyers* or cells will become the nuclei of the new order; and they may even prevent the transition from being unnecessarily violent and destructive." [6]

If Christian education is thus to focus on the basic reconstruction of the life of which Christians are a part, it is evident that in its processes it will often have to cut across age and class and racial divisions. An education centered upon instruction is necessarily an education graded according to age. In a more socialized form of education, there will be need for age groupings. But in many group relationships, such as the family, both old and young are involved. It will not be a fellowship of the Christian life if it is merely a place where parents provide necessities for their children. It will be such only as children and parents work together in the maintenance and the reconstruction of the life in which they are both involved in the family. Children and young people should be associated with adults in many aspects of the life of the church. Particularly should the young have a more vital part in the church as church. Further, the church cannot be a true Christian fellowship unless it is possible in a particular church to cut across racial discriminations and class divisions. The slogan, "Christian Youth Building a New World" is an illustration of a failure to realize that the building of a new world is not an enterprise of one age group, but must be a coöperative enterprise of all age groups. This is being recognized in the recent provisions for the coöperation of the United Youth and the United Adult Movements.

The problem of Christlike character is not solved by smaller Christian fellowships, in which the individual finds the opportunity for Christian expression in living, and in relation to which he has security and inspiration. If in his other relationships he yields submissively to the current practices, there is not only con-

[6] *Ibid.*, p. 61.

flict and division in his own personality, but the work of social reconstruction is hindered. Nor is it a solution of the problem, on the one hand, to adopt a philosophy that in everyday affairs the Christian must follow the established practices, even while he attempts in the church and in his smaller group relations to live the Christian life or, on the other hand, to turn to an other-worldly conception of religion in which the individual's attention is focused on relation to God and he is left to himself in his everyday affairs. Even more serious for Christlike character is the tendency to give the Christian label to whatever are the accepted practices and attitudes of respectable people or groups. Christians must seek to find individually and corporately those courses of action which, within the limitations of an un-Christian social order, as nearly as possible embody the Christian convictions. But they must do more. They must join with other Christians and with those who do not name the name of Christ but who believe in similar social goals in the remaking of the larger life of which they are a part, so that those convictions can be more fully realized. Christian education has a great challenge and opportunity to help individuals and groups to face realistically the problems of our world and to come to courses of action, practical and idealistic, by which Christians may influence human affairs in the direction of their convictions. There are enough church members in the United States to turn the tide of our present confused ego-centered competitive order toward a coöperative society in which love is more genuinely operative.

CHAPTER XII

The Educational Process and Christian Ethics

THE SOLUTION of the problem of Christlike character, suggested in the preceding chapter, is found through the enlistment of individuals in the reconstruction of the corporate life of which they are a part. Evangelical Christianity had confidence that divinely transformed individuals would result in a changed social life. But it did not recognize realistically the degree to which individual life is inevitably conditioned by social practices. Much of religious education has had this individualistic viewpoint. On the other hand, the social emphasis in the Christian movement and in religious education focused attention on bringing in the Kingdom of God on earth. There was confidence that changed individuals would come from improved social arragements. But there was failure fully to recognize that individuals determine the social arrangements. It is only in the integral relationship of the individual and the social that a realistic religious education can be developed.

There was often in the modern developments a failure to realize the seriousness of the human problem, both individual and social. The emphasis upon "judgment" and "crisis" in certain theological interpretations at the present time is a necessary corrective of the easy optimism with which religious educators often went about their work. But it should be emphasized that there is also, in this theological emphasis, a failure to recognize the degree to which. catastrophic crisis is the result of the failure to meet realistically the previous situations out of which tragic circumstances have developed. Serious discipline problems in home or school are the end results of the failure of parents or teachers to deal realistically and positively with previous crucial situations. Crisis in the relations of adolescents with their parents is not an inevitable characteristic of adolescence, but is directly the fruition of minor conflicts in the relation of parents and children which were not constructively resolved. The catastrophic crisis in Europe in 1939 is directly traceable, not only to the Treaty of Versailles, but also to one situation after another which was dealt with in such a way as to make the crisis inevitable. Crisis is an important and serious element in all situations demanding decision, but major catastrophic crises are the evidences of previous failures rather than of something inevitable in the nature of things. Because of human limitation, they probably cannot be eliminated from the world; but the emphasis should be on preventing them through realistic and positive dealing with the less serious situations out of which they grow, rather than on accepting them as the norm of human living.

The adoption by Christians of an educational approach and method in meeting the situations of life involves the utilization of Christian ethics, not only as a guide to individual practice, but also as the critique of established group practices and as the criterion for the reconstruction of group life, small and large. In other words, Christian ethics would be integrally related to an educational process which is centered in life situations. Such a vital and integral relationship has repeatedly been denied by those who praise Christian ethics in theory but doubt its practicability in the actual affairs of life. The common assumption that in this world one has to act according to the standards of the world is given support on theological grounds by interpreters of the neoorthodox type. For example, Emil Brunner says that in his "Calling" or particular status and work in life and in the "Orders" or the regulatory institutions for the preservation of law and order, the Christian has no methods with which to work different from a non-Christian. He has to use the instruments which have been developed in historical existence in a sinful world. But he says that sinful as they often are, these methods are God's gracious provision for the maintenance of life in the world and that God covers with his forgiveness any necessary activities of this sort. There seems to be in the very theological interpretation a recognition that in this world one has to follow the practices of the world.

Brunner amplifies this viewpoint both with reference to the "Calling" and the "Orders."[1] Even though in the economic sphere an individual may have to use the means which are available for economic activity, means which are not worthy when judged from the Christian viewpoint, he can still, according to Brunner, carry on his activities to the glory of God, for they are the only means available in historical existence and, in his mercy, God takes responsibility in such activities for everything which human beings cannot alter. It is true that the Christian, because of his love for his neighbor, will do something special, "by not always buying in the cheapest and selling in the dearest market, by treating his assistants, not only according to the economic point of view, but by drawing them, as his neighbors within the circle of his personal care."[2] But he must never fail to recognize that his primary responsibility is in the production of goods for the maintenance of life and that he must utilize the methods which will bring success in such an enterprise. This conception that unworthy means may be used for worthy ends is in contrast with the emphasis on an educational approach to the integral inter-relationship of means and ends. The very goals of the maintenance of life by the production of goods are being defeated in

[1] See Brunner, Emil, *The Divine Imperative*, Chapters XX and XXI.
[2] *Ibid.*, p. 259.

our civilization by the use of undesirable means in our competitive society. The religious educator believes that Christian ethics must be applied to the methods used as well as in the determination of goals, if the good life is to be realized.

Brunner also says that it is the obligation of the Christian not only to submit to the regulatory institutions of society, as represented in the "Orders," but also to take his responsibility in their maintenance. But he must recognize that these regulatory functions are always based upon compulsion and are in no sense an expression of love. It is true that the individual who is called upon to maintain order through the exercise of his "official" duty need not be completely "official." He can express his personal interest in and concern for the individual even within this framework, as for instance the personal attitude of a judge. But he must never allow this in any way to interfere with his official duty. The fact that it is for the maintenance of law and order means that it is good, but "as an order, owing to its necessary harshness, it is incurably loveless, and even—as such—contrary to the law of love." [3] In these "Orders" are most clearly revealed the contrast between the conduct of sinful humanity, in which Christians must share, and a life in the love of God. But the perception of this fact should not only lead to repentance, but also to a recognition that it is never possible to get rid of the contrast. We never "perceive the depth and the universality of evil, . . . until we are *obliged* to do something which, in itself, is evil; that is, we do not see this clearly until we are obliged to do something in our official capacity—for the sake of order, and therefore for the sake of love—which apart from our 'office' would be absolutely wrong." [4]

This conception of the "official" and loveless character of the maintenance of law and order is in direct contrast to an educa-

[3] *Ibid.*, p. 233.   [4] *Ibid.*, p. 227.

tional approach in which an effort is made to embody the law of love in these very arrangements. Brunner's conception of autocratic compulsion in "official" responsibilities in home, school, and state has evidently been influenced by his notion of the sovereign rule of God. In a true social conception, the father, teacher, judge, or other person who has responsibility is not an outside "official" whose business it is to bring loveless compulsion upon the members of a group to keep them in order. He is rather himself integrally a part of the group life since he is charged with executive or judicial responsibilities to carry out that which is recognized as necessary for the common welfare or that which has been democratically decided by the group.

Despite all the travesties which have been perpetrated in the name of self-government, the religious educator is not willing to abandon the utilization of an educational process in the determination of the will of the group for the conduct of its life. Indeed, it is in just this use of the educational process in what has been called discipline that some of the most significant things have happened. That this conception of official duty as being the expression of the will of the group rather than something imposed upon it, is not inapplicable even to larger social relationships, is seen in the fact that it is only those laws which really represent the will of the people which are obeyed in a democratic country. It has not been possible to devise instruments of compulsion which secure law and order along lines which the people consider undesirable, as was notably evidenced in the Prohibition amendment.

There is also challenge in an educational approach to Brunner's conception that all "official" duties must be loveless because they are centered in the maintenance of law and order and inevitably cannot be concerned with individuals as persons. It is just at this place that the most notable advance has been made. A parent or

teacher, it is true, is charged with responsibility for the maintenance of law and order so that the work of the group shall not be
hindered, but he is also obligated in his discipline of refractory
members of the group, who are threatening that order, to take the
personality and the personal welfare of the individual into full
consideration and to administer discipline in such a way that not
only will order be restored but the individual will be helped. Indeed, in these smaller group relationships, it is sometimes important to sacrifice law and order temporarily to the welfare of the
individual who is causing the disturbance. Instead of discipline's
being loveless and lacking in concern for persons, these are at the
very center of discipline from an educational viewpoint.

This emphasis is being increasingly recognized in larger
group relationships. In the administration of justice in the case
of juvenile delinquents, the court's attention is centered on finding an arrangement which will not only protect society but at the
same time will save the individual who has gone astray. Indeed,
in the juvenile court, saving the boy or girl seems often to weigh
more heavily in the decision than does the maintenance of law
and order. This is only beginning to be recognized in the case
of adult offenders, but there are evidences here and in other
countries that it may become a prominent factor in these cases.
Further government is no longer conceived simply in terms of the
maintenance of law and order. The social legislation in England
for old age and for unemployment, for example, and the tardy
enactment of such legislation in this country, are evidence of a
growing concern of government for the welfare of persons *as
persons*. Government, even in its present form in democratic
countries, is hardly the loveless manifestation of compulsion
which Brunner pictures.

It seems evident, therefore, that while interpreters of the neo-
orthodox type, like Brunner, recognize the significance of respon-

sibilities in this world in the Christian scheme, they fail to provide for the utilization of Christian ethics in the actual arrangements which are made for the preservation of life and for the maintenance of law and order. This is still more evident in the conception of these interpreters as to the place of Christian ethics in the improvement of the social order. Brunner says that a Christian is a member of human society and he is "justified in sharing the obligation to introduce a better order." His conception that disorder is worse than any system which maintains order, however unjust it may be, leads him to place careful limitations upon this reconstructive function. Great care must be given to the practicability of the changes which are proposed, to be sure that they do not result in disorder.[5] It is true, he says, that the "believer will see the injustice of the existing order more plainly than others, and will be more resolute in working for the introduction of the better order." [6] But a person who is not a Christian can see that a certain order is unjust and the working out of the better order is only indirectly a matter of faith. It is a concern of the human reason, as are all other natural moralities.[7] Indeed, "whatever is equitable—and thus truly righteous (right and equitable)—must be inferred by the healthy human moral sense, almost one might say by the moral instinct." [8] Thus while the Christian has the responsibility of aiding those who are working for a better order and of "setting in motion those forces which are required for this purpose," [9] it is a better order in the conception of which Christian ethics has not been utilized.

This viewpoint he makes quite explicit in his statement that "the ethical is not a constitutive but a regulative element in the world of the production and appropriation of goods." [10] By this

[5] *Ibid.*, pp. 229–230.
[6] *Ibid.*, p. 232.
[7] *Ibid.*, p. 232.
[8] *Ibid.*, p. 182.
[9] *Ibid.*, p. 232.
[10] *Ibid.*, p. 256.

he says he means that it is to be used in criticism of what *is* rather than in the construction of what *ought to be*. Therefore, while the Christian's experience makes him see the contrast between the established practices and those which are an expression of love, the law of love is not to be utilized in the reconstruction of these practices. This he also makes explicit in his discussion of the three-fold law which embodies the divine command.[11] There are, first, the laws of official duty, by which external community is maintained. These are the humanly determined practices by which order is maintained through compulsion and are loveless. Second, there is the absolute law, by which we recognize the lack of community or the expression of love in these official duties and are critical of them. But third, there is the law of love, whose function is not to guide the individual in these official duties but is to instruct the believer in his right personal relation with his neighbor. The prophetic message, according to Brunner, belongs to the second type. It cares not at all for what is possible but represents a proclamation of the absolute law and its significance "depends upon the fact that it is presented not as a 'programme,' but as a general challenge."[12] He thus gives scant recognition to the fact that prophets like Isaiah and Jeremiah were not challenging existing conditions in general but were speaking to definite historical events in which choices were being made, and were seeking to influence those choices.

No Christian educator with a social outlook can for a moment limit the rôle of Christian ethics to that of criticism. Nor can he agree that Christian ethics is applicable only in personal relations with others and is not pertinent for the construction and reconstruction of the common life. According to Brunner, the love of God, of which the Christian is a recipient as a gift, is expressed in personal relations to and personal service for other persons.

---

[11] *Ibid.*, Chapter XXII.   [12] *Ibid.*, p. 230.

Most of the "special things" which the Christian may do as Christian in his "secular" activities and his "official" duties are forms of this personal service. The judge can show personal concern and thoughtfulness for the prisoner; the employer can bring his employees, as neighbors, within the circle of his personal care; the individual can restrict the use of his savings upon himself and his family and can have a remarkably open hand for his neighbors who are in want.[13] This restricts the application of Christian ethics to those personal expressions of thoughtfulness which have been found within the most unjust systems and makes no provision for the utilization of Christian ethics in the elimination of the injustices. Christian slave-owners often showed personal thoughtfulness for their slaves.

Even in these personal expressions, there seems to be no provision in Brunner's thought for a significant use of Christian ethics in determining the character of the personal service. He places dependence upon the experience of the Christian through which the barriers between him and his neighbor have been removed and he is able to see him as he is. Therefore, he will render personal service suited to his need.[14] He seems to forget that even if this Christian experience turns the Christian's attention to his neighbor and his need, he will interpret that need in accordance with the outlook and emphasis which is current. There is nothing in such an experience to make him go beyond the accepted altruistic practice. The Christian experience may change the expression of the Christian from one centered upon himself to that reaching out to others, but it does not furnish the content for such expression. That can only come through a genuine educational process. It is true that Brunner emphasizes the illumination and guidance of the Holy Spirit which comes by way of the samples of that which the law of love demands as found

---

[13] *Ibid.*, pp. 228, 259.   [14] *Ibid.*, pp. 54–57.

in the Ten Commandments and the Sermon on the Mount. But this is to form the background and approach to the particular decision rather than being used in it.[15] Indeed, he says quite explicitly that the law of love cannot be used as a principle.[16] Further, the organ for determining what shall be done for one's neighbor is not reason but faith. God has some very special thing that the Christian is to do in relation to his neighbor and this is made evident to faith. Such an emphasis in fact denies the use of the Scriptures and of the Christian emphasis in significant manner even in decisions about personal relations. As a matter of fact, there is abundant evidence from the life of sincere Christians, even of Brunner's type of religious experience, that the illumination of the Holy Spirit as to what kind of service should be rendered to the neighbor is strangely like the best accepted practice.

Even this personal expression of love which the Christian will render to his neighbor is distinctly limited by Brunner. It is not something which is done for another, as in the indirect relationships of ordinary activities, but it is *showing* love. This cannot be expressed to people in the mass. Even where more than one other person is involved, the impersonal character of attitude and action begins to appear. As a matter of fact, according to Brunner, it is only in the Church, the Society of the Redeemed, that this can be fully expressed, because it is there only that the individual is completely united to his fellows in true community. This is possible because all are directly related to God in the new life they have found through Christ.[17] Therefore, while he recognizes that through secular work both in the production of goods and in the maintenance of law and order, the Christian is indirectly expressing the law of love in that he is doing something for his neighbor, he limits distinctly Christian activities

---

[15] *Ibid.,* Chapter XIII.   [16] *Ibid.,* p. 117.   [17] *Ibid.,* pp. 301–302.

to personal relationship and service to individuals and holds that this is found in its complete manifestation only in relationship to other believers in the Society of the Redeemed, the Church.

A basic difficulty in Brunner's thought grows out of the fact that even though he repeatedly uses the words "social" and "community," his viewpoint is not social but individualistic. Community is not used in the social sense, but as a personal relationship between individuals: husband and wife, parent and child, teacher and pupil, friend and friend, Christian and Christian. His chapter on Christian sociology [18] is not on sociology in any accepted sense of that word, but upon the personal relationships between individuals. Thus community in his conception is entirely a face-to-face, person-to-person relationship. With such a conception of community, it would be inevitable that his emphasis should lack true social significance.

Brunner not only does not seem to hold any organic conception of community but he criticises what he calls the Romantic theory where, he says, "the individual is subordinate to the whole, the individual is only a member of the whole community, whose duty it is to serve the community." [19] There would be agreement with Brunner's criticism of an organic conception in which the individual is completely subordinated and sacrificed to the social group, small or large. This is the "totalitarian" solution of the problem of social life and is not true community. But Brunner seems to have no conception of that type of community or social organism in which the life of individuals is intimately bound up with, not subordinated to, the life of the whole and in which the life of the whole is an expression of the life of individuals and their relationships with each other.

Brunner's failure to find relevance for the law of love in the ordinary life of human beings arises not only because of his lack

[18] *Ibid.*, Chapter XXVII.   [19] *Ibid.*, p. 299.

of a true social concept, but from his conception of love itself. He rightly draws the distinction between *eros,* spontaneous human love for another, and *agape* which is distinctively a New Testament word and is employed to designate affection, goodwill, love, or benevolence which is the fruit of the Christian experience. It is true, also, as Niebuhr emphasizes, that love of this sort is enjoined by Jesus on the ground that God treats human beings in this way, bringing his sunshine and causing his rain to fall upon both the evil and the good. But Brunner makes of *agape,* not love which is enjoined because of God's love, but love which is like God's. He says that God does not need or expect love in return. He expects rather that man shall express his love for him by love of his neighbor. But God's love, according to Brunner, is without condition, without mutuality. It is the complete giving of himself. Therefore the love which the Christian is to express to his neighbor is selfless love, the affirmation of the life of the other *rather* than one's own, an expression which expects nothing in return. Certainly such an expression of love can be approximated only in most limited areas and conditions of life and could hardly be relevant in social relationships in the form in which Brunner expresses it.

There seems, on the surface of the evidence, to be no reason for giving *agape* this extreme meaning. In the Sermon on the Mount, the same verb is used in speaking of the Old Testament conception of loving your neighbor and hating your enemies, as in Jesus' injunction that one should love his enemies. The emphasis of Jesus here seems not to change the character but to extend the range of this love. Jesus seems to make a connection between a human father's concern for his children and God's attitude toward humanity. The commandment is love one's neighbor *as* one's self, not *rather than* one's self. The emphasis would seem to be on consideration for others, irrespective of station or attainment or personal attitude toward one's self, but just on the basis of the fact that they are human beings. It would seem that the Christian conception of *agape* is goodwill in the rich meaning of that word rather than selfless love.

In this connection, it is interesting to note that Reinhold Niebuhr makes a definition of *agape* somewhat similar to Brunner's, but at the same time he insists on the relevance of the law of love to ordinary ethical problems. Niebuhr says that the "natural man" is under obligation to "emulate the love of God, to forgive as God forgives, to love his enemies as God loves them. Love as natural endowment, *eros*, is transmuted under this religious tension into *agape*." [20] While he calls it an impossible ethical ideal, he insists "on the relevance of the ideal of love to the moral experience of mankind on every conceivable level." [21] He gives various illustrations of how every type of moral code and every philosophy of morals is grounded, however imperfectly, in the ideal of love which "enjoins concern for the life and welfare of the other and seeks to restrain the unqualified assertion of the interests of the self against the other." [22] He insists that while this is an ideal, impossible of realization by human beings in history, the striving after this idea under the impulse of Christian experience distinctly raises the level of human life. It is true that his conception of the strength of the egoistic impulses of man as organized and directed by reason in the will-to-power of collective life seems to lead him to expect this will seldom go above the level of justice in collective life and even there will be realized with difficulty. He seems not to recognize the full possibilities of this idea even under human limitations. But nevertheless he is unequivocal in his insistence upon the relevance and the power of the love ideal.[23]

[20] Niebuhr, Reinhold, *An Interpretation of Christian Ethics*, p. 211.
[21] *Ibid.*, p. 104.   [22] *Ibid.*, p. 106.   [23] *Ibid.*, Chapter VII.

The Christian educator believes that love, in the sense of concern for the life and welfare of the other, of goodwill even to one's enemy, of efforts to establish a kind of life in which others as well as one's self have a full chance, is relevant to a religious educational process. He believes that the ideal of love can be made both the goal and the dynamic of such a process. There is no thought of a cold intellectual procedure in which the individual or the group seeks to find what the law of love would mean in human relations, if an attempt were made to approximate it, but has no expectation of acting upon the conclusion reached. In the last analysis, love as an ideal becomes a dynamic for living only as it is experienced. Such experience is not unrelated to the educational process but is its incentive and often also its fruition. Christian ethics is to be utilized in the educational process, not only as a guide to individual practice but also as the critique of established group practices and as the criterion for the reconstruction of group life.

The discussion thus far has been concerned with the relevance of Christian ethics to an educational process. But many, who would recognize the pertinence of Christian ethics in the solution of social problems, would make an entirely different objection. They would question the effectiveness of an educational process for the solution of social problems. The query is based in part upon the slowness of such a process. It does not seem suited to meet the crises of on-going events. But it is also based upon a conception of education as something removed from the actual situations of life through which individuals or groups become intelligent about social issues and decide what they would do if they could do anything. Decisions under such circumstances are arm-chair choices and are not made through a realistic facing of the actual situations. Something of this latter viewpoint is reflected in Emil Brunner's criticism of committee discussion:

The nature of this "better order" cannot be settled theoretically by sitting round a committee table and drawing up programmes. Nothing is easier than to devise a "better order" on paper; but nothing is so difficult as to find the better order which, under actual internal and external conditions, will become a *real* order. To construct ideological programmes is not only useless, it is harmful, because it breeds illusions, deflates moral energy, and makes the person who gives himself to this business an arrogant critic of the world around him.[24]

This viewpoint is in part influenced by Brunner's extreme emphasis upon law and order in accordance with which he thinks that any arrangement which preserves order is better than even a more ideal one which would result in disorder in the process of its realization. But it also reveals a false notion of the relation of those who are considering a better order to the life of the "order" itself. He seems not to recognize the possibility that those who are integrally related to a social grouping might themselves form the committee for the reconstruction of their own corporate life. This is the conception which is emphasized in a social theory of religious education.

In the more complex social situations, where conflicting groups and interests are involved, the educational process is that of conference. Even though the method of conference is in disrepute because of its prostitution in the Munich Pact and other decisions, it is still the only human alternative to that disastrous use of force, which, while it may temporarily stop the aggressor and secure a modicum of justice for one of the conflicting parties, never solves any problem. The conditions under which conference is possible are not easy to secure and they are often impossible. It is necessary that those who enter a conference leave "their arms outside the room where they confer," and this applies to dogmatism in convictions as well as to physical armament. Even where there is seeming willingness to confer, conflicting interests and deep-

[24] Brunner, Emil, *The Divine Imperative,* p. 230.

seated fears and prejudices make the conference method difficult. But the difficulties do not change the fact that without the recognition and utilization of the educational process of conference, there is no hope of any approximation of Christian ethics in social relations. This is not to say that life can become so ideal that there will be no necessity for the coercion of recalcitrant individuals or groups. It is only to emphasize that the coercion which is necessary to make the results of conference effective is far different from that coercion of individuals or groups by other individuals or groups involved in non-educational procedures.

Religious educators are open to definite criticism because they have not always put their theory into practice in the areas of life over which they have direct control such as the family and the church. Too often one group in a church has made a decision without conference with others involved and has taken steps to persuade or to coerce individuals or groups to follow this decision. Too often the leaders have decided what they thought would be good for children or young people, and then have sought by various forms of persuasion and coercion—those which were sugar-coated being none the less coercive—to try to put it into effect, without having paid the price of conference with those involved in the decisions. Frequently the church group have attempted to make decisions for those not in the immediate constituency of the church, such as labor or racial groupings, and then have sought by propaganda and in other coercive ways to put their will into effect. If the educational process of conference is ever to become recognized and effective in the larger relationships of life, it will first have to be embodied in those less complex conditions over which educational leaders have control in order that there may be developed both confidence and skill in the process.

The possibilities of an educational process in the solution of social problems are not realized, when a Herbartian method is followed. This procedure has dominated the churches for the past twenty-five years and is still the most common method. Since in the Herbartian procedure, the Christian principles are arrived at apart from their meaning in practice, it is comparatively easy to reach an agreement upon the principles. Apart from what they might involve if put into practice, any set of resolutions embodying the social ideals of the Hebrew prophets or the ethical principles of Jesus, if stated in the general terms of the Herbartian procedure, would probably receive a unanimous endorsement in most labor gatherings, rotary clubs, industrial associations and political gatherings as well as in religious assemblies. There is rather widespread agreement in the United States that human life is sacred and personality should be respected, that life should be managed so that human welfare is conserved and so that the common good is furthered. It is in the meaning of the principles in specific conduct that the differences emerge. Exactly opposite courses of action are often defended on the basis of the same principle. Since in a Herbartian procedure, the main emphasis is placed upon determining the principles, the real issue of their meaning when put into practice usually does not receive adequate consideration.

There is, however, an even more fundamental difficulty in the Herbartian method. There is an assumption that once the principle has been arrived at, the action which would be in line with the principle will be clear. Brunner seems to have this misconception of principle. He says that "the Christian conception of the Good differs from every other conception of the Good at this very point: that it cannot be defined in terms of principle at all. Whatever can be defined in accordance with a principle—whether it be the principle of pleasure or the principle of duty—is legalistic. This means that it is possible—by the use of this principle—to pre-determine 'the right' down to the smallest detail of conduct." [25] From this quotation it would seem that he equates a principle with a law.

This idea that a principle predetermines the course of action is due to a misunderstanding of the relation of principles to an educational process or to life's decisions. Principles represent points of emphasis, considerations to be taken into account, values which should be conserved, and therefore focus attention upon important considerations in a decision as to what to do. A principle is a sign or a symbol and has meaning only as what it involves in action is determined. Like other symbols, it has little meaning or significance except as it is embodied in concrete experience. But it is also true that the same symbols or principles have very different meanings for different people. An individual's principles are the reason for his action, but the principle does not predetermine the conduct. The principles are the "why" of the conduct.

The identification of the principle with some particular kind of conduct is easier in simple forms of individual conduct than it is in more complicated social situations. Honesty may be interpreted as giving correct change or refusing to receive or give help in examinations. But principles are often in conflict in the same situation. The principle of honesty would lead a child not to give help in an examination, but the principle of thoughtfulness for the other person would lead him to give help to a person in need. Thus children and young people often are dishonest on principle; that is, they follow the principle of being thoughtful for another person in need rather than that of being honest. The difficulty in trusting principles as unmistakable guides to conduct becomes increasingly evident in proportion as situations become complicated. Thus, while ethical principles are of prime importance, their utilization in the educational process is far

[25] *Ibid.*, p. 82.

more complicated and difficult than seemed to be assumed when the Herbartian procedures were followed.

The use of a thorough-going educational process in the consideration of ethical issues in contemporary Christianity involves several important changes from the educational practice as often followed in the churches. First, instead of being focused on a study of the Christian principles, this process would center in the actual situations that are being faced by Christians, not only nor chiefly within the church, but in homes, schools, community relationships, economic affairs, racial relationships, political decisions, and the like. These situations would be explored and the important factors brought to understanding so that the group in the church would be facing the situation realistically. This would eliminate the pious platitudes in regard to what is ideally desirable and would lead to a facing of the situations as Christians meet them in the world in which they live.

Second, in a thorough-going educational process, *all* of the alternatives for action which are being followed or being seriously proposed would be considered by the church group. Frequently, and perhaps usually, the church group considers only . the alternatives which the leaders think ought to be considered. Consequently, the alternatives which are actually operative in the life outside of the church, and even among Christians themselves, are never looked at. For example the alternative of giving or receiving help in examinations is never seriously explored, even though this is a live option which is being considered or followed by church children and young people. Drinking liquor under certain conditions is ruled out in favor of examining only total abstinence, even though again this fails to look at the alternatives as they face church young people. In race relationships, the alternatives of discrimination, which are actually practiced even in the church, are not examined. As a result, the educational process in the church is often of little help because, even if there is attempt to deal with actual situations, there is failure to face the situations realistically since certain alternatives are ruled out in advance.

Third, not only must all the alternatives be examined, but those which may be considered undesirable must be dealt with fairly. This means that the church group must look at them from the viewpoint of those who believe that they are the only practicable alternatives or that they are the desirable ones. In other words, the group considering the problem must have a chance to understand and to feel the conviction of those who believe in the supposedly undesirable alternative. This is an acid test of the thoroughness of the educational process. So often, even when all the alternatives are considered, certain are introduced only for condemnation. This is often true of proposals for radical reconstruction of life as well as of those which would involve lowering of standards. Consequently, the consideration is again unrealistic because the considerations which make these live options are never really faced by the church group. This stage in the educational process involves understanding what those who believe in an alternative think would happen if it were put into practice and why they believe this to be desirable.

The presentation of a supposedly undesirable alternative takes on the glow of reality best when it is given in person by someone who believes in it; but at times the group will be forced to depend upon the printed word, a report on which can be introduced into the process. In situations where there is conflict between groups, fairness is ensured by having those party to the conflict meet together in conference or at least by having present in the discussion a representative of the group which is not found in the church constituency.

Fourth, in a thorough-going educational process there will be honesty and accuracy in dealing with the facts. So frequently factual data are selected to prove that certain proposals would work out well and other proposals would work out undesirably. Honesty demands that the predictions of what would happen be checked on the basis of the best factual data of experience and experiment and that as accurate an account of the probable results of a proposed alternative be reached as is possible. This would demand much more thorough study than most church groups now engage in.

Fifth, in a thorough-going educational process, the attention will be focused on finding that which is most in line with Christian ethics. This involves two considerations. The first is the one discussed earlier in the chapter—that which is most Christian in any particular situation is not necessarily evident from the Christian principles. Sincere Christians disagree as to what is the course of action most in line with Christian ethics. It is a sobering fact to realize that if the Christian churches were given the right and the power to determine individual and corporate ethical conduct, they would be unable to act for they could not agree on what would be Christian. If there is any question on which Christian ethics would seem to be clear it is in regard to war; but the Oxford conference had to recognize three positions widely held among Christians. There are even greater diversities of conviction on economic, racial, and other social problems. On the face of the evidence, Christian ethics seems to offer nothing distinctive because Christians seem to represent a cross-section of the community in the range of their ethical beliefs.

Christian ethics does offer a distinctive emphasis and perspective in the educational process when the search for its meaning in any particular situation becomes an integral part of the process. This is accomplished not alone by using the Christian principles in the abstract as an emphasis in the search, but by a thorough study of other situations in the past and the present where the issue was similar and where effort was made to embody the Christian emphasis. The Bible contains material of paramount importance for such a search, not only because in it are the central records of the Christian religion, but also because its ethical teaching is integrally related to practical situations. For example, the Synoptic records of the life of Jesus are not a collection of his principles, but these are always associated as the reason for attitudes and action.

But a second consideration is also important. In the attempt to determine what Christian ethics would demand in any particular situation, an absolutist position hinders, if indeed it does not defeat, the realization of this goal. There are two reasons for this. When an individual takes an absolutist position on some one Christian principle or value, he rules out all other values involved and so makes an educational process which takes account of all the values impossible. For example, if he takes an absolutist position on the use of force in international or labor disputes, then he rules out all questions of justice in relation to these situations. Another reason that an absolutist position makes a thoroughgoing educational process difficult if not impossible is the fact that there are often limitations in the situations themselves, over which Christians have no immediate control, however much they may work for the change of those conditions. In the meantime, they have to act, if they are to act at all, in as Christian a manner as possible in a world which has many un-Christian limitations. Consequently, while there must not be the easy compromise by which the established practices are accepted uncritically, it is necessary to be realistic and to seek to find those practicable courses of action which most nearly approximate Christian ethics under the limitations Christians face and will always face in the world.

Sixth, in a thorough-going educational process, Christian ethics itself is not assumed but is subject to critical examination. In the emphasis upon the search for what is most Christian, there is an assumption that the members of the group are already committed to the Christian way of life and wish help in discovering what it involves in the particular situation. But if the educational process is to be of help to those within the churches who are doubtful as to the practicability or even the desirability of Christian ethics and particularly if it is to bring within the Christian educational process those who are not now committed to the Christian religion, there must be provision for critical examination of the ethics itself. Within the church are many, perhaps a majority, who believe in Christian ethics in theory but have no confidence as to its practicability in life. There are others who really believe that other philosophies of life are necessary in the world as we face it. Many have frankly committed themselves to an anti-Christian or a non-Christian attitude and practice and they do not come to the church because they do not find there any willingness to examine the Christian ethics itself. In a situation where Christian ethics is not accepted in most aspects of our own life as a nation and in which entire nations have repudiated it, there must be recognition of this situation in the educational process, if it is to deal realistically with these situations. Christians have confidence that a genuine exploration of the meaning of Christian ethics would result in a conviction as to its practicability and desirability in individual practice and group relationships; but they must show their confidence by a willingness to subject it to thorough-going examination.

Seventh, in a thorough-going educational process, there is opportunity to put decisions into practice. This is ensured in part when the situations considered are those which individuals or groups actually face, in which they must act in one way or another. However, unless there is careful consideration of the ways and means of putting decisions into effect, proposals for action different from those commonly accepted and followed will never get a chance. It takes realistic and resourceful planning to ensure that anything practical eventuates from the educational process.

The careful consideration of means for putting the decision into effect is important, not only because otherwise the educational process may end in pious hopes and make no difference in conduct, but also because of the close relationship between the goals of endeavor and the means by which they are attained. There is a common assumption that once the course of action and the goal of the endeavor are determined, the effectiveness of the means used is the only relevant concern. Brunner seems to have fallen into this error. In his emphasis that means must be those of historical existence and that the chief consideration is their practicability in attaining the ends, he seems to leave little place for a criticism of these means from an ethical viewpoint. Indeed, he offers the Christian a way of escape by saying that God has taken the sin upon himself and thus sanctified unholy means. But unless the means are consistent with the goals of the endeavor, they may defeat, and indeed are likely to defeat, the goals. This is seen, for example, in the discussion as to whether or not it is possible to use methods of force and violence to attain the goals of coöperation and goodwill. There may be times when only by such methods can sufficient restraint be placed upon evildoers to protect innocent victims from their ravages, but the goals of coöperative relations cannot be attained by methods which deny the principles of coöperation. The means for attaining the course of action decided upon must be consistent with the goals of the endeavor or the goals will be defeated.

In planning for action, there needs to be recognition both of the agreements and the disagreements in conviction as the result of the educational process. For example, a group may come to a united conviction as to what they as Christians believe should be done. In that case, they can carry the educational process through as a group into plans for action. But the members of the group may arrive at different convictions as to what would be Christian. In that case, each sub-group must have the chance to plan for action and the sub-groups must be encouraged to try out their convictions. The process will not be complete, however, except as the sub-groups are willing to compare the results of their separate experiments and evaluate them. Therefore, there must be provision within the churches for varieties of experiments in carrying out Christian ethics. The advice of Gamaliel should be taken seriously by religious educators: "Refrain from these men, and let them alone: for if this counsel or this work be of men, it will be overthrown: but if it is of God, ye will not be able to overthrow them; lest haply ye be found even to be fighting against God." [26]

This emphasis upon the experimental attitude toward various convictions regarding Christian ethics is particularly important in the policy of the churches in regard to economic, racial, and other more complicated social issues. The tendency at present is to seek to commit the church as a whole to an authoritative social program. Consequently, energy goes into efforts to secure adoption of certain proposals by majority vote by national or regional assembles or by local churches. But a majority vote does not mean a united conviction, so the divisions still persist despite the vote. But another consequence is more serious. Instead of using time and energy in experiments which put proposals into effect and in comparing and evaluating the results, groups use a disproportionate amount of time and energy in seeking to secure the adoption of resolutions. Further, experimental and coöperative search

[26] Acts 5:38–39.

is changed to competitive propaganda and political manipulation and an effective educational process is hindered. In a thorough-going educational process there will be frank recognition of the right and the obligation of minority groups to try out their proposals, not as the authoritative action of the church, but as the convictions of these particular groups. This will mean that, under the name of the churches, groups may be acting in diverse or even in opposite ways. They do not lose their connection with the church nor do they seek to say that they are acting for the entire church.

Eighth, in a thorough-going educational process, there is provision for comparing and evaluating the results of action on the basis of Christian ethics. Choices are made on the basis of the best prediction of probable consequences of a course of action. But there is no guarantee that the result will be as predicted. To refuse to adventure except where the empirical evidence is final and convincing would stultify the creative possibilities of an educational process. Faith lays hold of things as yet unseen. There is a sense in which an individual or a group, where there has been realistic facing of the situation and earnest search for the Christian solution, have an intuition of possibilities even before all the factors are clear. There is an adventure of faith in a true educational process. But whether the adventure is based on a false or a true insight will be only determined as it is carried out and evaluated. Whether the particular course of action is in line with Christian ethics can be determined only by trying it out and seeing what happens to the Christian values. Thus, the educational process is not complete until there has been earnest and critical evaluation of the consequences of choice and action. In both the process of choice in advance of action and in the evaluation of the results of the action, Christian ethics is in constant process of clarification and definition.

Improvement in ethical conduct is thus possible by the thoroughgoing use of an experimental educational process. As we have learned "methods of inventing" which have tremendously speeded up material progress, so we have methods by which ethical formulations and practices may be criticized and revised. By a critical examination of past and current history as well as by actual experiments, we can compare various types of action and the consequences of each. On the basis of such data, there is the possibility of a realistic consideration of ethical issues and the improvement of ethical practices. On this same basis, where the ethical situation is confused—where old standards have broken down, and new standards have not yet been formed—it is not necessary to wait for a slow and costly "trial and error" process for the development of new standards. The problems may be analyzed and attacked experimentally through the educational process and new standards worked out in the life of the group. But this involves the experimental attitude. Instead of attacking every variation from existing practice as a threat to the stability of the moral order, serious and sincere proposals should be given a chance and examined to see if they offer an improvement when tested by the Christian values.

Religious educators believe that the Christian ethics for any situation or any generation can only be determined by a thoroughgoing educational process. This is true not only because the meaning of Christian ethics is understood and is effective only as it is worked out in connection with circumstances where it is being utilized, but also because what is Christian is tested in the last analysis by the actual effects of any particular course of action upon the Christian values. Thus, the leaders in religious education would use an educational process both to determine and to embody Christian ethics. But they would trust only that educational process in which Christian ethics is central. Such a process does not ignore either Christian history or Christian principles. Instead, it utilizes the experience of the past as recorded in the Bible and in Christian history for an understanding of Christian ethics and brings it to bear upon present situations in the search for that which under present conditions most nearly expresses it. Christian ethics is integrally related to Christian education.

CHAPTER XIII

The Educational Process and Religious Experience

RELIGIOUS EDUCATORS of the neo-orthodox viewpoint criticize the developments in modern religious education because they believe that there is a tendency to identify religious experience with the highest forms of human experience found in man's devotion to ideal social ends and because they think that this results in there being no real distinction between religious education and the best forms of social education. "Religious education is conceived of as a sort of emotionalized social education" and "as a part of general education with no particular truth of its own." The focus of religious education upon the human scene and upon the social process of experience has resulted, in their judgment, in a failure to secure any vital experience of God. "To be sure, God may be mentioned, but God is conceived as immanent in the social process, as a part of nature, capable of being experienced in man's highest devotion to 'ideal social ends.' In short, the social 'religious attitude' is substituted for definite personal relations to a personal god. 'The beyond element' is swallowed up in present experience." [1]

It is important to note that the criticism that a social theory of religious education tends to minimize or lose the experience of God has been made not only by a neo-orthodox interpreter like Homrighausen, but also by a "liberal" religious educator like Wil-

[1] Homrighausen, E. G., "The Real Problem of Religious Education," in *Religious Education*, January–March 1939, pp. 13–14.

fred Evans Powell. The latter has made this criticism explicit in a book on the problem.[2] As a significant contribution to the process or method of religious education, he recognizes as desirable the increasing social emphasis which had its first definite formulation in 1917 in Coe's *A Social Theory of Religious Education*.[3] But he believes that a social theory of religious education tends "to give a one-sided emphasis to those aspects of religion concerned immediately with the improvement of our social relationships, and to minimize those other aspects that push out beyond the human realm to a reality that is felt to have supreme power or supreme worth."[4] He then reviews the writings of certain leaders in religious education in which the aims of the educational process are stated. He cites Coe's statement of aim, "growth of the young toward and into mature and efficient devotion to the democracy of God, and happy self-realization therein"; and Soares', "the development of persons devoted to the highest social well-being, which they identify as the will of God."[5] While these are "intended to differentiate this view from any merely humanistic conception," they nevertheless represent, he thinks, "certain tendencies in this social emphasis which, if followed to the end, might very well lead to the complete ignoring of the relation to God."[6] He is still more troubled about Ames' discussion in which he calls attention to the similarity between an experimental curriculum for religious education and the program of a progressive public school and in which he makes the distinguishing characteristic of religious education, not some peculiar content, but its approach and spirit, its idealization and evaluations.[7] Powell is no more satisfied with Coe's discussion (twelve

---

[2] Powell, Wilfred Evans, *Education for Life with God.*
[3] *Ibid.,* pp. 41–42.
[4] From *Education for Life with God* by Wilfred Evans Powell, p. 40. Copyright 1934. Reprinted by permission of The Abingdon Press.
[5] *Ibid.,* p. 45.   [6] *Ibid.,* p. 45.   [7] *Ibid.,* pp. 48–49.

years later) in *What Is Christian Education?* in which he feels that Coe makes "its radicalness" the distinguishing mark of religious education and focuses particular attention upon the "encouragement of free, creative, self-activity." [8]

Powell thinks that these would be "very satisfactory characterizations of a high type of moral and social education, and they include much that is essential in religion at its best, but they do not indicate clearly that the lifting of all of life to the level of a conscious relationship to God is fundamental to them." Further, "God seems sometimes to be not so much a metaphysical reality as a sort of symbol for the deepest, most truly shared, and most unselfishly motivated aspects of social experience." [9] These social conceptions, he says, are "indefinite as to whether the type of personality desired includes not only ethical and social attitudes, but also attitudes of dependence and worship"; they are not "clear as to whether the society to be created is one in which alone man's social aspirations shall be realized, or one in which also God's name shall be hallowed, and his kingdom come." [10] He thinks that there is in these current theories of religious education "a tendency toward the practical identification of religious education and social education." [11] Of course, he says, there is a recognition by all these leaders of a "something more" in religious education, but he feels that this "something more" is regarded as a "secondary consideration and its importance is greatly minimized." [12]

It should be recognized that the difficulty Homrighausen and Powell point out is a real one in all religious education that attempts to deal realistically with the life of children, young people, and adults in the human scene. The tendency of human beings is to become engulfed in the practical difficulties of the present

[8] *Ibid.*, p. 49.
[9] *Ibid.*, p. 47.
[10] *Ibid.*, p. 48.
[11] *Ibid.*, p. 50.
[12] *Ibid.*, p. 51.

situation and to accept uncritically the current standards of right and wrong, of desirable and undesirable conduct. In facing actual situations, it is difficult to secure any attention even to the "ideal social ends," which socially-minded educators would wish to have used in determining what to do in the present situation, and any kind of cosmic perspective is still more difficult to attain. Engrossed in the practical difficulties of living, adults as well as children tend to be governed by immediate practical considerations and ready-to-hand solutions of their problems. Further, with the present emphasis, not only in education but in all of life's activities, upon individual initiative and personal responsibility there is an inevitable danger that individuals will feel that they are the "arbiters of their fate." In an age of scientific achievement, there is a lack of appreciation of and reverence toward the given resources of the universe as they impinge upon human life and without which a human being could do nothing. This lack of trust and dependence is especially marked among the more favored groups who make up the constituency of the average church. What need do they have of God, so long as parents and the social order itself seem ready to supply their every need? Social as well as religious education faces the difficulty of securing any genuine perspective in the educational process.

The criticism of both Homrighausen and Powell that the conceptions of the goal of religious education have tended to be taken from educational theory in the general field is also in part justified. As already noted, the modern movement in religious education grew out of the general developments in education and was greatly influenced not only by experimental psychology but also by the developing theory and practice of education in the more progressive schools. There was little opportunity to study religious education, as such, for most of the seminaries had either no department or a very inadequate offering so that the training available was chiefly in connection with schools of education. A social viewpoint and social efficiency as the aim were prominent in the theory of general education. For Dewey and other leaders who formulated the philosophy of the newer education, the democratic way of life seemed the goal. Thus, his widely influential work, *Democracy and Education,* contained the viewpoint he advocated for public education in the very title. Since democracy, as conceived by Dewey, seemed in the days of the interest in the "Social Gospel" to contain many of the same points of emphasis which were found in the social hopes of the Kingdom of God, it was easy to identify the two without giving attention to the distinctively Christian points of emphasis in the conception of the Kingdom of God however interpreted. It hardly seems fair, as is often implied, to criticize Dewey and other leaders in general education for centering public education in social goals. In the separation of church and state in American education, there would have been no opportunity, however much there might have been a desire, to work out a philosophy of education in religious terms. In bringing a social emphasis into general education, they made it possible to utilize public education as a foundation and background for religious education and they enabled general and religious educators to work coöperatively.

Another and more fundamental factor was without doubt operative in the failure of religious education to have an adequate metaphysical grounding. The philosophy which seemed best to interpret both the spirit and the process of an experience-centered education was Experimentalism. John Dewey, who was the leading exponent of this philosophy, was also one of the most influential figures in the modern educational movement. In his book, *Reconstruction in Philosophy,* Dewey criticized classical philosophies for their attempts to rationalize or make intellectually respectable inherited points of view and insisted that the business of philosophy was to build a basis for the processes by which men and women actually live. In accordance with this emphasis, he sought to develop a philosophy which would interpret the use of scientific approaches and processes in social relationships. He considered the metaphysical problems which have engaged the attention of philosophy and theology as irrelevant, but at the same time he gave very little attention to the metaphysical assumptions and implications of his own philosophy. For this he was criticized, both by those not in sympathy with his viewpoint as well as by certain Experimentalist philosophers. For example, in a review of the evidence, John L. Childs showed that a world view is implied in Experimentalism and insisted that this world view should not only be admitted, but also be made more explicit than the Experimentalists had done.[13]

Dewey has in his recent writing given more attention to this aspect of his philosophy,[14] but even in these books, he has not carried his thinking to the point of indicating the metaphysical grounding of the ideal ends which he considers the goals of the educational process. Since so little attention was given to metaphysical questions in the philosophy which interpreted the educational process, it is perhaps not surprising that these should have been ignored by those who followed this philosophy in their educational theory or that even at times, as Homrighausen suggests, they should have adopted the "educational theories and methods without realizing or understanding their full implications." The corrective of this difficulty would not be, as some have suggested, an abandonment of both the educational process and philosophy, but rather more thorough attention to its metaphysical and to its religious meanings.[15]

The issue raised by Homrighausen and Powell is, however,

[13] Childs, John L., *Education and the Philosophy of Experimentalism,* Chapter III.

[14] Dewey, John, *The Quest for Certainty* and *A Common Faith.*

[15] This has been done by William C. Bower, one of the leaders in religious education, in his *Religion and the Good Life.*

more basic than would be involved if the situation were simply due to a neglect of the metaphysical grounding of a religious educational process. As a matter of fact, a comparison of the criticism and the defence of a social theory of religious education seems to show that the issue does not arise through lack of concern on the part of religious educators with a social viewpoint that an experience of God shall grow out of the educational process, but rather that it is due to differences of judgment as to *how* an experience of God is realized. The critics of a socialized religious education say that in the educational process, attention must be turned *directly* to God if it is to result in a religious experience in which God is fundamentally recognized. On the other hand, the defenders of a social emphasis say that a direct approach tends to separate God from human affairs and to make religious experience "other-worldly" and that it is only through a socialized approach that God will be experienced as a reality in human life.

The emphasis of the critics of a socialized religious education is revealed in the very title of Powell's book: *Education for Life with God*. After recognizing the degree to which children and young people may come to have consciousness of and response to God through experience in a Christian home, through the influence of teachers, and through facing the ordinary experiences of life, he says that these, in and of themselves, are inadequate and he proposes more direct methods for securing this end. The first method he suggests is a direct study of the Bible, because of "the power of the Bible to arouse a specifically religious response among those who have a sympathetic understanding of it." [16] What is needed, he says, is "to help pupils toward a sympathetic understanding of the Bible as a source of knowledge of God; to awaken in them a personal interest in its use; to cause them so to

[16] From *Education for Life with God* by Wilfred Evans Powell, p. 199. Copyright 1934. Reprinted by permission of The Abingdon Press.

enter into the experiences of its characters that they absorb something of their consciousness of God; and to lead them to discover that these experiences are reproduceable in their own lives." [17] But he makes worship the unique and distinctive method of a religious education which is focused on life with God. After rejecting Hartshorne's conception of worship as the criticism and redirection of experience and after insisting that worship does not take place in discussion groups, where experience is rehearsed and criticized and purposes are formed to give it a new direction, he confines worship to those experiences in which there is a direct and personal approach to God.[18]

In contrast to this emphasis upon a *direct* approach to God, certain religious educators believe that God can be experienced in a vital manner only in and through the social process. Coe deals with this problem in *What Is Christian Education?*.[19] After calling attention to the decline of "the realization of God as an actual presence and power," [20] he says that "either there is no such God as the Christian tradition claims there is, or else there is something so seriously defective in our religious technic that God cannot freely manifest himself through it." [21] He thinks the difficulty is in a "repetitious religion, a backward-facing religion" for "personality cannot fulfil itself by repetition either of one's own self or of other selves." [22] This is in direct contrast to Powell's emphasis upon the reproduction of the experiences of the Biblical characters. Coe says that "we ourselves must make a new demonstration of ethical love in human relations, or else lose our faith in

[17] *Ibid.*, p. 200.

[18] *Ibid.*, pp. 202–206.

[19] Powell does not refer to this analysis in his quotations from Coe, even though it is directly on the problem which he is discussing. This was probaby due to the fact that he quoted the aims of the various religious educators, but gave no attention in his discussion to the processes which they proposed.

[20] Coe, George Albert, *What Is Christian Education?*, p. 263.

[21] *Ibid.*, p. 267.   [22] *Ibid.*, p. 268.

God." [23] In reply to the fear lest the emphasis upon the social approach should invert the true order of teaching and leave the experience of God undeveloped, he says that "what leaves the experience of God undeveloped is, first of all, the endeavor of teachers and preachers to induce pupils and hearers to carry on dealings with God that are not at the same time dealings with men, as though God could be vitally apprehended otherwise than in the love that men have for one another. Then, in the second place, superficial handling of relations between men lends its own superficiality to faith in God." He insists that "the deepening of personal life (which is social), and the deepening of our faith in God, must take place at the same point, and through the same process." [24]

William C. Bower gives a similar emphasis, even though he phrases it in philosophical rather than sociological terms. Following his conception of religion as an evaluational process, with which Coe would agree, [25] Bower shows how in individual and corporate life there is the danger that some special set of values shall be made authoritative and final to the exclusion of other important values. This he thinks to be a danger even within religious experience itself. He sees "in religion the revaluation of all values whatsoever" and therefore something "vastly more than the summation of all the more or less particularized values. Through the process of revaluation a new and unique quality emerges within the religious aspect of experience that is not to be found in its disparate sets of values. It is at this point of fusion that for most religious persons God appears in human experience, not as something extraneously invading that experience from some 'supernatural' source as distinguished from the 'natural,' but as the most fundamental reality of our world moving creatively

---

[23] *Ibid.*, p. 268. [24] *Ibid.*, pp. 271–272.
[25] See Coe, George Albert, *The Psychology of Religion.*

within that experience." [26] He adds that "in the light of this fact of God, personal and social values become intensified, are subjected to the most searching criticism, and are set in their vast framework of universal and eternal relations in a personality-producing universe." In this process, "not only do the economic, social, intellectual, aesthetic, and ethical aspects of experience undergo reassessment and reconstruction, but life itself, both in its personal and its cosmic aspects, takes on fundamental meaning and worth." [27] The implication of this point of view is that religious experience is integrally related to other experience and that God becomes a reality to the individual in and through the experience of life. Religion brings to ordinary experience a distinctive quality and raises it to the religious level. "Wherever any experience of any sort whatsoever is seen and judged in its relation to the total meaning and worth of life in terms of its responsible relation to God, be it in the family, in industry, in vocation, in recreation, in intellectual pursuits, in aesthetic enjoyment, or in moral conduct, there experience takes on the religious quality." [28]

Homrighausen uses Hugh Hartshorne's emphasis upon character that eventuates in social functoning as an illustration of his contention that religious education involves a liberal theology in which the experience of God in a distinctive sense is lost; but he waives altogether Hartshorne's clear differentiation between ordinary "social functioning" and that which has the characteristic of religious experience. [29] Hartshorne says that functioning occurs at different levels. The lowest level of functioning is mechanical, illustrated in the activity of water in wearing down the hills or the operation of a man-made machine. Primitive social function-

---

[26] Bower, William C., *Character through Creative Experience*, p. 230.

[27] *Ibid.*, pp. 230–231.

[28] *Ibid.*, p. 249.

[29] Homrighausen, E. G., "The Real Problem of Religious Education," *Religious Education*, January–March, 1939, p. 14.

ing is seen in the activities of an ant-hill or a beehive. Much human activity, he thinks, is at this level, as in the case of an industry "where 'hands' are identified by their jobs" and "hardly more
than the ant does the individual worker understand the meaning
of the process." [30] Of similar type is the functioning of the soldier.

Hartshorne emphasizes that man is not limited to these primitive modes of social action. "Through other types of experience
he has developed capacities and interests which are genuinely
'social' and 'personal.' As generations have passed he has found
increasing opportunity to use his own intelligence in the guidance
of his conduct and in the determination of his goals." [31] Hartshorne says that this higher level of functioning is illustrated in
democratic forms of social organization, such as a well-conducted
committee meeting, an old-fashioned New England town meeting, a wisely managed family, a student council, a modern class
room, the free play of children. This is true social functioning
"at which level the individual has come into his own as a co-
operating whole, interacting freely with his group and discovering the meaning of his life in terms of the purposes of the
group." [32]

Hartshorne insists that to be truly meaningful, social functioning cannot be confined to the particular group in which it occurs,
but that the group itself "exists not for its own sake but for some
purpose which alone justifies its existence and its activity, and
therefore the activity of its members." Attention must be given
to this wider environment in relation to which social function becomes meaningful. This involves "either discovering or creating
some meaning for life as a whole in terms of which the activities
of groups and of individuals may be appraised." [33] But this wider
meaning of life, in Hartshorne's viewpoint, is not confined to the

[30] Hartshorne, Hugh, *Character in Human Relations*, p. 240.
[31] *Ibid.*, p. 241.   [32] *Ibid.*, p. 242.   [33] *Ibid.*, p. 243.

social significance of individual and group functioning. "Beyond the circle enclosing true social function," he says another is needed "which shall remain undrawn to suggest that there is no definite area to be included," because "from here on we are impinging on all reality" and a reality "within which the essentially personal factors of our experience subsist." [34] Character as the art of living is won "through the performance of daily activities in the light of their meaning for the largest or most inclusive reality of which one can conceive" and with a sense of relationship "with that in the universe which makes for the growth of personality." [35] This level he calls "cosmic functioning." Hartshorne interprets God in functional rather than theological terminology in this discussion, but it is evident that he not only believes that God is inevitably involved in every social act but that the conscious recognition of this fact is essential to true social functioning. He thus shows that it is in and through social functioning that the experience of God is realized.

A similar emphasis is found in the discussion of religious education in Wieman and Wieman's *Normative Psychology of Religion*. In this book, the authors say that the "ultimate objective of religious education is to awaken in the child dynamic loyalty to God" but that this "cannot be given to the individual, nor memorized into him, nor trained or inculcated into him in the direct sense, but it can be fostered by the provision of such conditions for his living as direct his sensitivities and responses into this distinctive way of behaving." [36] Therefore, in religious education the process is carried on "in such ways that the individual will develop loyalty to the absolutely supreme and inclusive value which is beyond all values known or conceivable through the

[34] *Ibid.*, pp. 243–244.
[35] *Ibid.*, pp. 249–250.
[36] Wieman, Henry Nelson and Regina Westcott, *Normative Psychology of Religion*, pp. 459–460.

present resources of society." [37] Later in the chapter, the authors make explicit their conviction that the experience of God grows out of meeting the concrete issues of life and that the educational process is important in realizing this end. They say that religious education "will tend to vitalize religion through keeping it close to the real issues which concern individual and group living. The young cannot deal in abstractions. They learn by doing. If religion is to be strong and healthy it must induct youth into such experiences as will engender dynamic loyalty to God in terms of issues vital to highest human fulfillment. In doing so, it will induct itself into those causes which foster more appreciative and valid discernment of the Supreme Value in those terms which are most meaningful for persons of the present time and place." [38]

In this connection it is pertinent to note that Paul Tillich, who recognizes his affinity with Brunner but who has often though quite incorrectly been called a Barthian, makes a similar emphasis in regard to the experience of God. Tillich as a philosophical theologian discusses the issue in philosophical rather than educational terminology. His point of view is found in his discussion of *Kairos* and *Logos*, a study in the metaphysics of knowledge. [39] The issue is phrased by him in terms of the relation of *Logos*, the timeless and pure form, to *Kairos*, "the moment of time approaching us as fate and decision." [40] He objects to the efforts both of Roman Catholicism and Protestantism to avoid the equivocal character of all decision for God. These are found in "the Catholic doctrine of the supernatural grace, which raises one out of unequivocal darkness into the world of unequivocal truth" and in "certain forms of radical Protestantism, which point to the tran-

---

[37] *Ibid.*, p. 461.
[38] *Ibid.*, p. 478.
[39] Tillich, Paul, *The Interpretation of History*, Part Two, II.
[40] *Ibid.*, p. 129.

scendant reality of God but rigorously deny his reality in this world." He says that in both the "decision-character of knowledge, the introduction of the knowing subject into the historical fate, is lost. Catholicism knows only two possibilities of an historical fate: to belong to the Church or not to belong to it. Radical Protestantism knows only the one historical fate: to stand under divine judgment." In opposition to these positions, he asserts that there cannot be a final decision for God but that every human decision with reference to God is equivocal.[41] He later says that history (by which he seems to mean something similar to that which has been called social experience in this chapter) exists "where there is decision, namely a decision which is concrete, on the one hand, and which is rooted in the depth of the Unconditioned on the other hand." He adds that decisions in the conditioned sphere, that is in human existence, mean nothing in themselves but get their meaning because they have an unconditioned element in themselves. He then states explicitly that this unconditioned meaning will be realized—that is, that God will be realized in human life—only in the *Kairos,* fate and decision in time. "If individuality is to have unconditioned meaning, it must be interpreted as the appearance of a concrete, genuine decision which transcends itself. That such individualism is possible nowhere else but in the personal sphere, that is, where there is freedom and where there is fate, requires no proof. Everywhere else individualization remains imperfect. Everywhere else the individual is subjected to the universal." [42] This, he says, is the true Protestant attitude: "to stand in nature, taking upon oneself the inevitable reality; not to flee from it, either into the world of ideal forms or in the related world of super-nature, but to make decisions in concrete reality. Here the subject has no possibility of an absolute position. It cannot go out of the sphere of decision.

[41] *Ibid.,* pp. 136–137.   [42] *Ibid.,* pp. 138–139.

. . . Fate and freedom reach into the act of knowledge and make it an historical deed: the *Kairos* determines the Logos." [43]

This review of the authors quoted by Homrighausen and Powell would seem to refute their statement that for these leaders in religious education there is nothing distinctive about religious education as compared with altruistic social education. For them the beyond element is not swallowed up in the present experience, but it finds its true realization in that experience. The "something more" in religious education is not regarded as a secondary consideration and its importance minimized, but the experience of God is central in the religious educational process. Whether or not there is agreement that this is the way that the experience of God is most vitally realized, there can be no question in regard to the conviction of these educational leaders as to the paramount importance of the experience of God in the educational process.

It is interesting to note what seems to be a basic agreement between those who have approached the problem educationally and those whose approach has been philosophical. Tillich, with terminology which is strange to the average American religious educator, and Coe in language with which the educator is more familiar, both say that God becomes apprehended and experienced only in the concrete situations of life where he is realized in the crucial act of decision. Both would seem to agree that this is defeated where attention is turned directly to a God so beyond and unrelated to the human scene that relationship to him is irrelevant to mundane affairs or where through authoritative creed or church he is used as the rationalization of some present belief so that decision is unnecessary. A socialized form of religious education would seem to be of fundamental importance, if God is to be dynamically and creatively experienced in human life.

[43] *Ibid.*, pp. 134–135.

The efforts to secure an experience of God by direct methods are likely to defeat the very ends desired. In so far as these methods succeed, they tend to separate relationship with God from the concerns of life. It is true that a direct approach to God, unrelated to the concerns of living, is possible for mature Christians in a form of worship, sometimes designated as communion with God; but such a level of experience is possible in a meaningful fashion only as the fruition of many experiences of worship directly related to human needs, just as the highest communion between human beings is the fruition of many concrete situations of life which have been met and shared.

There is an important place in religious education for taking children and young people back into Biblical times with a view to recapturing imaginatively these significant experiences. Such Bible study widens and enriches the present experience. But this is not the form of Bible study which is most likely to make the Bible a living force in present affairs or to make God a living reality in human life today. However much teachers may succeed in getting children or young people to enter imaginatively into the experiences of Bible characters and particularly of Jesus Christ, unless these experiences are brought to bear upon present-day situations and reinterpreted in terms of present-day problems, they are likely to remain interesting but not particularly pertinent to the life of today. The suggestion of Powell that children and young people should be encouraged to reproduce these Biblical experiences in their own lives seems perhaps the least effective way to use the Bible. All experience—and this is notably true of religious experience—has a distinctiveness of its own. It not only is related to particular circumstances, which can never be reproduced, but it also takes on the distinctive qualities of the experiencing persons. In other words, experience is always unique. Attempts to copy the experience of others are always questionable. The experiences of

Biblical characters are of great value, but their significance will be realized by individuals or groups today only as they, deeply conscious of their own problems and needs, go to the Biblical experiences for inspiration and insight to face their own problems and only as they come to their own solution of their problems and their own unique experience of God.

The same difficulty is found in the "direct" forms of worship. If worship is to have nothing to do with the criticism and redirection of experience, then there is grave danger that individuals will make their decisions without reference to God, and use worship merely to secure the forgiveness of their sins and to make their peace with God for the inevitable secularization of their everyday lives. As already noted, this is the danger in Brunner's emphasis. If worship is to have no integral relation to discussion groups, where experience is rehearsed and criticized and where purposes are formed to give it a new direction, and the conscious approach to God is to be reserved for separate experiences of worship, then inevitably individuals and groups will make their decisions unrelated to an earnest search to find God's will, and will use the worship experience to ask God's blessing upon decisions they have already made and to seek his power for purposes they have already formed. This is what makes for lack of vitality and even for hypocrisy in worship.

It is true, as Hocking emphasizes,[44] that worship is an alternation from life's activity, but it is not in isolation from it. It is an alternation in order to gain new perspective and new resources for the life's task. It is significant that the incidents recorded in the Synoptic Gospels of the prayer life of Jesus are all related to crucial choices or problems in his life, where he wrestled all night or for forty days in prayer, not in a direct approach to God apart from the experiences of life, but in the search for the Father's will. "My

[44] Hocking, William Ernest, *The Meaning of God in Human Experience.*

Father, if it be possible, let this cup pass away from me: nevertheless, not as I will, but as thou wilt." [45]

The meaning of this emphasis can perhaps be illustrated by the relation of parents and children. It is true that children may make direct approaches to their parents with requests and petitions and in expressions of affection; and parents may make direct approaches to their children in restraint and discipline and in manifestations of love and care. But these are not the relationships between parents and children in which the most vital experience takes place. They tend to make of parents either purveyors of favors or enforcers of legal regulations. Children come to have the most vital and meaningful experience of their parents only as there is opportunity to share life with them in and beyond the home. It is as they work *with* parents, not *for* them; as they share with their parents in experiences of recreation; as they feel the comradeship of their parents in facing their crucial problems, that parents come vitally to be experienced by their children. The experience of God is analogous. It is as God comes into vital relationship with individuals in the experiences and the choices of life that his resources are available and that he becomes a living presence.

The social process of religious education, which critics of religious education fear because they think it is centered too much in human life, is the very process which gives the largest promise of bringing about a vital experience of God. Vitality of religious experience is not realized by turning away from the problems and decisions of human life in efforts to find a direct relationship to God. It is only as individuals and groups are engaged in the enterprises of God on earth that they can truly find a relationship to him. Bible study and prayer and worship will not of themselves produce vital religious experience. It is only when these are utilized because of a concern for human life and because of a sense of need for resources

[45] Matthew 26:39.

beyond those which seem available in human endeavor that they lead to the vitalizing of religious experience. The experience of God is integrally related to a social process of religious education.

The social emphasis in what was known as the "Social Gospel" brought a new vitality in religious experience. Ordinary human affairs in business and profession, industry and politics, had been assumed to be secular, with which the Christian religion was not directly concerned. Walter Rauschenbusch's books, which appeared in the early part of this century, emphasized the vital concern of the Christian religion with the corporate arrangements of life, particularly in business and industry because these so definitely affected human welfare. The responsibilities of this world, where the welfare of human beings was at stake, became the opportunity to manifest one's love of God, and in turn out of this experience of comradeship with God in the enterprises of human life, there came renewed vitality in the experience of God. But the tendency was to abandon the Social Gospel as soon as real difficulties developed and to characterize it as a misinterpretation of the Christian religion. Indeed, some religious leaders are saying that the movement itself was a manifestation of man's sinful presumption in thinking he could do anything significant about human affairs.

Without doubt, in some of its manifestations, the social emphasis has represented over-optimism and lack of realism in facing the human problem. But difficulties are not a sufficient reason for an abandonment of the social emphasis. Indeed, such a retreat may be but the rationalization of our lack of faith. As long as the task of the Social Gospel seemed easy, it did not bring us into the full possibilities of the experience of God. Unaided human endeavor seemed adequate to the task. It is when difficulties arise and the cause seems hopeless that the experience of God should grow in vitality. Then it is that individuals come to realize that unless there are possibilities and resources beyond those which are evident, there is no hope of approximating the Kingdom of God in human affairs or making the love of God manifest in human life. Unless the Kingdom of God can take on some genuine significance as the goal and incentive of our human relationships and unless the law of love can be interpreted in terms which give it relevance to ordinary human endeavor, Christians lose one of the most significant sources of vitality in religious experience. In a social process of religious education, there is an integral relationship between the Kingdom of God and the efforts of Christians in the remaking of human life and between the experience of God and the endeavors of human beings to make the love of God manifest in human affairs. A social emphasis and an educational process are essential for a vital experience of God.

The integral relation of religious experience to the educational process can be understood only as religious experience is described psychologically rather than theologically. Waiving the question as to what distinguishes a true from a false religion, and looking at religious experience from the viewpoint of the individual or the group who has the experience, there are two related factors which may be said to determine what is the religion of an individual or a group: First, that to which the individual gives supreme devotion and for which he will sacrifice all else; and second, that on which he supremely depends and in which he places final trust and confidence. These represent his real religion, when viewed psychologically, whatever the individual may declare in his verbal statements. Viewed from the way it functions, an individual's religion is the organizing center of his life.

On the basis of these two criteria, nationalism is sometimes a religion. The state is the organizing center of life and the object of supreme devotion and supreme trust is placed in the resources and power of the state. For many individuals, business or professional success has been their religion and they have had supreme confidence in their own efforts to attain that goal. Such religions have been characterized as false because they involve an ego-centered humanism, in which the success of an individual or a group is the center of devotion and in which trust is placed in human effort; in other words, in which man is his own God. But this does not change the fact that they have and do function as religions in the lives of individuals and groups.

Approached from this psychological viewpoint, the more far-reaching and the more inclusive the goal or center of devotion, the nearer is it to an adequate religion. Internationalism would represent a more adequate form of devotion than nationalism. While supreme devotion to some social group, such as labor, a race, or a nation, is higher than a self-centered life which has no concern for others, it is still a tribal form of religion which the prophets criticized. Supreme devotion to some inclusive goal—the welfare of all races, a better economic order, a world-wide social order of justice and coöperation—is a higher form of religion than one with more limited goals. Likewise, trust in the contribution of all men, regardless of race or class or nation, for the realization of this goal and belief in coöperative endeavor are higher forms of religious expression than trust in individual or racial or national prowess.

Many would hold that all these are false religions; indeed, not religions at all because, however inclusive the goal or coöperative the effort, they center in man. For them, there can be no religion without God. Again speaking psychologically rather than theologically, this means attempting to view human life from the most inclusive and ultimate perspective possible, that of God. It is the effort to know for what man was created, what is the goal of human life, what is human destiny, on what can man really depend and in what can he ultimately put his trust. Christianity, approached from this viewpoint, is not a religion because of its particular beliefs. Systems with very different beliefs are also religions.

It is a religion because of the nature and grounding of those beliefs. There have been varied interpretations of the Christian religion; but whatever the interpretation, the basic emphasis has been that there is a meaning and goal for human life beyond present events and that there are resources for human beings beyond those immediately evident in human endeavor. As a result, human life has supreme worth and human destiny has a new perspective.

It will thus be seen that searching criteria must be used to determine whether education is religious education or whether a religious practice is the medium of a religious experience. Certainly the leaders in religious education would be ready to say that while they seek earnestly to meet the conditions in the educational process under which it may represent a genuine religious experience for those participating in it, all too often there is nothing genuinely religious about it. It does not follow that because a group is facing some important life situation and attempting to discover what to think or to do about it that it has reached the level of religious experience. The discussion of the problem may be just an exchange of prejudices or dominated by ego-centered or group-centered goals and considerations. Nor does it follow that because religious language is being used in Scripture reading, praying, or hymn-singing in the worship service that this is a religious experience. The words may not be the medium of expression of genuine commitment to the goals of religion or of actual experience of God in human life. Religious education becomes the medium for the realization of religious experience in proportion as the ultimate meanings and goals of religion are the organizing center of the process and in proportion as ultimate resources beyond those immediately evident are released. The distinctive characteristic of religious education is the fact that in it an attempt is made to meet the conditions under which the educational process reaches the level of worship and the educational experience is a religious experience.

CHAPTER XIV

Religious Education and Prayer and Worship

THE INTEGRAL relation of religious experience to an educational process was discussed in the last chapter, but no consideration was given to the bearing of educational principles upon the practice of prayer and worship. Certain basic assumptions of the historic forms of worship and of an educational process are different. The issues do not concern differences in the conception of God, as to whether he is transcendent or immanent or both transcendent and immanent, important as are these questions; but as in the case of the relation of religious experience to the educational process, the issues grow out of differences of conviction as to the relationship of God, whatever conception of him may be held, to human life and destiny. While *what* God is like is inevitably involved in *how* his resources become available in human life, the focus of the difference has been in the *how* rather than in the *what*. Perhaps it would be more accurate to say that the differences have turned not so much on the nature of the being of God as upon his behavior in relation to human affairs. The focus is the *operational* and *functional* aspects of God's being, and not the *theoretical* and *speculative* questions as to the nature of God which have so much occupied theological thinking.

Unfortunately for both historic forms of worship and for religious education, the issues in the area of worship have to a large extent been waived in the practical development of program in the churches, both nationally and locally. This has been accomplished practically by a division of the field: educational insights have been applied to the so-called *teaching* aspects of the program, while *worship,* not only in the services of public worship but also in the church school and the young people's society, has usually been conducted on the historic assumptions as to God's relationship to human life. Attempts have been made to correlate teaching and worship, but an examination of these reveals that this has not resulted in a genuine integration because the inter-relation has been one of content rather than of process. The teaching period and the worship service have been focused upon the same problem or subject matter, but the basic differences as to process have continued. This attempted solution of the problem by a division of the field may be responsible for the lack of dynamic in much religious teaching and for the lack of meaning in a great deal of worship. Instructon in religion which does not reach the level of an earnest search for Christian truth in regard to the purposes and the resources of life and which does not result in the realization of this truth in Christian experience is coldly intellectual and without significance in life experience; and worship which is isolated from this effort to find an answer to the problems of life is either coldly formal or insignificantly otherworldly. Teaching and worship are integrally a part of one process in any significant program, and method, in the sense of an attempt to understand and meet the conditions under which genuine religious experience takes place, is as important for worship as it is for teaching.

Historically, prayer and worship in all forms of religion have had to do with the Beyond; in terms of the Christian religion, with God. But the vitality of worship has depended upon the Beyond's having some significant relationship with the here and now. The problem of prayer and worship has arisen, not so much from a disbelief in God, as from a growing lack of vital relationship of God to the everyday life of human beings. In the childhood of our grandparents there was no problem. They grew up in homes and in communities where God was very directly related to that which happened in human affairs. Every aspect of life was the subject of prayer. If prosperity came or health was maintained, it was God's blessing and he was thanked. If adversity came or sorrow entered the home, it was the visitation of God either for wrong-doing or it had some purpose in God's relationship to human beings, and there was submission to God's providential will. In times of difficulty and perplexity, God's direction and guidance were sought. God was an immanent factor in human life, and prayer and worship were the recognition and expression of this fact. That which was true of our grandparents was to a great extent true of our parents, but is much less true of our children.

Two opposite factors have contributed to remove God more and more from vital relationship with human beings in their everyday affairs. One has grown out of the attitude of the Christian religion in the face of an advancing science, and the other has arisen in the developments in the scientific movement itself of which education has been a part. In the mediaeval world, as is well-known, there was no conflict between science and religion because the prevailing scientific and religious interpretations were consonant with each other. The Ptolemaic astronomy was consistent with the interpretations of revealed religion. Copernican astronomy caused difficulty because it was inconsistent with the interpretations of the universe of prevailing religion, and Copernicus was attacked not on scientific but on religious grounds as a heretic. In an advancing science, a naturalistic description of what happened in the world of nature was increasingly made and therefore nature was removed from the realm of the *direct* action of God which had formerly been assumed in both science and religion. This is not the place to trace the conflict between science and religion, but it does not seem an oversimplification to say that the Christian religion eventually attempted to solve the problem by granting the operation of natural law in the physical world and by retaining for religion the direct providential action of God in human life and destiny.

This solution of the problem succeeded until science invaded the realm of human affairs. In the developments in education and psychology, attempt was made to bring human life under this same realm of orderly events. There was, therefore, invasion of what had been the unique area of God's relationship to human life. As long as education confined itself to the mind and emphasized the intellectual aspects of personality, there was still possible the reservation for religion of the area of the human spirit. But in the developments of mental hygiene, God's relation to that aspect of human personality and destiny was also threatened. The dilemma is illustrated by the experience of two pious maiden aunts of a practicing psychiatrist. When they found with what kind of problems their nephew was dealing, almost in horror they protested, for, they said, these are matters of sin with which only a clergyman has the right to deal.

It is with the practical effects of this development upon prayer and worship that we are particularly concerned. If physical nature is the realm of the operation of natural law and not directly concerned with God's relationship to human life, then those who are laboring in such areas are engaged in "secular" affairs and they no longer have the sense of a vital relationship to God in their everyday endeavors. With the advance of technological science, more and more of the processes which made up daily life were relegated to the secular, and men and women were increasingly divorced from any sense of direct relationship to God in their everyday affairs. This came to be the interpretation on the part of Christian leaders of the work of those who were dealing with human beings within the realm of an advancing science. For example, the physician was considered to be doing scientific work. It was true that prayer might be of some service in supplementing his efforts, but his work as such was scientific and thus secular. With the separation of church and state and the divorce of the direct teaching of religion from the schools, education became secular. It was dealing with the training of the mind, but was not considered as responsible for character and religion. Social work came in the same category. In short, there was recognized by the church a division of life into two categories: the secular and the sacred. This was seen in the life work decisions of students in conferences of a generation ago, when the issue was whether or not they should go into a "sacred" calling like missionary work or the ministry, or into a "secular" calling like business or medicine or law. There was little or no recognition of the "sacred" character of all vocation. Thus God was removed from any vital relationship to so large a proportion of the life of individuals that prayer and worship could at best touch only limited aspects of human experience, even though these were held by the followers of the Christian religion to be all-important areas. God was divorced from direct relationship to the common life by the leaders of religion themselves. Small wonder then that prayer and worship lost in pertinence and vitality.

It was the glory of the liberal movement in religion and in religious education that its leaders refused to admit this solution of the problem. They resisted this division of life into "sacred" and "secular" and insisted on God's relationship to all of life. They met the problem by insisting that God worked in and through the orderly processes of nature and that he was directly related to individual life through the procedures of human search and reflection. But unfortunately they did not carry their interpretations to the point of a radical revision of the practices of prayer and worship. The public worship, even when conducted by ministers who made this personal interpretation of God's relationship to human life, was carried on with the historic forms, the language of which spoke of relationship to a God of direct action rather than to one who worked in and through the processes of life. Since this was the conception in the Bible, in the hymns and in the stately historic ritual which was available, it is perhaps not surprising that they did not remake the worship service so that it was more consonant with their actual beliefs. While they personally could use these historic formulations because they reinterpreted them in terms of their present conceptions of religion, they forgot that the rank and file of their congregations did not make this reinterpretation. They were living in the midst of a world in which all of their activities were carried on with recognition of the orderly processes of nature and they were left without any adequate medium of expression of the deep religious faith which underlay these processes.

Leaders in religious education share in responsibility for this situation. Only a few of them gave attention to the reconstruction of worship necessary for the expression of the deep religious faith on which confidence in the educational process is based. This may have been due to their preoccupation with the remaking of the educational process itself. The fact that conduct of worship was considered by the minister as his unique function, the invasion of which was difficult and aroused much emotion, may have been a factor. In any case, it is true to the facts to say that over and over again where an educational process has been used which was deeply religious and had in it the elements of worship, the experience did not find this expression, but was frustrated by efforts at worship which in reality denied the religious character of the educational process. In so far as religious educators confined the application of their theory to the reconstruction of the teaching process and did not include with it a fundamental reconstruction of worship which would integrate the worship experience with the teaching experience, they contributed their part to the removal of God from significant relationship to the educational process. Since the educational process was more and more centered in human experience, this failure on their part contributed to the removal of God from significant relationship to human affairs.

But a second, and opposite influence, grew out of the scientific movement itself. The Age of the Enlightenment, which embodied the spirit of the new science, was a protest against religious obscurantism and an ardent affirmation of the right and possibility of human intelligence. In the scientific developments, man's discoveries and his achievements have been emphasized. It is not surprising that this emphasis upon the possibilities of human life took on the appeal of religion and enlisted something of the type of devotion which has characterized religion. With the growing achievements of man, there seemed to be no limit to human possibility, and therefore men took on the dimensions of God and made God seemingly unnecessary. For the rank and file of individuals, this divorce of God from ordinary affairs was not a matter of philosophy but of practical experience. In a scientific age, man found his physical needs supplied by an advancing technological science, his health difficulties met by a developing medical science, his educational needs by the growing provision for education. In more and more areas of life did he cease to look to the church and the minister for help. Instead, he turned to the physician, the teacher, the expert in a particular vocation. With the coming of mental hygiene, many people turned from the minister to the psychiatrist and the psychologist for help on personal problems. Since the church made no provision in its interpretations of religion and in its worship for the relationship of God to these allied vocations, it is not surprising that the life of the ordinary man became secularized, and, in so far as he had a religion, it was one of trusting himself or, perhaps, trusting science as found in these various representatives of science. It is not surprising, also, that those who were interested in the philosophical problems should have developed thorough-going interpretations of the new developments, interpretations which were in conflict with those of the Christian religion in that no place was left for God in the historic sense of the term. So naturalism became the religious interpretation of the new confidence in science, and humanism that of the new confidence in man. But in neither was God's relationship to human life recognized in any significant manner, and for those of this conviction worship in the historic sense of finding one's relationship to the Beyond was not a part of experience.

There is no question but that human beings in the midst of the present tragic breakdown of human endeavor, in the presence of the frustration of individual life and of the disillusionment in regard to their social hopes, need that courage in the presence of defeat and that calm in the face of tragedy, which the experience of the providential relation of God to human life and destiny in historic prayer and worship supplied. Unless worship can be truly a part of the educational process, religious education will not make a significant contribution to the solution of human problems at this or any other time. The danger is that religious education wil not make that contribution because it will come under the domination of one or the other of the opposite extremes in the present developments. It will not make the contribution if it allows itself to abandon its sense of human responsibility, and joins the present theological trend which, as Maritain, the French Roman Catholic theologian, expresses it, attempts to turn humanism upside down by the "annihilation of man before God." However much it may prove a solution for some individuals to admit the complete impotence of man and to pass all responsibility to a God who is so completely other that man cannot ever find out anything about him by human knowledge, it will not solve the problem for those who cannot accept such a theology; and these probably represent a majority of people in the United States. In any case, even if it were possible to persuade human beings to accept worship on this basis and find a personal solution of their problems in this way, it would be a tragedy for humanity.

Nor will it solve the problem to take the opposite extreme and equate worship with any type of education in which man faces his human situation, reflects upon his problems, and comes to decisions as to his courses of action. The difficulty with this type of worship is that it tends to annihilate God before man. It does not recognize the degree to which man is dependent, even for life itself, upon "given" elements for which he is in no way responsible and without which he could not live for a moment. It does not emphasize sufficiently the resources within and beyond himself, which again are the "given" resources of life, upon which he may call and which are available in times of tragedy as well as in times of prosperity. It does not deal realistically either with the depth of the "demonic" forces in man himself, in human society, and in nature with which he must deal, nor on the other hand, with the constructive, creative, and healing forces which are also available. It tends to turn man in on himself destructively because it offers nothing in which he can put his trust except his own unaided effort. A God who has been *completely* democratized as a part of the social process is a denial of the very conditions upon which the process depends; a finite God who is engulfed in the struggle of good and evil may give consolation as a fellow-sufferer, but he does not offer real help for the solution of the problem; a God who is completely identified with the processes of nature gives no sense of relationship with those pervading and distinctive characteristics of nature on which man's life depends.

If worship is to be integrally related to the educational process, it must not be of a type which ignores or denies that process, as has been true in the parallel programs of religious education and worship. It must not be of a kind which ignores or denies the processes which embody the best insights of how man takes responsibility in the world, if it is to express significant relationship of God to the everyday life of human beings. It does not solve the problem to think of education as a human process which is to be supplemented by a divine experience in worship, or of reverent human endeavor as a human process which is to be supplemented by divine aid. There must be a more definite inter-relation of the human and the divine if God is to be vitally related to everyday affairs and if worship is to be significant for daily living.

As already indicated, the liberal movement in religion and in religious education started upon a development which brought the human and divine into a creative inter-relation, but did not carry through the readjustments so that they affected the process of worship. What is needed at present is not an abandonment of that development and a reaffirmation of earlier interpretations of God's relationship to human life. It is necessary, on the one hand, that there shall be a correction of the unrealistic aspects of the former developments in which there was not adequate recognition of the seriousness of the human problem; and, on the other hand, a reconstruction of the worship process so that it is built on the basic assumptions of God's relation to human life which are found in the educational process and in other forms of reverent human responsibility.

There are two points of emphasis in the "liberal" movement which need to be reaffirmed and made operative in the process of worship. The one is the *immanence* of God. There were differences among those of the liberal tradition as to whether God is transcendent and becomes immanent in the world or whether he represents distinctive and pervading characteristics of the universe as it impinges upon human life, characteristics upon which man can count and in relation to which he lives his life. Were this a book on the philosophy of religion, a discussion of these differences in interpretation would be important; but for the question at issue they can be waived. Whether that which we call life, on which growth in all aspects of the world depends, is bestowed by a transcendent God or is one of the pervading characteristics of the universe is not the question; it is the fact that it is a manifestation of God. As to whether healing power, which is found in nature and in the human body, is bestowed by a transcendent God or is an immanent characteristic of the universe, it is manifest in this world and is available. As to whether love is bestowed by God through some divine work of Christ or whether Christ manifested the most transforming characteristic of the universe incarnate in human beings, its possibilities in human life have never been fathomed.

The important point is that God is not confined to some special relationships with human life, but the Given, which we call God, is the basis of all human endeavor. Man does not create anything; he simply utilizes that which he finds here. That which sustains his life, by which he lives, in connection with which his purposes are formed, is God. This immanent conception of God recognizes the many ways in which the Given, by which we live and on which we depend, manifests itself in the world. There is no new discovery in science, no new cure for disease, no new technological invention which is not dependent upon some distinctive given characteristic of this universe, as it impinges upon the world, and man's so-called creations are really discoveries and utilizations of these powers and possibilities. Such an emphasis recognizes in a significant and creative manner God's relation to human life. It makes every aspect of life sacred, for it is related to powers and possibilities, the mystery and wonder of which every scientific discovery enhances rather than destroys. It gives the true basis for a reverent attitude toward all of life.

But the emphasis in the liberal movement upon man's part is equally important and it is this aspect which was never thoroughly incorporated in the reconstruction of worship. In the emphasis which liberal religion made upon God's working in and through orderly processes, there was recognition that the given resources of God are not available at the whim of man, even when that whim is expressed in ardent petition to God. God is an impartial and dependable God, whose sun shines on the evil and the good and whose rain descends on the just and the unjust. His resources are available for the solution of human problems and for the reinforcement of human life and endeavor, only as man meets the conditions for their release.[1] An examination of the evidence seems to show that this is fundamental in God's relation to human life.

The most evident examples are in the two tragic conditions which face the world today—widespread economic difficulties and the outbreak of war. Until recent years it was assumed that the poor we would always have with us, because somehow in God's management of the universe he rewarded some with riches and others with poverty. Now we know that there is a sufficiency in actuality or potentiality so that everyone in the world could have enough. An economy of plenty instead of scarcity is possible. We have had to admit, however, that this problem will not be solved except as men and women meet the conditions of living together in such a way that these potential resources are available and can

[1] Compare Hartshorne, Hugh, *Character in Human Relations*, Chapter XVII.

be distributed and used. Verbal petitions to Deity do not avail; and yet God has not failed man, for these resources are in this world. But the prayer for plenty will be answered only as man is willing to do his part in discovering and meeting the conditions of enough for all.

Enough progress has been made in the relations of man to his fellows to make evident that love, the dominant characteristic of God as manifested in human life, when trusted even to the level of good-will, can be counted on in the relations between human beings. We do not go around each one carrying a gun to protect himself against his neighbor, because we have been willing to meet the conditions under which this degree of love can be released in the world. But the nations of the world do not trust love and are unwilling to meet the conditions of love, which include justice as well as good-will. As a result, the nations are in danger of destroying whatever civilization we have attained in devastating combat. Verbal prayer will not meet the situations. It will be met only as nations are willing to meet the conditions under which love is released in the relationship between nations.

This is equally true in the more intimate relationships of life. Christian parents have desired that their children should grow up as individuals of worthy Christian character. They have prayed most earnestly for them. But it is a sobering fact that parents who have not met the conditions in their relations with their children and in their conduct of the home have not had their verbal prayers answered. Pious parents have ruined their children. It is only the prayer which is the verbal expression of the earnest effort to find and meet the conditions which is answered. Christians have believed and desired that they might have the guidance of God in their own lives. Again guidance is possible, but seems to come only to those who pay the price of earnest search for the answer to their problems.

While discovery of the conditions is an important part of the process of releasing the given resources, which are God, fortunately each individual does not have to do his own discovering. The discoveries and insights of history are available and can be utilized in the process. Jesus Christ made manifest in human life, more vividly and perfectly than has ever been done, a God of love. The record and interpretation of his life, as found in the New Testament, make evident this resource in human life in so commanding a way that it has captured the life and practice of countless thousands.

When medical science discovered the germ origin of disease and when Pasteur found that there was in nature that which would kill disease, he made a discovery about the resources of God as manifested in human life, which became a base line for all future efforts to find and meet the conditions for the cure of disease. When it was recognized that the healing power was in nature itself and that all the physican could do was to meet the conditions for the release of this power, there were new possibilities for health that were not available before that discovery. It is on the basis of this kind of discovery that the reverent search for the answer to the problems of health goes forward. Cancer is one of the diseases that has not been fully conquered. But physicians who are working on this problem are seeking to find the source of cancer with the confident assumption that a cure can be discovered. But like the cure of other diseases, it will not be something which man creates but which he discovers and utilizes. Disease is not inevitable, but it will be eliminated only in proportion as the causes and cure are discovered and man is willing to meet the conditions under which the cure is available.

Man is not forced to meet the conditions for the release of the resources which are God. Recognition of this fact is important for worship. Man is free to reject them. This is true even in human relationships. A mother soon reaches the limit of what she can do for a child, a husband for a wife, or a friend for a friend. The mother can give the baby nourishment only as he does his part in suckling. Crying is useful only as a symbol that he wants to do his part. A child can have the advantages of home and education and all the things which are available only as he meets the conditions through his own attitudes and action. One of the tragedies of life is the helplessness of parents, ready to make the good things of life available to their children, but powerless to give these to them because the children will not meet the conditions for their availability or because they reject them altogether. The response of love comes only through meeting the conditions for the release of love. The most elaborate protestations of love bring no response from the object of affection unless they are the symbol of attitudes and action which express love and regard. God seems to be under this same limitation in his relationship to human life.

But it is possible for man not only to reject the resources of God which would enrich and reinforce his life, but it is also possible for him to release the opposite. He not only can refuse to meet the conditions for the cure of disease, but he can also meet the conditions under which disease develops. He not only can refuse to meet the conditions of love, but he can also meet the conditions under which love is turned into hate, so that all the forces of hate are released in the relations between individuals, between groups, and between nations. The "demonic" possibilities of life are not inevitable, but are released in the same way as are the "divine,"—by meeting the conditions under which they are released.

It is thus seen that if religious education is to make a contribution to the relationship of God to human life, it will need to embody in worship the recognition of three facts: first, that whatever the interpretation of God, his manifestations and resources are immanent in his world; second, that these resources are available only as man discovers and meets the conditions for their release; and third, that man is free to reject these resources or indeed to meet the conditions for the release of just the opposite. There must be recognition of the fact that the problem of worship is not with God. God is more ready to give than parents are to give good gifts to their children. The problem of worship centers in man. The best insights of religious history, confirmed by the data of science, in regard to this world and God's relation to it would seem to show that the answers to human problems are available; that they are not created by man, but he finds them given in his world; but that the solutions are available only by reverent search to discover them and by willingness to meet the conditions by which they become operative.

The educational process and the process of worship are similar. Man does not face the situations of his world and decide what to do and develop skills for carrying out his decisions, and then add an experience of worship of an entirely different sort. Indeed, the great historic forms of worship, even though they have had a different conception of God's relation to human life than that which is outlined here, have followed the steps of an educational process: first, a recognition of sin or inadequacy or need; second, an acceptance of the answer to this need in the forgiveness or the guidance of God; third, the commitment to a new life; and fourth, the utilization of the resources of God in carrying out the new commitment. The approach here suggested would not differ in the steps of a worship process, but in the fact that it would recognize more fully man's responsibility for reflective search in the examination of possible courses of action from the viewpoint of the values at stake and the goals of endeavor, and also for meeting the conditions under which the available resources would be released.

There are distinct differences in the process which has reached the level of worship from the ordinary effort to solve human problems or to find the resources for human endeavor. The first is in the recognition of the degree to which man's solution of his problems is dependent upon the given elements of the universe; in other words, in his recognition of God. This changes the whole attitude in the use of the process. It destroys pride in one's own ability or achievement and makes one humble and reverent in the presence of the mysteries of God. It is not man's freedom and responsibility which have made him proud and assertive; it is his illusion that he creates that which he achieves.

The second difference is in the focus of the search. An individual whose attention is focused on his own security and success is likely to lose it for himself as well as others. A search for private reward or aggrandizement ends in defeat, for only as the resources of the universe are sought in the interests of others as well as of one's self, in the interests of the most inclusive social goals, is solution possible either for the individual or for others. This is true of corporate worship, where the search is for a group or for a nation. True worship is fundamentally social worship.

The third difference is related to the second. The process which has reached the level of worship is carried on from an inclusive rather than a limited perspective. In religious terms, it is from the perspective of God rather than of man. But in the actual operation of worship, it represents those most inclusive perspectives upon the human problem that human beings of deep religious insight have been able to attain.

All life should be carried on in the spirit and on the level of worship; that is, in a recognition of man's dependence upon God and in a sense of relationship to him. But this will not be attained unless there are alternations from life's activities. There is both a retrospective and a prospective aspect of these alternations of worship. In the retrospective type of worship, there is opportunity to review past experiences, to evaluate them critically, and thus to recognize failings in a mood of confession and achievements in a mood of thanksgiving. By reliving past experiences either in thought or symbolism and by meditation upon them in the atmosphere of worship, they are seen in their perspective, relationships emerge, failures become more evident, new meanings are seen, and the significance of these experiences is more vividly felt. They are gathered up in their wholeness, and their meaning for present life is more clearly seen. A large element in worship has been reliving through some form of ritualistic expression significant experiences in one's personal history, in the corporate experience of a group, or in the history of religion, and thus laying hold anew of past sources of confidence and strength as well as of corrective to human life and endeavor. Some writers on worship have made this element of "Celebration" the dominant factor of worship.

But the prospective aspect of worship is also important. In this there is an opportunity to look to the future through finding, in a consideration of immediate life situations and problems, guidance as to what to do and renewal of strength for the responsibilities involved. Worshipful meditation is of definite help in coming to the right decisions. First, the meditations are carried on in an atmosphere which puts one's highest aspirations and most basic purposes into control. Consequently it becomes in the most genuine sense a search for the highest, which, in terms of historic religion, has been called the will of God. Second, in the mood and the atmosphere of worship, there is a heightening of the sensibilities and powers of the individual, so that important elements in the situation and possibilities of solution become more vividly felt. Third, in the quiet, away from the pressure of life's events, it is possible to review the factors and to look at them in perspective, in their relation to each other, so that important elements stand out in greater relief while unimportant, though often irritating and insistent ones, sink into the background. Fourth, the hectic effort in which no clear thinking is possible and the worry which distracts true decision are gone, and in the relaxation of the mind there is strength.

For worship to be thus of service, there must be a direct relationship between the alternations of worship and the experiences of life. It is true that the atmosphere should be different from that of the daily round of activity. This is the reason that the tired business man who wants rest and assurance objects to the appearance of the week's problems in his worship, just as he wants to forget office and business when he goes for a week-end in the country. But worship is more than a vacation from life's responsibilities. Individuals should find not only answers to life's problems but also inspiration and strength to carry out their new purposes. Hence, the alternation of worship is but an aspect of a larger process of living. For worship to be most rewarding, the individual must bring to the quiet and meditation the concerns of life and the data out of life's activities, that he may gain new insights and new purposes which he will try out in the laboratory of experience. What the worshiper does before the worship and what he does afterwards are really part of the complete process of worship. It is an alternation from activity and leads back again to activity.

Psychologically, an important element in the strength and inspiration which the worship experience may bring is the new conviction reached or the new purpose formed, as one has sought his way out of the perplexity or problem facing him. We are so made that everything we have in the way of resources and ability is thrown into drive and the whole set of the personality is changed by something in which we come to believe with conviction and toward which we have set ourselves with abandon. Convictions reached and purposes formed in the atmosphere of worship, connected as they are with the most ultimate convictions of life and destiny, are supremely·of this kind. Worry, anxiety, and bafflement set into operation the protective elements, flight and fighting; purpose, commitment, conviction, set into operation all the positive elements of personality. Further, in such a positive atmosphere, there is also the incentive to reëxamine one's purposes in the light of the most ultimate meanings life has for the individual, so that a reconstructive element enters into worship. The "revaluation of values," on which Professor George Albert Coe has laid emphasis, is an important factor of worship.[2]

When one has come to a conviction as to what he should and purposes to do, he then comes to the last step in the process of worship—facing what is involved in putting his purpose into effect in life. This sets him upon an active search for an understanding of the given resources, which are God, on which he can count in his endeavor and for the conditions under which these resources will be available. As they are understood and laid hold of by the individual in meditation and plans are made for their utilization in actual fact, the available resources of the universe become concentrated upon the situation in hand and God becomes a living reality in relation to these immediate affairs. In this period of worship, he makes the adjustments by which the resources in the "Other" are made available to him.

The difficulty of securing so fundamental a worship experience within the forms of worship as usually followed is evident. They have been developed, not on the basis of an earnest and reverent search, but as authoritative answers to human problems, either through the sacrament of the Mass or through the authoritative interpretation of the Word of God. They are based also upon God's help being secured through petition rather than through a

[2] Coe, George Albert, *The Psychology of Religion*, Chapter XIII.

reverent search for the conditions under which those resources are available. Therefore, it is difficult to develop a worship experience of the type which has been described within the pattern of historic forms of worship. In so far as the public worship is simply a setting in which the ritual carries one along in the steps of a worship process and each worshiper can furnish his own content of problem and experience, it is possible for the church and its service to be utilized by those who find in it an emotional setting and a useful guide to private worship; but that is using the ritualistic service for a different purpose from its primary one. As to whether the Protestant nonliturgical service, with its focus in the pulpit and the message of the minister, can furnish help on a worship process of the type described depends upon the minister. If his sermon seeks to make the problem clear, presents the alternatives the individual is really facing, raises the considerations of importance in a truly religious solution of the problem, and gives his own convictions as testimony rather than authority, then it can be of genuine help to the private meditation of the worshiper in the pew.

In services of public worship, such as the Protestant, with a wide age range in the congregation and with people out of varied experiences, there is always a problem where the content is furnished by the minister. Therefore, it is essential that worship be not confined to the large services of public worship, but that there be more opportunity for smaller group worship. For this the Quakers can give us more help than either the liturgists or the preachers. The process will be more that of a meditative group conference than one of direct personal meditation. Further, since individuals are involved in corporate life, it is important that more opportunity be given for worship in functional groups where individuals involved in the same situation or problem may meet together. The groups will be larger or smaller depending upon the number of those concerned in the specific problems. Sometimes they might represent certain types of responsibility, such as parents, high school teachers, business men; at other times, they might represent certain types of problem, such as life work, governmental, racial problems. Many such groups around specific needs should be provided in the church.

Worship for various age levels and groups can probably be furnished best in integral relationship to the educational groups of the church. In this way, the spirit and attitude of worship can be combined with real study of the problems and of the resources out of religious history which are available. The worship will then have a depth and a content not possible where the process is carried through more superficially. In one sense, it may be said that worship of this sort would simply be the educational process brought to the level of worship. But in setting the conditions under which this may be accomplished definite periods of worship in the educational process may be of help. The so-called opening exercises might well set the mood in which the search goes on in groups. It should lead to a recognition both of God and of man's dependence upon him and of the possibilities in reverent search for the will of God. When a group or a number of groups, facing the same problem, have come to the place where there is a real concern about the problem or a real sense of sin and inadequacy, this should be focused and given more definite expression in a period of worship which should end in the mood and attitude of search. When they are baffled as to what to do or have definite differences of conviction which are in danger of turning the process from one of reverent search to argumentative debate, they could follow the practice of the Quakers in their business meetings of having a period of worship in which the purposes which unite the group and the perspective which the Christian religion brings are more definitely focused. When conviction is reached, either individually or corporately, this should be brought to emotional focus and religious recognition in worship, and attention should then be centered upon the resources of God which are available and upon discovering and meeting the conditions under which these resources are released. When the group has come to some conclusion from its study of the resources which are available and the conditions under which they may be released, the commitment to the meeting of the conditions might be made vivid and meaningful in a period of more definite worship.

Retrospective worship of this integral type is also desirable after attempt has been made to act on decisions made. Such action should be reviewed, evaluated, and enriched in the atmosphere of worship. Such retrospective worship is valuable in relation to all types of activity. When a group has been on a hike together in the beauty of the out-of-doors, or has had a social evening of genuine fellowship, or has engaged in some project beyond their private welfare for some social cause, the meaning and significance of this experience can be gathered up in a worship period of the celebration or retrospective type.

It is thus evident that while the entire process of education will be meaningful only if it reaches the level of worship, this may be aided by definite periods of worship as alternations to the process of study and search. If this is to be accomplished, there must be provisions for adjustments in schedule. Probably much of such worship will need to come incidentally and integrally as a part of the work of any group, although there are possibilities along this line in departmental worship where several groups are engaged in similar processes.

One caution needs to be made. The discussion of this chapter may sound as if the experience of worship was something which could be made to order. In the attempt to discuss the conditions under which worship has more possibility of taking place, there is no thought that any individual can cause others to worship. Many, perhaps most, of the provisions for worship do not reach the level of worship experience; and sometimes a real experience of worship takes place at unexpected places and under unforeseen circumstances. But this does not change the fact that there are conditions under which the worship experience has more chance of happening than others and there are other conditions under which one may be almost sure it will not be realized. The function of the religious leader in regard to worship is the same as in regard to other aspects of religious education. He is to seek to provide the conditions under which worship may be realized.

The main problem of worship is to have it related to the important on-going processes of living. Worship represents not so much a special aspect of life as the mood and attitude in which all the processes of life are carried on, and the alternations of definite worship are useful only as they help to secure this mood in all of life. It represents a recognition of man's dependence upon God and reverent search to discover and meet the conditions for the release of his resources. It represents a recognition of man's responsibility for his life and that of his fellows, and attention to the determination of purposes to which his endeavors will be given and of values which are worth while because they are in line with the more ultimate purposes. It helps to determine to what men give themselves and upon what they will depend.

CHAPTER XV

The Meaning of Christian Education

THAT THE QUESTION as to whether religious education can be Christian involves basic issues in regard to religion and education and their inter-relation has become increasingly evident as the various aspects of the problem have been explored. The conclusions must now be summarized in their bearing upon a philosophy of Christian education.

The term "religious education" cannot be identified with education in any particular religion, such as the Mohammedan, Jewish, or Christian. It is an inclusive term which could be applied to any and all education in religion. But this does not mean that religious education is a vague sort of education in religion in general. As a matter of fact, all education takes place in a particular cultural situation and is influenced by it. This contemporary culture has a history and represents accumulated experience. Education "takes place in the growing generation where historical culture and contemporary living meet." [1] This is true also of special aspects of education. Education in democracy is oriented to particular situations where democracy has been or is being tried; education in citizenship always assumes citizenship somewhere; education in morals has meaning only as it is related to attitudes and behavior in particular situations. Religious education also is carried on at a particular time and place, and is influenced both by contemporaneous cultural conditions and by current religious attitudes and practices.

[1] The International Council of Religious Education, *Christian Education Today*, A Statement of Basic Philosophy, p. 15.

The religious situation in most countries is not a unified one. There are diverse religious groupings, each with its own history and distinctive points of emphasis. Even where religious education takes place independent of a particular religious grouping, it cannot be intelligently carried on except with understanding of the historic strands and the distinctive differences in religious emphasis. When the education is of inter-faith type, as when Christians meet with Hindoos or Mohammedans in the Far East or Jews and Christians in the United States meet in conference together, recognition of distinctive elements is important for a significant educational experience. While it is true that there are certain distinguishing characteristics of religion, wherever and however manifested, these have become known only by the study of particular religious manifestations and have meaning only in relation to a definite orientation.

There are elements in the religious situation in the United States which affect the cultural orientation of religious education. In any consciously defined sense of the term, religious education has been almost entirely eliminated from publicly supported schools in the interests of religious liberty. As a result, definitely organized religious education takes place for the most part within each of the three great faiths—Jewish, Catholic, or Protestant. While religious education can never be divorced from the wider cultural and religious influences, it does in the United States tend to have the orientation of a particular religious grouping. But similar orientation within a particular religious faith is found in other countries. In other words, that which is more definitely in evidence among the Jews, where culture and religion are integrally inter-related, has been to a certain extent true of all great faiths. Religious groupings tend to be cultural groupings.

It is thus seen that religious education does not imply a general search for truth independent of any definite cultural or religious orientation, and that Christian education connotes an education which has its orientation within the Christian religion. That orientation requires full recognition of the historic origin and continuity of Christianity. The long religious development among the Hebrew people as recorded in what the Christians call the Old Testament forms the background of the Christian movement. The term "Christian" itself implies the centrality of Jesus Christ in the Christian religion. His life and teachings are of prime importance in coming to an interpretation of the Christian religion for today. But there are more than nineteen hundred years of Christian history with diverse interpretations of the meaning of Jesus Christ and of the Christian religion. The interpretations in the New Testament writings belong approximately to the first century, but during the centuries since Christianity has come in contact with diverse cultural situations and varying ideologies and has both influenced and been influenced by them. The Christian religion, as it is known today, is therefore the product of a long history with various of these historic strands manifested in our current life. Religious education which is Christian cannot be unmindful of these historical interpretations. "In its essential nature, present experience cannot be dissociated from the traditions of historical experience without distortion, nor neglect the great Christian heritage without becoming superficial and unimportant." [2]

The present issues do not concern the importance of the Christian heritage in religious education which is Christian. They concern rather how that heritage is to be used. The neo-orthodox interpreters select from this long and diverse development a certain definite stream and identify this as true religion. For them, all others are false or misrepresentations. This stream does not represent a process of growth but one of adaptation to changing

[2] *Ibid.*, p. 15.

conditions. The truth was made known once for all in the interpretations of Jesus Christ in the New Testament. For the religious
educator, this Christian heritage represents a process of both
adaptation and growth. As Christianity has come into contact
with diverse conditions and new knowledge, it has itself under-
gone both reinterpretation and enrichment. Religious education
which is Christian is a part of this century-long process. "Here
the accumulated traditions of the past are undergoing re-testing,
re-appraisal and reconstruction in the light of expanding experience; and at the same time contemporary experience is undergoing interpretation, appraisal, and re-direction in the light of
our historic Christian heritage." [3] Religious education therefore
is not an education with a fixed and predetermined content.
There is no one true interpretation of the Christian religion
which it is its function to transmit. Rather, religious education
is an enterprise in which historical experiences and conceptions
are utilized in a process by which individuals and groups come
to experiences and convictions which are meaningful for them
today.

It is thus evident that for those with an educational approach,
an experience-centered religious education is far more than an
improved methodology for making a certain religious interpretation understood so that it may be appropriated by individuals
or groups. It represents their conviction as to the process through
which the Christian religion has developed and through which
Christian experience has been realized. "Learning in and through
experience" is not a pedagogical slogan, invented by progressive
educators. It is rather a statement of the way mankind has found
out everything which is known and has made whatever progress
has been attained. All knowledge has grown out of man's experience with nature and with human beings. All the ideas of man-

[3] *Ibid.*, p. 15.

kind are conclusions from and interpretations of experience. Science is no exception. It represents a more accurate and more controlled method of experience than that of the man on the street. Scientific conclusions grow out of experience and scientific interpretations are based upon it. Man has had to learn how to manage affairs in his world and any progress he has made has come only as he has taken responsibility, made decisions, and acted on those decisions. He has had to discover and to learn how to utilize or release the resources available for the maintenance of his life and for the solution of his problems, all the way from the resources of physical nature to the limitless possibilities of love. Ethical standards and social arrangements are the product of a long experience process. Mankind has learned in and through its experience.

Religion is no exception to this dependence upon learning through experience. Everything that man knows about God has grown out of his experience in the world and out of his reflections upon the manifestations of God in nature and in human life. God did not become known by some single and complete revelation. The record of the Hebrew-Christian religious development is an example of the long and slow process of growth from the primitive ideas of God and of religion in the early Old Testament records to the fullness of meaning in the New. That process did not cease with the New Testament period. The history of Christianity is the record of the continuance of this process in the developments within the Christian movement. The interpretations of Jesus Christ are not the creation of the human mind nor direct revelations unrelated to human experience. They are based upon the life of a person who lived in this world at a definite time and place and have grown out of the experiences of individuals with that person. Forms and methods of worship have been the product of man's effort to find his way in his world. Commencing with the primitive efforts to propitiate the forces which seemed to threaten his life, worship has grown to the level of reverent recognition of the degree to which all man is and may become is dependent upon the given resources of life. An educational process seems fundamental in God's relation to human life. It may be said that God is an educator, for it is in and through an educational process that religion has developed in the race. It is only through such a process that God becomes known or that an experience of God is achieved.

The individual is dependent upon this same experience process for his own development. Each child has to learn everything in and through his own experience as he tries himself out in his world. Fortunately for human beings, they are not dependent upon first-hand experience alone. They can utilize the experience of others in the past and in the present, and they are able to increase the range of their own immediate experience by imaginative participation in the experiences of others. In the human economy parents and teachers are available to coöperate with the young in this learning through experience. Further within this experience process is included mental as well as physical activity as the individual reflects upon and interprets his experience. It is nevertheless true that each child has to do his own learning and that this learning takes place through his own experience.

The development of the Christian life is dependent upon this same experience process. Children and young people come to a knowledge of God in the same way that the race has come to its understanding, viz., by their experience with the manifestations of God in human life. Parents and teachers can help in the interpretations of that experience. They can increase its range by providing for youth significant experiences in the present or out of the past. But it is only the manifestations of God which enter the experience that are significant for the individual. The same is true of the meaning and significance of Jesus Christ for the individual. The organization of religious education around the life situations of children, young people, and adults is therefore more than a pedagogical device for motivating subject matter. It is fundamental to the significance of religious education. Since learning takes place in and through experience, a significant educational process must be related to these situations where the learning is taking place. Otherwise attitudes and habits will be developed and ideas will be formed in the "trial and error" learning of life, without the contribution which the Christian religion might make.

From an educational viewpoint nurture or growth in Christian life and experience is not a fad of modern religious education. It represents the fundamental method by which the Christian faith has grown in the individual and the race and by which Christian experience has been realized. An individual does not become a Christian all at once through some single experience of conversion any more than he becomes an adult by some special experience. He starts, whatever his age, as a little child in the Christian life, and it is in and through his experience that he grows more and more toward maturity in Christian experience. Religious educators, therefore, emphasize human responsibility for meeting the conditions under which growth in Christian life and experience is possible and think of Christian education as the process through which this takes place. "Christian education is a reverent attempt to discover the divinely ordained process by which individuals grow in Christlikeness, and to work with that process." [4]

The life situations of children and youth are thus the center of the educational process, and the purpose is to help in meeting these situations. The church will furnish for children, young people, and adults many experiences of its own which will enrich

[4] Harner, Nevin C., *The Educational Work of the Church*, p. 20.

and supplement those in other relationships of life; but religious education has a definite function in relation to experience in home, school, and community beyond the confines of the church. Experience involves not only the activity in which one is engaged, but also the decisions as to what to do and the evaluation of the results of that activity. The function of religious education is to help children, young people, and adults to consider the problems involved in the situations they are facing with a view to discovering what is the Christian course of action or the Christian solution of the problem, and to make plans for carrying out these decisions in individual and group life. In turn, it has the function of examining and evaluating current action from the viewpoint of the Christian religion.

A series of decisions have to be taken into account in religious education. In an educational process, there is the assumption that human beings have the capacity for choice and that growth takes place through making choices, through acting upon these decisions, and through evaluating the consequences of action. All of these decisions are not in the moral or ethical realm. Christian practices, such as prayer and worship, and fundamental beliefs of the Christian religion are also involved. While infants are born with the capacity to choose, they have not developed such an ability any more than they have learned how to walk or talk. The choices and the conduct of infants and of very little children are determined in large part by their parents and other adults who are responsible for their care. But if children are to grow to maturity in the Christian life, they must increasingly develop in the ability and the willingness to take responsibility for their decisions and for their conduct. If parents and other adults try to make all their decisions for them and try to protect them from the consequences of their action, they keep them immature. This does not mean that children are left without guidance or help to make their own decisions, but rather that parents, teachers, and other adults seek to meet the conditions under which children grow in their ability to choose and act on those choices. In Christian education, they try to ensure that they face the Christian issues in such choices and feel the Christian possibilities. There is definite recognition of the limitation upon Christian education as upon all education. No adult can make a child a Christian any more than he can educate him in any other way. A Christian is one who has become such by his own choice.

The danger in Christian education is at this point of personal decision and responsibility. If parents and other adults persist in their domination of children and young people, they may prevent them from having a vital Christian experience of their own. Children trained in the religious beliefs and practices of their parents and of their parents' church may accept these, as they do other attitudes and practices of the adult generation, without question and without ever making them really their own. This seems especially likely to happen when religion is taught on an authoritarian basis, as is assumed in the neo-orthodox type of religious education. As a result, children may grow up with second-hand moral standards which lack the strength of personal conviction and a second-hand religion which lacks the vitality of personal experience.

Those with an educational approach emphasize that while there are differences in the importance of choices which are made, growth in Christian character and experience does not depend upon one supreme choice. It is rather a series of choices with action or attitude involved in each. While the individual does not have to make a choice in every situation and can establish attitudes and ways of acting which are operative in similar circumstances, there are always new situations which demand new choices. So the individual has to face over and over again what it means to be a Christian and whether or not he will make the Christian choice. Crucial times for Christian education come when the individual moves into a new set of circumstances and relationships, when he goes from the protection of the family circle to the play and the school group, or when he makes the final adolescent transitions from his parents' home and relationship to a home and vocation and a more independent life of his own as a young adult. There are also strategic times of decision in the life of adults. But in all these, the central fact, from the viewpoint of religious education, is that both the meaning of the Christian religion and loyalty to it are involved.

Subject matter in such an experience-centered process is recognized as the record and interpretation of significant experience in the area under consideration or as data pertinent to understanding or solving the immediate problem, to be understood and used in its bearing upon the situation of the individual or the group. The Bible is recognized as a record of experience in meeting life's situations with significant insights as to the meaning of life and religion, indeed the most significant record of religious experience available. On the one hand, the purpose in the use of the Bible is to enable children and young people and adults to relive this experience, to recapture it imaginatively so that it does not consist of facts to be learned or verses to be memorized, but becomes alive in the present. In this way, their experience is widened and enriched. On the other hand, the purpose is to use this experience of the past to give help in meeting present situations, particularly to bring perspective and emphasis and point of view for current decisions and attitudes.

From this viewpoint, the experiences of prayer and worship do not take place alone, or even chiefly, in formal practices; but they represent the dominating spirit and attitude of this experience process, as individuals and groups seek to find the will of God for their lives and the resources of God for their endeavors, and as they evaluate their conduct on the basis of what they have discovered to be God's purpose and will in human life. Indeed, the so-called formal practices of prayer and worship are seen to have meaning and vitality only as they are alternations from life activity and are integrally related to life situations.

An experience-centered educational process does not imply lack of conviction. It only indicates how convictions are held. Convictions represent what seem to individuals or groups to be best. They act as if those convictions were final, but at the same time they take toward their action a critical attitude and seek ways of improving it. The two are not inconsistent. A physician acts on whatever he already knows with a confidence that has elements of finality, and yet he is continually searching for improvements in his theory and practice. So standards and practices which have been arrived at through the educational process should be followed with conviction, but should not be considered as rigidly fixed. They should be held as hypothetical and tentative, not in the sense that one cannot act because he is not sure, but in the truer sense that they are to be "tested and confirmed and altered through consequences affected by acting upon them." [5]

An experience-centered educational process is inconsistent, however, with positions dogmatically and finally held. This is the source of much of the opposition to religious education and is also the cause of a conflict within education itself. There has often been a tendency for each religious faith to consider its own the only true religion. This results not only in the unwillingness to learn from other faiths, but also in the practice of branding them as false and untrue. Under these circumstances the followers of each faith feel the necessity of defending and propagating their own faith as the true religion. The search for truth is turned into

[5] Dewey, John, *The Quest for Certainty*, pp. 263–264.

dogmatic defense and counter-defense of a particular set of truths. Divisions arise and the fellowship of a true educational process is at an end. Religious education becomes a means for indoctrinating children and youth in a particular set of Christian interpretations or the propaganda by which others are influenced to accept that particular set of dogmas as the only true faith.

Religious leaders are not the only individuals with dogmatic certainty. Those who are at the extreme right in social and political outlook and wish to maintain the *status quo,* and those who have moved to the extreme left and wish to overthrow the existing order are often as dogmatic in their certainty as to the final right of their beliefs as are some of the followers of religion. Those at the right wish to use education to maintain the *status quo* and they oppose free discussion of current problems as zealously as they do the direct teaching of radical notions. Those at the extreme left would like to use education for the propagation of their proposed theories and they also are opposed to free consideration of these problems. Thus, a true educational process is being challenged both from the extreme right and the extreme left. It is not surprising to find that those of a religious outlook who move to a dogmatically held extreme left in economic and political theory should at the same time move to a dogmatically held extreme right in religious faith, for the extreme right in religion and the extreme left in economics and politics are often alike in dogmatic certainty. The conflict then is not alone between authoritarian religion and experimental education. It is rather a more fundamental cleavage between those of dogmatic certainty in ethical and religious beliefs, and those who take the experimental attitude toward life and who are convinced that ethical standards and goals of endeavor as well as religious beliefs are worked out by the same educational process as the means for their attainment. A true educational process is denied as soon as education is made the servant of any dogmatism, whether in religion or in any other area. The freedom of individuals and of groups to search for and find their own meaningful interpretations of life and destiny is important in religious education which is Christian. This liberty is in line with the spirit of the New Testament. It was a cardinal principle of the Reformation. It is true to the scientific spirit and method. It is that which gives Christian experience its vitality.

The issues in regard to religious education center in the source of authority. Those with an authoritarian approach seek to find authority for their interpretations outside of human responsibility in some direct revelation of God. Those with an educational approach recognize that while God has not left himself without witness, man has not been given any direct revelation of the meaning of these manifestations. He has been left to discover these manifestations and to make his own interpretations of them. It is true that man has by his own efforts produced nothing. His very capacity to take responsibility in his world is given him in his native equipment, and the resources upon which he depends he finds in his world. But it is also true that he is dependent for the development of his own capacities and for the discovery and utilization of these resources upon human responsibility and effort. Much of his learning has been "trial and error." True education of the social type represents conscious and effective ways by which human beings have met situations, have made decisions, have discovered and utilized available resources, and thus have taken responsibility in their world. Education is not something which is confined to the school. It is the fundamental method open to man for solving the problems of his world. It is the process used wherever significant responsibility is taken by man, whether in personal decisions and relations, in family life, community relations, or economic and political affairs. It is the basis for the conviction that individual growth and social progress are no longer at the mercy of circumstances, but become a possibility though not an inevitability. Therefore the source of authority is in the educational process itself. In saying this, there is recognition of the fact that it is only by such a process that man can determine what to do or can discover on what he may and must depend.

Trust, however, can be placed in an educational process only when it reaches a genuine religious level. Such a process is controlled by inclusive and even ultimate goals and purposes beyond the private welfare of any individual or group, and is grounded in discovery and utilization of the resources upon which man's life depends. The source of authority for the Christian is in that educational process which is guided by Christian purposes and is grounded on the Christian's confidence. The contribution of the Christian religion to reverent human responsibility is not realized when the emphasis is limited to a sense of guilt for failure and to an offer of forgiveness for sin. What is needed is both confidence and direction for a different kind of responsibility from that which has brought defeat. An experience-centered and socially organized educational process would seem to furnish the medium for the utilization of these positive contributions of Christian faith and experience. There is full recognition of finite limitations and of the human possibilities of evil as well as of good, and there is realistic appraisal of the tragic seriousness of the human problem; but at the same time there is integral in such an educational process what seems to have been Jesus' confidence in the unrealized possibilities even of plain and humble persons and groups. While it is dominated by the Christian emphasis upon the worth of persons and upon mutual respect and brotherly relations between them, it is centered in family, school, church, community, and other corporate groupings where the choices and responsibilities of individuals are intimately bound up with the social groups of which they are a part. Therefore, the goal is truly social, for it is that approximation which is possible to human beings in their social arrangements of the Kingdom of God in which love is manifested in all social relationships. Confidence in the success of these human endeavors is based upon the Christian belief in the limitless resources of God which are available to individuals and groups who meet the conditions for their release. Thus, Christian faith and experience are integrally related to an educational process which is Christian.

If confidence is to be placed in the educational process, the Christian purpose and confidence must be more than a matter of intellectual assent. It is only as individuals and groups have been captured by the possibilities of love made manifest in Christ, as the goal of the Kingdom of God has become the dominating purpose of their lives, and as fellowship with God has become an actual experience, that the educational process can be trusted. There is hope of the beginning and the growth of such living experience when individuals join with their fellows in the enterprises of God on earth.

BIBLIOGRAPHY

Chapter II. PROTESTANT INFLUENCE IN AMERICAN
RELIGIOUS EDUCATION

BETTS, GEORGE HERBERT, *The Curriculum of Religious Education,*
The Abingdon Press, New York, 1924.

BUSHNELL, HORACE, *Nature and the Supernatural,* Charles Scribner's
Sons, New York, 1858.

—— *Views of Christian Nurture, and of Subjects Adjacent Thereto,*
Edwin Hunt, Hartford, 1847.

CHENEY, MARY BUSHNELL, ed., *Life and Letters of Horace Bushnell,*
Harper and Brothers, New York, 1880.

CUBBERLEY, ELLWOOD P., *The History of Education,* Houghton Mifflin
Co., Boston, 1920.

CULVER, RAYMOND B., *Horace Mann and Religious Education in the
Massachusetts Public Schools,* Yale University Press, New
Haven, 1929.

HARKNESS, GEORGIA, *John Calvin; The Man and His Ethics,* Henry
Holt and Co., New York, 1931.

HUNT, ROBERT N. CAREW, *Calvin,* The Centenary Press, London, 1933.

JACKSON, JEROME K., and MALMBERG, CONSTANTINE F., *Religious Education and the State,* Doubleday, Doran and Co., New York,
1928.

McGIFFERT, ARTHUR CUSHMAN, *Martin Luther, The Man and His
Work,* The Century Co., New York, 1911.

—— *Protestant Thought before Kant,* Charles Scribner's Sons, New
York, 1911.

MYERS, A. J. W., *Horace Bushnell and Religious Education,* Manthurn
and Burack, Boston, 1937.

STEWART, GEORGE, *A History of Religious Education in Connecticut to* the *Middle of the Nineteenth Century,* Yale University Press, New Haven, 1924.

SWEET, WILLIAM WARREN, *The Story of Religion in America,* Harper and Brothers, New York and London, 1939, Revised Edition.

TYLER, BENNETT, *Letter to Dr. Bushnell on Christian Nurture,* privately printed, 1847.

—— *Letters to the Rev. Horace Bushnell, D.D., containing Strictures on his Book, Entitled "Views of Christian Nurture, and of Subjects Adjacent Thereto,* Brown and Parsons, Hartford, 1848.

Chapter III. THE DEVELOPMENT OF AN EDUCATIONAL APPROACH

BETTS, GEORGE HERBERT, *The Curriculum of Religious Education,* The Abingdon Press, New York, 1924.

BOWER, WILLIAM CLAYTON, *The Curriculum of Religious Education,* Charles Scribner's Sons, New York, 1927.

BROWN, ARLO AYRES, *A History of Religious Education in Recent Times,* The Abingdon Press, New York, 1923.

COE, GEORGE ALBERT, *A Social Theory of Religious Education,* Charles Scribner's Sons, New York, 1917.

DEWEY, JOHN, *Democracy and Education,* The Macmillan Co., New York, 1916.

—— *How We Think,* D. C. Heath and Co., Boston, 1910.

HALL, G. STANLEY, *Adolescence,* D. Appleton & Co., New York, 1904.

HARTSHORNE, HUGH, and MAY, MARK A., *Studies in the Nature of Character:* I. Studies in Deceit; II. Studies in Service and Self-Control; III. Studies in the Organization of Character, The Macmillan Co., New York, 1928-1930.

INTERNATIONAL COUNCIL OF RELIGIOUS EDUCATION, *Christian Education Today,* A Statement of Basic Philosophy, Chicago, 1940.

—— *The Development of a Curriculum of Religious Education* (Educational Bulletin 101, rev. 1930), International Council of Religious Education, Chicago, 1930.

JAMES, WILLIAM, *Principles of Psychology* (Two volumes), Henry Holt and Co., New York, 1890.

—— *Talks to Teachers,* Henry Holt and Co., New York, 1899.

KILPATRICK, WILLIAM H., *Foundations of Method,* The Macmillan Co., New York, 1925.

—— *The Project Method,* Bureau of Publications, Teachers College, Columbia University, New York, 1918.

KNIGHT, EDGAR W., *Education in the United States,* Ginn and Co., New York, 1929.

KÖHLER, WOLFGANG, *The Mentality of Apes,* Harcourt, Brace and Co., New York, 1925.

THORNDIKE, EDWARD L., *Educational Psychology* (three volumes), Teachers College, Columbia University, New York, 1913.

WHEELER, RAYMOND H., and PERKINS, FRANCIS T., *Principles of Mental Development,* Thomas Y. Crowell Co., New York, 1932.

Chapter IV. RELIGIOUS EDUCATION AND THE INTERPRETATION OF THE CHRISTIAN RELIGION

BARTH, KARL, *The Doctrine of the Word of God,* trans. by G. T. Thomson, Charles Scribner's Sons, New York, 1936.

—— *Evangelium und Bildung,* Verlag der Evangelischen Buchhandlung Zollikon, 1938.

BRUNNER, EMIL, *The Divine Imperative,* trans. by Olive Wyon, Lutterworth Press, London, 1937; The Macmillan Co., New York.

COE, GEORGE ALBERT, *What is Christian Education?,* Charles Scribner's Sons, New York, 1929.

THE COMMISSION ON APPRAISAL, WILLIAM ERNEST HOCKING, CHAIRMAN, *Re-Thinking Missions, A Laymen's Inquiry after One Hundred Years,* Harper and Bros., New York, 1932.

COMMITTEE ON THE STATE OF THE CHURCH, JOHN A. MACKAY, CHAIRMAN, *The State of the Church,* Federal Council of the Churches of Christ in America, New York, 1939.

HOMRIGHAUSEN, E. G., *The Real Problem of Religious Education,* in Religious Education, Chicago, January-March, 1939.

—— *The Minister and Religious Education,* in Christian Education, Washington, April, 1938.

INTERNATIONAL COUNCIL OF RELIGIOUS EDUCATION, *The Development of a Curriculum of Religious Education,* Chicago, 1930.

—— *Christian Education Today,* Chicago, 1940.

JERUSALEM CONFERENCE, I.M.C., VOL. II, *Religious Education,* International Missionary Council, New York, 1928.

KRAEMER, HENDRIK, *The Christian Message in a Non-Christian World,* Harper and Bros., New York, 1938.

LEWIS, EDWIN, *The Faith We Declare,* Cokesbury Press, Nashville, 1939.

McGIFFERT, ARTHUR CUSHMAN, *A History of Christian Thought, Vol. I.,* Charles Scribner's Sons, New York, 1932.

SMITH, SHELTON, *Theological Reconstruction in Religious Education,* in Christendom, Chicago, Autumn, 1939.

VIETH, PAUL H., *Objectives of Religious Education,* Harper and Bros., New York, 1930.

Chapter V. RELIGIOUS EDUCATION AND THE USE OF THE BIBLE

BARTH, KARL, *The Knowledge of God and the Service of God,* trans. by J. L. M. Haire and Ian Henderson, Charles Scribner's Sons, New York, 1939.

—— *The Doctrine of the Word of God,* trans. by G. T. Thomson, Charles Scribner's Sons, New York, 1936.

BOWER, WILLIAM CLAYTON, *The Living Bible,* Harper and Brothers, New York, 1936.

BRUNNER, EMIL, *The Mediator,* trans. by Olive Wyon, Lutterworth Press, London, 1934; The Macmillan Co., New York.

CADBURY, HENRY J., *The Peril of Modernizing Jesus,* The Macmillan Co., New York, 1937.

DEISMANN, ADOLPH, *Paul, a Study in Social and Religious History,* George H. Doran Co., New York, 1926.

GRANT, FREDERICK C., *The Growth of the Gospels,* The Abingdon Press, New York, 1933.

HOSKYNS, SIR EDWIN and DAVEY, NOEL, *The Riddle of the New Testament,* Faber and Faber, Ltd., London, 1931.

KRAEMER, HENDRIK, *The Christian Message in a Non-Christian World*, Harper and Bros., New York, 1938.

LAKE, KIRSOPP and SILVA, *An Introduction to the New Testament*, Harper and Bros., New York, 1937.

LAKE, KIRSOPP, *Paul, His Heritage and Legacy*, Oxford University Press, New York, 1934.

LEWIS, EDWIN, *The Faith We Declare*, Cokesbury Press, Nashville, 1939.

—— *A Christian Manifesto*, The Abingdon Press, New York, 1934.

MCGIFFERT, ARTHUR CUSHMAN, *A History of Christian Thought*, Vol. I., Charles Scribner's Sons, New York, 1932.

MACKINNON, JAMES, *The Gospel in the Early Church*, Longmans, Green and Co., London, 1933.

PORTER, FRANK CHAMBERLIN, *The Mind of Christ in Paul*, Charles Scribner's Sons, New York, 1930.

STREETER, BURNETT H., *The Four Gospels, A Study of Origins*, Macmillan and Co., London, 1924; The Macmillan Co., New York.

Chapter VI. HUMAN KNOWLEDGE AND RELIGIOUS EDUCATION

BARTH, KARL, *The Knowledge of God and the Service of God*, trans. by J. L. M. Haire and Ian Henderson, Charles Scribner's Sons, New York, 1939.

BRUNNER, EMIL, *The Christian Understanding of Man*, in an Oxford Conference Book of the same title, Willett, Clark and Co., Chicago, 1938.

EDDINGTON, A. S., *The Nature of the Physical World*, The Macmillan Co., New York, 1929.

MILLIKAN, ROBERT ANDREWS, *Evolution in Science and Religion*, Yale University Press, New Haven, 1927.

PORTER, FRANK CHAMBERLIN, *The Mind of Christ in Paul*, Charles Scribner's Sons, New York, 1930.

SCOTT, ERNEST F., *The Fourth Gospel, Its Purpose and Theology*, T. and T. Clark, Edinburgh, 1920.

Chapter VII. RELIGIOUS EDUCATION AND THE HUMAN PREDICAMENT

AUBREY, EDWIN E., *Present Theological Tendencies,* Harper and Bros., New York, 1936.

BARTH, KARL, *The Knowledge of God and the Service of God,* trans. by J. L. M. Haire and Ian Henderson, Charles Scribner's Sons, New York, 1939.

BRUNNER, EMIL, *The Christian Understanding of Man,* in an Oxford Conference Book of the same title, Willett, Clark and Co., Chicago, 1938.

—— *God and Man,* trans. by David Cairns, Student Christian Movement Press, London, 1936; The Macmillan Co., New York.

—— *Man in Revolt,* trans. by Olive Wyon, Charles Scribner's Sons, New York, 1939.

—— *The Mediator,* trans. by Olive Wyon, Lutterworth Press, London, 1934; The Macmillan Co., New York.

—— *The Theology of Crisis,* Charles Scribner's Sons, New York, 1929.

—— *The Word and the World,* Student Christian Movement Press, London, 1931.

HORTON, WALTER M., *Contemporary Continental Theology,* Harper and Bros., New York, 1938.

Chapter VIII. RELIGIOUS EDUCATION AND SIN AND GUILT

BENNETT, JOHN, "The Causes of Social Evil" in *Christian Faith and the Common Life,* An Oxford Conference Book, Willett, Clark and Co., Chicago, 1938.

BREADY, J. WESLEY, *England: Before and After Wesley,* Harper and Bros., New York, 1938.

CALHOUN, ROBERT L., "The Dilemma of Humanitarian Modernism" in *The Christian Understanding of Man,* An Oxford Conference Book, Willett, Clark and Co., Chicago, 1938.

NIEBUHR, REINHOLD, *An Interpretation of Christian Ethics,* Harper and Bros., New York, 1935.

RANK, OTTO, *Will Therapy,* Alfred A. Knopf, New York, 1936.

STARBUCK, EDWIN D., *The Psychology of Religion,* The Walter Scott Publishing Co., London, 1899.

SWEET, WILLIAM WARREN, *The Story of Religion in America,* Harper and Bros., New York, 1939, Revised Edition.

TILLICH, PAUL, *The Interpretation of History,* Charles Scribner's Sons, New York, 1936.

Chapter IX. HUMAN NATURE AND RELIGIOUS EDUCATION
Chapter X. A SOCIAL STRATEGY OF RELIGIOUS EDUCATION
Chapter XI. RELIGIOUS EDUCATION AND CHRISTLIKE CHARACTER

ALLPORT, FLOYD H., *Social Psychology,* Houghton Mifflin Co., Boston, 1924.

ALLPORT, GORDON W., *Personality, A Psychological Interpretation,* Henry Holt and Co., New York, 1937.

CALHOUN, ROBERT L., *What is Man?,* Association Press, New York, 1939.

COLE, STEWART G., *Character and Christian Education,* Cokesbury Press, Nashville, 1936.

BIDDLE, WILLIAM M., *Propaganda and Education,* Bureau of Publications, Teachers College, Columbia University, New York, 1932.

COE, GEORGE ALBERT, *A Social Theory of Religious Education,* Charles Scribner's Sons, New York, 1917.

HENDRICKS, IVES, *Facts and Theories of Psychoanalysis,* Alfred A. Knopf, New York, 1934.

HORNEY, KAREN, *The Neurotic Personality of Our Time,* W. W. Norton and Co., New York, 1936.

—— *New Ways of Psychoanalysis,* W. W. Norton and Co., New York, 1939.

McDOUGALL, WILLIAM, *Social Psychology,* Methuen and Co., London, 1922.

MEAD, MARGARET, *Sex and Temperament in Three Primitive Societies,* William Morrow and Co., New York, 1935.

NIEBUHR, REINHOLD, *Beyond Tragedy*, Charles Scribner's Sons, New York, 1937.

—— *An Interpretation of Christian Ethics*, Harper and Bros., New York, 1935.

—— *Moral Man and Immoral Society*, Charles Scribner's Sons, New York, 1932.

—— *Reflections on the End of an Era*, Charles Scribner's Sons, New York, 1934.

PLANT, JAMES S., *Personality and the Cultural Pattern*, Commonwealth Fund, New York, 1937.

SMITH, J. W. D., "The Crisis in Christian Education" in *Church, Community and State in Relation to Education*, An Oxford Conference Book, Willett, Clark and Co., Chicago, 1938.

SHERRINGTON, SIR CHARLES S., *The Integrative Action of the Nervous System*, Charles Scribner's Sons, New York, 1911.

THORNDIKE, EDWARD L., *Educational Psychology*, Vol. I, The Original Nature of Man, Teachers College, Columbia University, New York, 1913.

WATSON, JOHN B., *Behaviorism*, rev. ed., W. W. Norton and Co., New York, 1930.

Chapter XII. THE EDUCATIONAL PROCESS AND CHRISTIAN ETHICS

BRUNNER, EMIL, *The Divine Imperative*, trans. by Olive Wyon, Lutterworth Press, London, 1937; The Macmillan Co., New York.

ELLIOTT, HARRISON S., *The Process of Group Thinking*, Association Press, New York, 1928.

NIEBUHR, REINHOLD, *An Interpretation of Christian Ethics*, Harper and Bros., New York, 1935.

NIEBUHR, H. RICHARD, *The Kingdom of God in America*, Willett, Clark and Co., Chicago, 1937.

Chapter XIII. THE EDUCATIONAL PROCESS AND RELIGIOUS EXPERIENCE

BOWER, WILLIAM CLAYTON, *Character through Creative Experience*, University of Chicago Press, Chicago, 1930.

—— *Religion and the Good Life,* The Abingdon Press, New York, 1933.

CHILDS, JOHN L., *Education and the Philosophy of Experimentalism,* Century Co., New York, 1931.

COE, GEORGE ALBERT, *The Psychology of Religion,* University of Chicago Press, Chicago, 1916.

—— *What is Christian Edudcation?,* Charles Scribner's Sons, New York, 1929.

DEWEY, JOHN, *A Common Faith,* Yale University Press, New Haven, 1934.

—— *Democracy and Education,* The Macmillan Co., New York, 1916.

—— *Reconstruction in Philosophy,* Henry Holt and Co., New York, 1920.

—— *The Quest for Certainty,* George Allen and Unwin, Ltd., London, 1930.

HARTSHORNE, HUGH, *Character in Human Relations,* Charles Scribner's Sons, New York, 1932.

HOCKING, WILLIAM ERNEST, *The Meaning of God in Human Experience,* Yale University Press, New Haven, 1912.

HOMRIGHAUSEN, E. G., *The Real Problem of Religious Education* in Religious Education, Chicago, January–March, 1939.

POWELL, WILFRED EVANS, *Education for Life with God,* The Abingdon Press, New York, 1934.

SOARES, THEODORE G., *Religious Education,* University of Chicago Press, Chicago, 1927.

TILLICH, PAUL, *The Interpretation of History,* Charles Scribner's Sons, New York, 1936.

WIEMAN, HENRY N., and REGINA WESTCOTT, *Normative Psychology of Religion,* Thomas Y. Crowell Co., New York, 1935.

Index

Absolutist position, 254

Adult religious education, importance of, 226

Allport, Gordon W., 190

American Sunday School Union, 20–21, 24

Ames, Edward Scribner, 262

Anthropology, 186–187

Authoritarian, *see* Protestantism, authoritarian emphasis in, and Religious education, authoritarian conception of

Authoritative conceptions, 151–154, 161–163, 166–168, 234–237

Authoritative conceptions of education, 167–168, 317–319

Authority, source of in religion, 12–16, 68–69, 71, 72, 78, 80–84, 90–91, 97–98, 112–113, 142–145, 149–150, 151–154, 319–321

Barclay, Wade Crawford, 56n.

Barnes, Mrs. J. Woodbridge, 36, 38n.

Barth, Karl (Barthianism), 80, 92–94, 113, 124–125, 132, 142–143, 149, 151, 162

Bennett, John, 172–174, 196

Betts, George Herbert, 23n., 34, 35n., 36n.

Bible, authority of, 12–15, 81–84, 90–91, 112–115, 119–120, 309–310; historical approach and criticism, 10, 34, 38, 91–95, 98, 100–101, 111–112, 116–119, 140; human knowledge in interpretation of, 128–132; interpretation of, 12–14, 90–115, 119; neo-orthodox viewpoint on, 90–97; study of, 34, 91–95, 113–115, 116–119, 267–268, 276–277; use of in religious education, 3, 5, 12, 20, 23–24, 39, 47, 52–53, 59–62, 81–84, 97–98, 115–120, 241–242, 254, 260, 267–268, 276–277, 309, 316

"Biblical Psychology," 125–126, 129, 141–142

Bible Study Union and Publishing Co., 35n.

Blakeslee, Erastus, 35

Bower, William C., 57, 60n., 62, 69, 86, 269–270

Bready, J. Wesley, 163

Brown, Arlo Ayres, 36n., 38n.

Brunner, Emil, 71–74, 79–80, 90, 93–97, 112–115, 125–126, 129, 130, 141–146, 151, 234–236, 237–243, 246–247, 249–250, 277

Bushnell, Horace, 27–33, 39, 45, 52, 228; criticism of views of, 31–32

Cadbury, Henry J., 113n.

Calhoun, Robert L., 168, 195, 219–220

Calvin, John, 14–16, 84

Catechism in Sunday Schools, 23, 25

Childs, John L., 266

Character Education Inquiry, 46–47

Character, development of, 28–30, 45–48, 57–59, 156–157, 191–197, 208–213, 310–316

Children and young people, religious education of, 25–26, 28–30, 36–38, 41–43, 52–56, 61–62, 70–71, 79, 87–88, 165–168, 225–226, 228, 231, 276–277, 278, 312–316

Choices, *see* Decisions

333